experience

2ND EDITION

WORKBOOK

B2

First for Schools

CONTENTS

Listening	Use of English	Speaking	Writing	Review
topic: supertasters **task:** sentence completion	key word transformations (p9) word formation (p10)	**topic:** comparing activities **task:** long turn	**topic:** local events **task:** review	unit check 1
topic: reading lists **task:** multiple choice	open cloze (p19) multiple-choice cloze (p20)	**topic:** holiday preferences **task:** interview	**topic:** a memorable journey **task:** article	unit check 2
topic: visiting a parents workplace **task:** multiple matching	key word transformations (p29) multiple-choice cloze (p30)	**topic:** benefits of volunteering **task:** collaborative task	**topic:** effective learning **task:** essay	unit check 3 Use of English units 1–3 (p34)
topic: out and about **task:** multiple choice	open cloze (p41) multiple choice cloze (p42)	**topic:** city vs. country life **task:** discussion	**topic:** local changes **task:** email	unit check 4
topic: floorball **task:** multiple choice: longer text	key word transformations (p51) Word formation (p52)	**topic:** team sport **task:** long turn	**topic:** coping with stress **task:** article	unit check 5
topic: mapping with sound **task:** sentence completion	key word transformations (p61) word formation (p62)	**topic:** local wildlife **task:** collaborative task	**topic:** accuracy of information **task:** essay	unit check 6 Use of English units 1–6 (p66)
topic: entertainment **task:** multiple choice: short texts	open cloze (p73) multiple choice cloze (p74)	**topic:** how we use entertainment **task:** discussion	**topic:** short stories **task:** story	unit check 7
topic: group activities **task:** multiple matching	key word transformations (p83) multiple choice cloze (p84)	**topic:** things that affect relationships **task:** collaborative task	**topic:** sharing in the community **task:** email	unit check 8
topic: giving up social media **task:** multiple choice	open cloze (p93) word formation (p94)	**topic:** shopping styles **task:** long turn	**topic:** making choices **task:** essay	unit check 9 Use of English units 1–9 (p98)
Listening (p110)		Speaking (p113)		

Wake up your senses!

READING

1 Complete the text with these words.

cosy dismiss dull overwhelming pigeonhole
pretty reluctant willing worthwhile

Small change, big difference

Is life feeling ¹... and boring
right now? Are you ²... to
get out and try something new? Then change. But
this doesn't mean taking on huge challenges that
become ³... . The key to
shaking up your routine is to start small. Look for
ways of changing the stuff you do every day: take
a different route to school or college, download a
song by a band you've never heard before, talk to a
student you don't normally mix with. These things
might sound ⁴... basic but
don't ⁵... them. For one thing,
they help to make day-to-day life a bit more fun.
And they really can be ⁶...
because they make you start to think differently.
It's easy to ⁷... yourself with
fixed roles and routines. Making a change every
day helps you escape in a risk-free way. And if
you're ⁸... to step out of
your ⁹... routine in small
ways, you're much more likely to take on bigger
challenges.

2 Read the article on the right quickly. Choose the
quotation (1–3) that best fits the main message of
the text.

1 Whoever said money can't buy happiness simply
didn't know where to shop

2 Have stories to tell, not stuff to show

3 Good advice comes from bad experiences

3 Read the article again. Choose which sentence (A–G) best fits
each gap (1–6). You do not need one of the sentences.

A A description of a difficult situation can over time turn into a funny
story that becomes part of the speaker's identity.

B While the happiness we get from objects fades over time,
experiences define who you are.

C Firstly, the memory of an experience stays with us for a long time,
much longer than the excitement you get from buying an object.

D So don't give up buying objects completely but invest in some great
experiences, too.

E There's nothing wrong with objects: some are necessary, others are
beautiful.

F He has been studying the link between money and happiness for
over twenty years.

G They seem to regret missing an experience more than losing out on
an object.

Extend

4 Complete the questions with the correct prepositions. Check your
answers in the article.

1 What three objects are most important .... you?

2 Have you ever been left .... feelings of disappointment after
buying something? What?

3 How many people are you connected .... on social media?

4 What's happened this week to make you feel positive ....
life?

5 Complete the comments (1–6) with the correct form of these pairs
of words.

regret / miss   last / keep   possession / stuff

Objects OR experiences?

Sarah Add message | Report

I guess objects. I often ask 'Why do I have all these ¹........................... ?'
But then I'm not very good at getting rid of all my old ²........................... !

Hayley Add message | Report

Both. The only thing I ³........................... is not getting tickets to see
my team but I really ⁴........................... seeing it live.

Liz Add message | Report

I think both. Experiences give you memories that ⁵........................... ,
but ⁶........................... objects also brings back happy times.

The search for *happiness:* to have or to do?

I magine you could have either the object of your dreams or the experience of your dreams. Which would make you happier for longer? Most people would choose the object. It's logical. You can keep the object for years but the experience may be over in days, hours or even minutes. Well, according to recent research, if you want to be happier for longer, choose the experience.

Thomas Gilovich is Professor of Psychology at Cornell University in the United States. [1] .... His research suggests that people who spend money on experiences are generally happier than those who buy physical objects. So why are experiences more important to our wellbeing than possessions?

[2] .... Although the majority of people think it's better to spend money on something physical, Professor Gilovich has found that the opposite is true. People tend to believe an experience will come and go. They feel they will be left with very little when compared to owning an item.

But in reality we remember experiences long afterwards, while we soon get used to our possessions or even bored with them.

The research also looked at other differences, including how people felt before a purchase or experience. Professor Gilovich says that people look forward to enjoying an experience more than owning an object. So before getting a new smartphone, for example, it's exciting to think about owning the object itself. But more pleasure comes from thinking about what you can do with the object and how you can share experiences with others. Another area of the research was how people felt after choosing not to do or buy something. [3] .... So you may feel worse about not going to see a band with friends than not buying a new pair of jeans.

Perhaps one of the most important results from the research was the effect on identity. [4] .... Professor Gilovich believes that who we are isn't a direct result of the things that we own. He says that our experiences are a bigger part of ourselves and that even though you can really like your material things, they are separate from who you are. In other words, they aren't a part of your identity. He adds however, that we are connected to our experiences.

If experiences make a person, they also make a community. They are very often shared with family and friends, face-to-face and on social media. Even if they last only a very short time, they become part of the stories that we tell each other. They can be remembered across different communities and generations. Even if an experience has made someone unhappy, describing what happened can make that person feel more positive about things. [5] ....

So we connect more with other people when sharing experiences than when comparing objects. The next time you're bombarded by adverts on TV, online and on the streets, maybe take a moment to decide how you want to spend your money. [6] .... But you won't enjoy them forever. And your friends probably want to hear more about where you went in your new trainers than about the trainers themselves. ■

GRAMMAR

present tenses

Choose the correct meaning (A or B) for each sentence.

1 My dad works nights so we don't see much of him in the week.
   A This is true just this week.
   B This is true every week.

2 Why are you wearing your coat in the house?
   A I'm asking about this moment.
   B I'm asking about a changing situation around now.

3 Why are things going up in price?
   A I'm asking about this moment.
   B I'm asking about a changing situation around now.

4 You're always taking my bike without asking!
   A You've got my bike now and I want it back.
   B You do this a lot and it annoys me.

5 So, she shows me her phone and she's laughing. I read the text and I feel like crying. Then she just walks off!
   A This happened in the past but I want to make my story more real.
   B This is happening now, so it's a real story.

6 You've cut your hair. It looks great.
   A I can see the result of a past change.
   B I know when you changed your appearance.

7 You've been chatting on that phone for hours.
   A You've talked to your friends already today.
   B You're still talking.

Find and correct four mistakes in the sentences. If the sentence is correct, write 'correct'.

1 We don't know each other for long, but we get on very well.

2 How long have you been learning to play the bongo drums?

3 You're always criticising me! It's just not fair!

4 I'm hot because I run round the park.

5 I broke my phone two days ago so I don't message my friends for ages.

6 Have you checked out that new video yet?

7 All my friends are spending every Saturday afternoon at the football.

8 To be honest, I'm a creature of habit. I don't often try new things.

Choose the correct words to complete the conversation.

A: Oh, this ¹looks / is looking fun!

B: What ²are you looking / do you look at?

A: One of those personality quizzes: 'How adventurous are you?' Shall we do it together?

B: Hmm, ³I'm not really enjoying / I don't really enjoy quizzes like that.

A: Oh, come on! We ⁴haven't done / don't do anything like this for ages. It'll be a laugh. The first question is about food: How many new types of food ⁵have you tried / have you been trying so far this year? One to five, six to ten or eleven to fifteen?

B: Maybe one to five. ⁶I've never been / I never am very adventurous with food.

A: OK. The next one is about meeting new people: You ⁷stand / are standing alone at a party. How do you make contact? Walk over to a group and say hi, find one friendly person, or…?

B: I'm sorry but I ⁸get / I'm getting a bit bored with this quiz already.

A: Oh, don't be like that! It's only a bit of fun.

B: Yes, but ⁹I've had / I've been having enough now. I think I'll go home.

A: Oh, ¹⁰you've always been walking / you're always walking off like that.

B: That's not true! I just don't always like what you like.

🔊 1.1 Listen and check your answers to Ex 3.

Complete the blog with the correct form of the verbs in brackets. Use short forms where possible.

How common is common sense?

People ¹................................ (always / tell) me to use my common sense. It's so annoying! What ²................................ that even .... (mean)? A dictionary definition ³................................ (say): the ability to behave in a sensible way and make practical decisions. OK, so it's common sense to check for traffic when you ⁴................................ (cross) the road. I get that. But what about when it comes to studying? We ⁵................................ (work) on a design project at school for the last few weeks. It ⁶................................ (not go) too well at the moment, so I asked my dad for help. All he said was, 'Just use your common sense.' I ⁷................................ (try) to work out how that's helpful ever since. Great advice, Dad, thanks! ⁸................................ anyone .... (ever / say) that to you? What do you think common sense ⁹................................ (mean)? How ¹⁰................................ it .... (help) with your schoolwork up to now?

VOCABULARY

describing experiences and feelings

1 ◀ 1.2 **Listen to eight speakers. How does each person feel? Number the adjectives (A–H) in order (1–8).**

A thrilled ....   **E** determined ....
B petrified ....   **F** sympathetic ....
C tense ....   **G** offended ....
D relieved ....   **H** moved ....

2 **Replace the highlighted words in the conversations with these adjectives.**

anxious   insulted   strong-willed   terrified   understanding

1 A: We used to be best friends but she never listens to anyone else's problems.
   B: You're right. She's never been very sympathetic.
2 A: What was the matter with Gemma yesterday?
   B: I think she was feeling a bit tense before the match.
3 A: Can you believe Joe said I always get what I want?
   B: Well, you are pretty determined when you want to be.
4 A: Have you signed up for the school trip yet?
   B: Rock climbing? Are you joking? I'm petrified of heights!
5 A: Why isn't Lisa speaking to Dan?
   B: She felt offended when he laughed at her new glasses.

3 **Complete the adjectives. Then answer each question for you.**

On a scale of one to ten ...

1 How i _ _ _ _ _ _ d would you be if someone called your local football team rubbish? ☐

2 How u _ _ _ _ _ _ _ _ _ _ _ g would you be if your best friend forgot your birthday? ☐

3 How t _ _ _ _ _ _ _ d would you be if a tarantula touched your hand? ☐

4 How a _ _ _ _ _ s would you feel if you had to take a long flight by yourself? ☐

5 How s _ _ _ _ _ _ _ _ c would you feel if your brother/sister was unfollowed on Instagram? ☐

6 How d _ _ _ _ _ _ _ d would you be to win a new tennis racquet? ☐

4 **Complete the article with the correct form of these verbs.**

add to   get across   miss out   put off   take off   try out

Smells like you've got a text

We experience so much of today's world through smartphones and computers, but only in an audio-visual way. You can see and hear, but not much else. What about our other senses – do they need to ¹............................? A computer scientist, Adrian David Cheok, is asking the same question. He hasn't been ²............................ by the limitations of the online world. He's been ³............................ new ways of sending sense messages over the internet. A new device called Scentee has been developed that allows you to send a smell message! The device connects to an app on your smartphone and the smell is activated when opening a text. Professor Cheok is also developing ways of ⁴............................ touch and taste messages .... using digital transmission. Who knows how quickly these ideas will ⁵............................,' but just think how your sense of smell, touch and taste could ⁶............................ your whole online experience.

Extend

5 **Change the adverb or preposition in bold to give the meaning in brackets.**

1 give **up** → give .... (surrender; stop fighting)

2 take **off** → take .... (be similar to in character or looks)
→ take .... (return, e.g. to a shop)

3 try **out** → try .... (see if clothes fit/suit you)

4 get **across** → get .... (recover from, e.g. an illness)
→ get .... (have a good relationship)

5 put **off** → put .... (tidy; put something in its correct place)
→ put .... (stop something burning, e.g. a fire)

6 add **to** → add .... (calculate the total of several numbers)

LISTENING

🔊 1.3 **Listen to the podcast. What is the presenter's aim?**

A to show listeners how to test their sense of taste

B to compare his sense of taste with the average person

C to give information about a special category of people

🔊 1.4 **Listen again and complete the sentences with a word or a short phrase in each gap.**

A science podcast

▶ The first podcast in the series on senses talked about **1**............................... .

▶ Supertasters have more **2**............................... for processing taste than an average person.

▶ The presenter was surprised that being a supertaster can **3**............................... your diet.

▶ Approximately a **4**............................... of the population are supertasters.

▶ People tend to lose their sense of taste and smell after the age of **5**............................... .

▶ The majority of people don't understand that the nose and mouth are both needed to produce a **6**............................... variety of tastes.

▶ The 350 receptors in the nose work by detecting the **7**............................... structure in the smell of what we eat.

▶ It is estimated that human beings can distinguish up to **8**............................... different smells.

▶ Many people from the Science for Life office **9**............................... .

▶ The presenter was disappointed to have **10**............................... result in a taste test.

Extend

Match these adjectives with the types of food (A–D). There's one extra word you do not need.

bitter   salty   savoury   sour   sweet

Choose the correct words to complete the sentences (1–5).

1 Any non-sweet food can be called **salty / savoury**.

2 Food with a lot of or too much flavour is described as **great / strong**.

3 An apple without much flavour can be called **watery / fruity**.

4 Dishes with a lot of chillies can be called spicy or **burning / hot**.

5 Someone who refuses to eat many types of food is called a **bossy / fussy** eater.

Choose the correct words to complete the text.

A matter *of taste*

I have an identical twin sister, but we couldn't be more different when it comes to food. She loves cakes and biscuits whereas I don't eat many **1sweet / savoury** things. She's definitely a milk chocolate fan, but I prefer the **2fruity / bitter** flavour of dark chocolate. It's the same with coffee: mine is **3strong / sour** and full of flavour, hers is all **4salty / watery**. And she never wants to eat my curry! I love chillies so it's much too **5fussy / spicy** for her, but for me, the **6hotter / bigger**, the better!

USE OF ENGLISH 1

Choose the word in each sentence that is not needed.

1 I have a younger sister, but she's more taller than me.
2 The third film in the series wasn't as good as than the first two.
3 I can't eat this curry. It's too much hot!
4 You're a so far better runner than I am.
5 The too earlier we get there, the easier it'll be to find seats.
6 I'm not as old enough to ride a scooter.
7 Of all the concerts we've ever done, we played most worst last night.
8 The book got more and much more complicated as the story went on.
9 Only the most of skilful players get selected for the first team.

Choose the correct words to complete the review of a school show.

Our year's got TALENT!

Year Eleven's talent show was [1]**more / much** ambitious [2]**than / as** last year, with a total of fifteen performances. For some reason the audience wasn't [3]**as big as / so big than** last year, but it was still a fun evening.

Alex Clark's band 'SoundScape' played first. Simon didn't sing as [4]**well / good** as he can, but he said he felt [5]**most / more** nervous than usual performing in front of his classmates. We then had some sketches from the drama group. To be honest, I think they went on a bit [6]**too long / long enough** and the audience lost interest. The last act before the break was Emma Mason singing *Hello*. It was as if Adele was in the room. I really think Emma's voice is [7]**good enough / too good** for her to go professional. But the surprise act of the night was Sam Kumar. He started with some impressions of the teachers and he just got [8]**better and better / more and more better** as he went on. By the end everyone was laughing [9]**more loud / so loudly** you couldn't hear his jokes.

Complete the post with the correct form of the words in brackets. You need to add extra words to some answers.

A laugh a minute

Did you hear about the teenager who wanted an iPad? Look at what her parents gave her! 😂😂😂

Her parents must have a good sense of humour. So that got me thinking – what's [1] .... (funny) thing you've seen recently?

Max — Add message | Report

That must have been [2] .... (disappointing) day of that kid's life! Imagine the look on her face! But [3] .... (even / good) than that was what I saw yesterday. A guy from my school who thinks he's [4] .... (good) at everything was walking and texting at the same time. There was a lampost just ahead of him. [5] .... (close) he got to it, [6] .... (convinced) I was that he'd look up and walk round. I called out to warn him, but he [7] .... (not / near) to hear me. The next thing I saw was the guy walking straight into the lampost! He walked away [8] .... (as / quick) he could and pretended nothing had happened. But he definitely looked [9] .... (lot / cool) than he usually does!

Complete the second sentence so that it has a similar meaning to the first sentence, using the word given. Use between two and five words, including the word given.

1 You are a more fluent speaker of Russian than me.
SPEAK
You .... than I do.

2 We didn't leave early enough to catch the school bus.
TOO
We .... to catch the school bus.

3 There's no difference in height between Max and his sister.
AS
Max .... his sister.

4 He's the kindest person I know.
ANYONE
I .... than him.

5 Jo is by far the fastest runner on the team.
CAN
Jo .... the rest of the team.

6 As smartphones become cheaper, they get more accessible.
THE
The cheaper smartphones become, ... get.

USE OF ENGLISH 2

Complete the table.

	adjective	noun
1	fit	....
2	deaf	....
3	childish	....
4	different	....
5	lazy	....
6	....	fashion
7	....	hope
8	....	enthusiasm

Complete the notices with the correct form of the words. There is one word you don't need in each set.

1 athlete   enthusiasm   impress

Feeling the need for a challenge? Want to improve your .... ability?

Come to our .... new Leisure Centre on Market Street.

---

2 artist   science   vision

Tickets now available for the Brainwave Festival

See groundbreaking presentations by the best .... brains on the planet.

Join us for a wide range of musical and .... events.

---

3 fool   happy   move

Wanted: your worst pictures!

A picture of your dad doing his robot .... on the dance floor?

You feeling .... in fancy dress?

Share and we'll pay £25 for the best – or worst! – snaps.

🔊 1.5 Listen to five short conversations and complete the sentence for each one.

One of the speakers doesn't have much sense of:

1 ....   **4** ....

2 ....   **5** ....

3 ....

Read the article and complete it with the correct form of the word in capitals.

Lost and Found ✕

My last school had a very good reputation for music, with a
¹ .... orchestra and choir.   **SUCCESS**

I was never much good at music, but I enjoyed singing. That was until the music teacher heard me.

'Who is that with the truly
² .... voice? Please   **DREAD**
don't sing, just mime the words.' And on that day I stopped singing. I wasn't
at all ³ .... with   **COMFORT**
people hearing my voice.

But about a year later, I came across a singing class for non-singers called 'You can speak, so you can sing.' We started just by playing with different sounds. Working in a
⁴ .... way helped   **REPEAT**
to build our ⁵ ....   **CONFIDENT**
I've now done a singing course with the same tutor and it's been great working
in a ⁶non- ....
environment. So the big question is,   **COMPETE**
'Has it made a difference?' Well, I'm no opera singer, but there's certainly been
an ⁷ .... And the   **IMPROVE**
most important thing is that it's made
music ⁸ .... to   **ACCESS**
me. I feel I lost my voice and now I've found it.

SPEAKING

🔊 1.6 **Listen to five students. What went wrong for them in the speaking task? Match the speakers (1–5) with the phrases (A–E).**

A not using a range of language   Speaker 1 ....

B not comparing both photos   Speaker 2 ....

     Speaker 3 ....

C asking the teacher for vocabulary   Speaker 4 ....

D hesitating a lot   Speaker 5 ....

E asking the other student questions

Make notes to compare photos A and B.

How might the people be feeling about their chosen activity?

Similar	Different
location	number of people

Feeling:

....
....
....

Complete one student's answer to the task with these words/phrases. There are two words or phrases you do not need.

achievement anxious celebrating better differences direction showing energetic show similar similarity whereas

Both pictures **1**................................. people outside, standing on the top of a hill. The pictures are **2**................................. because they both show young people out walking during the day. Another **3**................................. is that they are all wearing practical clothes like jeans, shorts and boots that are suitable for hill walking. In both pictures, the weather looks dry, although there are some clouds in the sky. One of the main **4**................................. is that the first picture shows a group, while in the second one there's a girl alone. In the first picture, you can't see the people's faces, **5**................................. in the second one you can see the girl's expression. The people in the group seem to be enjoying themselves. They have their hands up in the air, as if they are **6**................................. . Perhaps they have a sense of **7**................................. after climbing up the hill. But in the second picture, the girl seems more tense. She could be feeling **8**................................. about getting lost. Perhaps she doesn't have a very good sense of **9**................................. . I'd say that the group in the first picture are definitely having a **10**................................. time than the girl.

Read the question. How could you compare these pictures?

Why do you think these people have chosen to do these activities?

Record yourself answering the question in Ex 4. Time yourself and try to speak for one minute.

WRITING

a review

Do you know how to write a good review? Try the quiz and find out.

Get writing right! ✓

1 What's the most important aim of a review? To:

A entertain the reader ☐

B help the reader make a choice ☐

C give the reader instructions ☐

2 What three things might put the reader off?

A a chatty and informal style ☐	D one solid paragraph of text ☐
B a lot of repetition ☐	E an interesting title ☐
C a variety of language ☐	F very formal language ☐

3 Number the review content in order (1–4).

A the reviewer's recommendation ....

B brief details about the subject ....

C the reviewer's experience ....

D more information / examples ....

Read the extracts from six reviews. Match the subjects (A–F) with the extracts (1–6).

A	music festival	....	D diving course	....
B	games design day	....	E language course	....
C	art class	....	F dance lesson	....

1 The cost of the paper and paint isn't included. For a half-day course, ...

2 The tutor teaches you the steps really slowly, so .... much previous experience.

3 The range is amazing. If you fancy trying Mandarin, Japanese or Russian, I .... this centre.

4 It's a great place to check out new bands. If you get a chance to go next year, you ....

5 If you're already a strong swimmer and you want to be pushed out of your comfort zone, ...

6 You progress really quickly to create great graphics. The coding is complex, though, so .... a beginner.

Complete the extracts in Ex 2 with these phrases. Separate the words and add the correct punctuation.

itsnotreallyworththemoney   itsperfectforanyonewithout   itswellworthtrying
iwouldn'trecommenditto   thoroughlyrecommend   wontregretit

Complete the compound adjectives. Some words (1–6) can be used more than once.

class   conditioned   day   fashioned   inclusive
known   lit   organised

1 air- ....

2 all- ....

3 brightly- ....

4 first- ....

5 old- ....

6 well- ....

Choose the noun in each group that doesn't go with the adjective.

1 three-day festival / instructor / ticket

2 all-inclusive location / ticket / package

3 brightly-lit studio / theatre / atmosphere

4 well-known performer / presenter / audience

5 air-conditioned transport / activity / bus /

6 well-organised event / cost / workshop

7 first-class service / problem / accommodation

Replace the highlighted text with these more interesting descriptions.

absolutely delicious   extremely dull   really dreadful
totally terrifying   truly fascinating

1 The food they serve is very nice.

2 The talk was really interesting.

3 The organisation of the event was quite bad.

4 I found the speaker very boring.

5 The rollercoaster ride was very scary.

Read the task. Write your review in 140–190 words, using an appropriate style.

TEENAGE ✗ EXCHANG

Tell us what you think!

We organise trips for groups of international students. We're looking for reviews of events that young people can go to in your area.

Tell us about an event you have been to. In your review describe your experience, positive or negative, and say whether or not you would recommend it to people of your age.

UNIT CHECK

1 🔊 **1.7 Listen and complete the anecdote. Use full and short forms as in the recording.**

So I [1]........................... home and this girl [2]........................... my name. The next thing I [3]........................... she's there in front of me and she [4]........................... . She [5]........................... to know where her iPad is. And I [6]........................... to her, "I [7]........................... you. What [8]...........................?" So then she just [9]........................... . And I [10]........................... there thinking, "What [11]...........................?"

2 Complete the blog post with one word in each gap.

Putting the **sense** in **sensitive**

I've just started a novel and it's [1]........................... silliest thing I've ever read. All the girl characters are a [2]........................... more sensitive [3]........................... the boys. They're always saying and doing the right thing. As I read, I got more and [4]........................... frustrated. Why wasn't the writer imaginative [5]........................... to create true-to-life characters? Everyone knows that the [6]........................... interesting stories are when characters do the unexpected. If the next part of the book is [7]........................... bad as the first, I'll give up. Life's [8]........................... short to read bad books!

3 Rewrite the sentences using the word given. Use between two and five words, including the word given.

1 Your marks are improving as you practise more.
   BETTER
   The more you practise, ... are getting.

2 The sports challenge was far more difficult than the reviewer said.
   AS
   The sports challenge .... the reviewer said.

3 I'm not nearly as adventurous as you.
   FAR
   You .... me.

4 You're too young to go and see a band by yourself.
   ENOUGH
   You .... to go and see a band by yourself.

5 There's no better time to pick up a bargain.
   THE
   This .... to pick up a bargain.

4 Complete the online article with the correct form of these verbs.

add to   get across   miss out   put off
take off   try out

Have you ever smelled a food advert or heard your dinner?

Don't be [1]........................... by these ideas – businesses are using multi-sensory techniques to [2]........................... their message .... Food companies have been [3]........................... 'smell-vertising' – advertising through the sense of smell. A UK company wanted a new potato product to [4]........................... in the market. It installed special adverts at bus stops. You pressed a button and it gave off the smell of a warm baked potato straight from the oven.

Restaurants [5]........................... also .... their customers' experience. Some spray scents just as a dish is served to connect the customer with positive memories. And your other senses don't need to [6]........................... . One UK chef is famous for a fish dish made to look like a beach; as you eat, you listen to the sounds of the sea through an MP3 player.

5 Write the words with the correct suffix. Make any necessary spelling changes.

1 **verb → noun:**
   achieve → ....
   excite → ....

2 **verb → noun:**
   differ → ....
   exist → ....

3 **adjective → noun:**
   lazy → ....
   tired → ....

4 **verb → adjective:**
   compete → ....
   create → ....

5 **noun → adjective:**
   enthusiasm → ....
   sympathy → ....

6 **noun → adjective:**
   knowledge → ....
   change → ....

2 On the bucket list

READING

Complete the sentences with these pairs of words.

awe-inspiring / live up to expectations   boom / freak out   exotic / superb
feature / have access to   medieval / appeal to   vast / incredible

1 We've had a .... in tourists since a celebrity came to live near here. They all .... when they get near the house and start taking selfies.

2 The advert described the waterfall as an .... sight, but I was disappointed. It didn't ....

3 More and more adventure movies are filmed in .... locations with .... scenery.

4 A tour of the .... castle in the Old Town might not .... children and teenagers.

5 I love visiting places that .... in my favourite films. To .... these locations brings back all the best scenes.

6 Watching the sunset over the .... mountain peaks was an .... sight.

Read the article on page 15 quickly. Which would be the best category for it?

A travel tips

B true-life stories

C family and lifestyle

Read the article again. Match the questions (1–10) with the teenagers (A–D).

Which teenager:

1 hasn't told their parents that they don't want to go on the family holiday? ....

2 complains of being bored during recent holidays? ....

3 mentions a difficult relationship with someone near their age? ....

4 received a very strong negative reaction to the idea of missing the family holiday? ....

5 asks if they can stay with a relative over the summer? ....

6 suggests their parents don't have confidence in their behaviour? ....

7 refers to activities done to please others? ....

8 wanted to earn some money during their holiday? ....

9 mentions using technology to contact people when away from home? ....

10 states that their parents haven't agreed on whether to accept their holiday plans? ....

Extend

Find phrases in the article for these definitions. (Clue! All the answers contain the words *in* or *out*.)

1 take part (introduction) ....

2 choose not to do (something) (text A) ....

3 don't include me (text A) ....

4 makes arrangements for (text B) ....

5 be about to experience something enjoyable (text B) ....

6 asked if it's OK with (someone) (text B) ....

7 relax (text C) ....

8 undecided (text C) ....

Complete the conversation with the correct form of the phrases in Ex 4. There is one phrase you do not need.

A: I've been thinking about the summer and I wanted to ask you something.

B: Oh?

A: Well, I'd like someone of my own age to have fun and [1] .... with. So how do you feel about [2] .... with our family holiday?

B: Wow! I don't know what to say!

A: Well, we've booked an amazing house right on the beach. There's lots to do there, so if you came, you [3] ....

B: It sounds fantastic, but [4] .... you .... your parents yet?

A: Yes, and they're more than happy. They've agreed [5] .... all your travel arrangements.

B: That is so kind. And of course I would love to, but my parents would never say yes. They like us to be together over the summer, so I can't [6] .... of my family holiday, I'm afraid.

A: But I really want you to come. Listen, I won't [7] .... straightaway. Just ask your mum and dad. You never know, they might say yes.

2.1 **Listen and check your answers to Ex 5.**

Do I *have* to come with you?

Summer holidays are all about family time and sharing experiences. But what happens when one child in the family doesn't want to join in? We hear from four young people with different ideas for the perfect summer break.

A Michelle, 16, USA

My parents own a small summer house on the New Jersey coast. We've been going there since I was a kid. I have amazing memories of swimming, fishing and camping on the beach there. But that's been my vacation: the same two weeks in August, the same destination. So this year, I thought to myself, 'Is there any way I can opt out of this?' In the last couple of years, the trip has been pretty tedious because it's tough finding fun things to do. So I took a deep breath and said to my mom, 'I was thinking of working over the summer, just to top up my allowance. So maybe count me out for the vacation.' I had no idea what was coming next. My mom freaked out. Her final words were, 'No way!' So, New Jersey here I come.

B Lily, 17, UK

In our house, planning the family holiday is a two-person project. My dad sorts out the travel and accommodation, and mum plans the day-to-day activities. She tries to come up with things that will appeal to everyone but that's tricky. I'm the eldest at seventeen, but there's quite a gap between me and my sister, who's thirteen, and my brother, who's just seven. Last year, I found myself at a space museum to keep my brother smiling and a farm for my animal-mad sister! This year I'm hoping to be in for a treat. My best friend has invited me to spend a fortnight in Greece with her parents. She's an only child and so needs someone of her own age to go away with. The only problem is I haven't checked it out with my family yet. I'm trying to pick the right moment …

C Ritchie, 15, USA

Usually, it's just mom, dad, my sister and me on vacation together, and that's always worked pretty well. This year, my aunt Ellen and her family are joining us from Canada. The plan is to rent a place for both families to chill out together. The problem is that time with Ellen is anything but relaxing. She's competitive and bossy. She's always comparing my sister and me with her kids. And I have never gotten along too well with my cousins, even though we're all in our teens. Today Ellen emailed over a list of chores for the rented house. Week one, I do the dishes and take out the garbage. When I saw the list, I said to dad, 'You call this a vacation? Can I please go to grandma's instead?' Dad said yes and mom said maybe so things are still up in the air.

D Ed, 13, UK

I get on well with my family when we're away, but I miss my friends. We message each other all the time but it's not the same. Last year my friend, Adam, went to an activity camp. He posted all the different things he was getting up to. Cool stuff like kite-surfing and canoeing, as well as team sports and days out. I showed mum and dad all his posts in the hope they would let me go too. All they said was, 'Maybe when you're older.' I mentioned it again last week, but I'm still not allowed to go. My parents are convinced I'm too young to be away without them. Maybe they think I'll do something stupid. So now Adam is off to the camp again. It's so unfair.

GRAMMAR

past tenses

Complete the sentences with the correct ending (A or B).

1 I first went abroad

    A twice already this year.

    B two years ago, when I was thirteen.

2 While I was taking a selfie,

    A a girl suddenly put her face in the picture.

    B a girl was putting her face in the picture.

3 He didn't really join in. He

    A was always playing computer games instead of enjoying the trip.

    B 's been playing computer games instead of enjoying the trip.

4 We were going to get tickets for the water park

    A and it was great fun.

    B but it was closed on Sunday.

5 Dad was due to join us for the second week

    A but he was ill and couldn't make it.

    B and he loved the area too.

6 There was no one to help us. We got to the hotel after midnight and

    A the receptionist went home.

    B the receptionist had already gone home.

7 I was happy, but really tired after

    A we've been exploring the city all day.

    B we'd been exploring the city all day.

Complete the sentences with the past form of these verbs.

| going to + skype / be   read / miss / have to   swim / step |
| take off / wait   used + spend / would + collect   walk / crash |

1 We .... along the beach when suddenly a huge wave .... over the rocks.

2 By the time the plane actually ...., we .... on the runway for an hour.

3 I .... home, but the signal in the hostel .... hopeless.

4 My sister .... already .... out to the rock by the time I .... into the water.

5 I .... on the bus, so I .... my stop and .... walk 5 km back to the campsite.

6 As I young child, I .... a week with my aunt and uncle near the coast. I .... shells and stones from our walks along the beach.

Find two sentences in which 'would' can replace 'used to'.

1 I look really different from my passport picture. I used to have long hair.

2 We used to build a campfire every night and tell ghost stories.

3 We have a house on the mainland now, but we used to live on a small island.

4 My family and all our cousins used to stay in a big farmhouse every summer.

5 My aunt has been all over Europe. She used to work as a tour guide.

Match the sentence halves (1–6) with (A–F).

1 I used to be petrified of flying,

2 We couldn't believe how crowded the Tokyo underground was,

3 My friend doesn't want to come on the adventure holiday,

4 I hated the cold showers at the campsite at first,

5 I couldn't eat the first curry I tried in Thailand,

6 The tourist season used to finish in September,

    A as she isn't used to cycling long distances.

    B but I'm not so scared of it now.

    C as I'm not used to eating spicy food.

    D but I got used to them quite quickly.

    E but people seem to travel all year now.

    F but we're getting used to it now.

Complete the chatroom posts with the correct form of the verbs. Use short forms where possible.

| **Ali** | Add message \| Report |

I **1** .... (go) to Croatia last month to stay with a girl I met online, Nika. I **2** .... (never/travel) abroad without my parents before and I really **3** .... (miss) them. Nika and I **4** .... (not/get on) from Day 1. It was strange because we **5** .... (write) to each other for ages and we seemed to like the same things. I **6** .... (be due/stay) three weeks and I lasted only one! 😆

| **Tanya** | Add message \| Report |

Last summer holidays I **7** .... (go/have) a week in Boston with my best friend's family. I **8** .... (look forward) to it for ages, but then suddenly my parents said no. They **9** .... (used/have) us all together over the summer. I **10** .... (already/make) loads of holiday plans, but dad **11** .... (not think) it was fair on my brother! 😖

VOCABULARY

travel anecdotes and apps

1 Complete the conversations with the correct form of a phrasal verb with 'up'.

1 A: Where are you going all .... like that? You normally wear jeans and a hoodie.

B: We're going to a wedding. I begged my mum to let me wear jeans, but she said we had to .... everyone's expectations and look smart.

2 A: Have you seen this competition for the trip of a lifetime?

B: No, what do you have to do?

A: .... a slogan to go with this travel ad.

B: But the place in the picture looks really ordinary. It (not) .... the idea of luxury or adventure.

3 A: Did you persuade your parents to let you go to the music festival?

B: I tried several times, but they said no, so I .... in the end.

A: So what will you do?

B: I .... probably .... watching it online.

2 Choose the correct answers to complete the sentences.

1 He's .... the .... because he's just got A-grades in all his exams.
(moon, over, above, planet)

2 I can't wait to go round the world. Travel is so .... on the .... of things I want to do.
(timetable, high, important, list)

3 Hearing the match had been cancelled left us all feeling .... in the ....
(low, down, rubbish, dumps)

4 We'd never heard such amazing guitar playing from a young kid. We were just .... by his talent.
(exploded, away, blown, up)

5 As soon as I saw the new phone, I .... in .... with it. I knew I had to have it – and soon!
(dropped, like, love, fell)

6 Changing colleges was one of the hardest things I've ever done. I didn't know where to go or who to make friends with, but slowly I've .... into the .... of things.
(swing, got, balance, become)

3 🔊 **2.2** Listen to six people answering questions. Complete the questions they are answering with the idioms from Ex 2.

1 Why are you so .... ?

2 What made you .... it?

3 How long did it take .... ?

4 What was it about their performance that .... ?

5 What's happened to make you .... ?

6 What's .... for the summer holiday?

4 Complete the extracts from an article on holidays. For each gap, use a word from A and a word from B.

A cheap extremely make (x2) package

B helpful reservations sure tours travel

Holiday highs and lows ✈

I was planning a trip earlier this year. I'm a student without much money, so I was over the moon to come across an app for **1**... . With World4less you can **2**... for flights and accommodation of course, but the app is for people under eighteen, so the holidays and **3**... are to places that appeal to younger people. The app is constantly checking prices so you can **4**... you're getting the best deal. It was **5**... in saving me time and money.

A enter improve keeps takes travelling

| **B** all the details a record light |
| my travel experience such a long time |

I'm hopeless at **6**... . I always pack at least two big suitcases. It drives my dad mad because it **7**... to collect my luggage after a flight. Imagine how I felt when we arrived in the south of Spain last month, but my bags ended up in South Africa! It was a nightmare filling in the lost luggage forms. You had to **8**... of what was in the bags in three different forms. How am I supposed to remember? Who **9**... of what they put in their suitcase the night before? Maybe taking just a backpack would **10**... !

LISTENING

🔊 2.3 **Listen to a young person talking about a book club. Match the book titles (1–4) with the places (A–F). There are two places you do not need.**

A Zimbabwe

B Australia

C Spain

D Cuba

E India

F Greenland

1 Life of Pi ....

2 The Old Man and the Sea ....

3 First Light ....

4 The Shadow of the Wind ....

🔊 2.4 **Read the questions and underline the key words. Listen again and choose the correct answer (A, B or C).**

1 What does Samira say about the majority of reading lists?

  A They appear on too many websites.

  B They are based on age or topic.

  C They have books for people of all ages.

2 What does Samira say about the books in her reading list?

  A They are all based in different locations.

  B They all have travel as their main topic.

  C They are suitable for holiday reading.

3 Samira's group selected the order of books on their list by

  A alphabetical order.

  B geographical location.

  C group and personal choice.

4 What does Samira say about *Life of Pi* and *The Old Man and The Sea*?

  A They are both very exciting stories.

  B They weren't equally popular with the group.

  C They both feature people and wildlife.

5 When asked about the book *First Light*, Samira says

  A she wants to avoid telling people too much about the story.

  B she didn't like the characters or the story very much.

  C she's already been to the place where the book is set.

6 Why was *The Shadow of the Wind* Samira's favourite book?

  A It wasn't as long as some of the other books.

  B It helped her with her language skills.

  C The story was extremely exciting.

7 For Samira, what's the most important thing about her reading list?

  A You can read books in different languages.

  B You can find out about locations around the world.

  C You can see the world through other people's eyes.

Extend

Choose the correct words to complete the phrases.

1 be taken to the far **areas** / **corners** of the globe

2 go on a round-the-world **excursion** / **trip**

3 **pack** / **put** a suitcase

4 be a great **beginning** / **starting** point

5 join somebody on an **expedition** / **experiment**

6 **have** / **get** adventures

7 get a **globe** / **global** view

Complete the conversation with the correct form of the phrases from Ex 3.

A: Oh, I'm bored. I wish we could just
¹ .... with enough stuff for a month, get on a plane and start
² .... somewhere exciting.

B: I know. I'd love to travel more. Wouldn't it be brilliant to ³ .... on a
⁴ .... , visiting every country on the planet?

A: Oh, that's my dream! You know where would
⁵ .... ? The Arctic.

B: The Arctic? You'd begin your journey of a lifetime in snow and ice?

A: Absolutely. It's just so different. Imagine
⁶ .... scientists
.... to find out all about the area. There's an international research station there, so you'd really ⁷ .... by meeting people of different nationalities.

B: Hmm, I was thinking more of surfing in Australia!

USE OF ENGLISH 1

Find and correct six mistakes in the sentences. Tick any sentences that are correct.

1 I'll never forget sitting round the fire with the moon shining down on us.

2 That was an airline that lost all our luggage.

3 Where's best place you've ever visited?

4 You find out so much about a place if you explore on the foot.

5 The travel apps we bought weren't particularly helpful.

6 New York's Fifth Avenue is the perfect destination for shoppers.

7 Have you ever been to Netherlands?

8 I love the travel. I wish I could go abroad more often.

9 We stood for ages listening to a street musician playing the guitar.

10 It's great to get away for the weekend once in the while.

Choose the correct words to complete the sentences.

1 Travel is no longer just for **a / an / the / –** wealthy. Access to **a / an / the / –** other countries is open to nearly everyone.

2 The guide offered **a / an / the / –** bus or **a / an / the / –** walking tour. I'm glad we chose **a / an / the / –** walking tour. We saw so much.

3 Working in **a / an / the / –** travel industry, my brother goes abroad several times **a / an / the / –** month.

4 Diego is **a / an / the / –** boy I was telling you about. He's **a / an / the / –** tutor at the sports camp we stayed at.

5 **A / An / The / –** Swiss are known for producing some of **a / an / the / –** best chocolate.

6 I've tried skiing **a / an / the / –** couple of times, but I don't think I'll ever be good enough to ski in **a / an / the / –** Alps.

🔊 2.5 Complete the travel announcements with 'a', 'an', 'the' or zero article (–). Then listen and check your answers.

1 Ladies and gentlemen, we have just landed at .... Pulkovo Airport in .... St Petersburg, where .... local time is 20:30 and .... temperature is 6°C. We hope you have enjoyed your flight with .... International Airlines and we wish you .... very safe journey to your final destination.

2 .... train on .... platform one is .... 8.22 service to .... York. .... train is made up of six coaches. .... first coach, coach A, is for .... first-class ticket holders only.

3 This is .... security announcement. Please do not leave .... luggage unattended in .... station at any time. .... left-luggage facility is located on level two. .... facility is open twenty-four hours a day.

Complete the article with 'a', 'an', 'the' or zero article (–).

TRAVEL: MAKING PASSPORTS PRETTY

The majority of passports are in fairly conservative colours: dark blue, burgundy or black. But now [1].............. Scandinavians have rejected that tradition and have made their passports pretty.

Norway's latest passports have [2].............. range of brightly-coloured covers: white, turquoise or red. [3].............. Oslo design studio won [4].............. competition to redesign the document. They took as their inspiration [5].............. 'Norwegian Landscapes'. And they hid [6].............. secret inside. If you put a page of [7].............. passport under ultraviolet light, the landscape changes and [8].............. Northern Lights suddenly appear.

The Finnish passport also reveals a playful love of [9].............. design. It features [10].............. moose on the bottom of each page. If you're feeling bored while waiting for your flight, flip the pages quickly and watch [11].............. animal stroll across the passport.

Are these [12].............. coolest passports ever? Possibly. But one thing is certain. They will bring [13].............. smile to their owners as they travel around [14].............. world. And maybe even to [15].............. airport security officer at passport control. Now that would be a pretty sight.

USE OF ENGLISH 2

Choose the correct words to complete the sentences.

1 Global **heating / warming** is an enormous international challenge. It is thought to be the cause of a number of natural **disasters / disastrous**.

2 Many iconic sites such as the Great Wall of China are struggling to cope **from / with** the effects of mass **tourists / tourism**.

3 Litter can cause severe **damage / wrong** to the environment and **get / have** a huge impact on wildlife, so **remember / think** twice before you drop an empty packet or bottle.

4 I finally **achieved / succeeded** my goal of running a marathon **in / on** my third attempt.

5 **To / At** the first sign of bad weather, turn back. It's **none / no** use putting yourself in danger.

Replace the highlighted text with these words or phrases.

---

collapsing   done a lot of harm   foreign visitors
make a living   quality of life   run into problems
taking such a risk   tourist season

A report has shown that a number of houses along the British coast are in danger of ¹falling into the sea. Severe storms have ²created damage to the rocks which has resulted in coastal erosion in several areas. At the time most owners bought their dream house by the sea, they didn't realise they were ³putting themselves in so much danger.

The ⁴period for visitors in many cities has extended beyond just the summer with ⁵people from abroad flocking to major capitals across the whole year. This allows more local people to ⁶earn money from tourism, but also puts their city under pressure. Many places have ⁷had difficulties balancing the need for local housing and building new tourist accommodation. Some locals complain that such high levels of tourism affects their ⁸general wellbeing.

Extend

Which preposition fits with the words/phrases in each set?

1 deal / cope / disagree   ....
2 congratulate / decide / concentrate   ....
3 be scared / ashamed / afraid   ....
4 ask / pay / prepare   ....
5 complain / care / worry   ....

🔊 2.6 Listen to five short recordings. Complete the sentences with the correct verb and preposition from Ex 3.

1 The man forgot .... his food.
2 The boy .... the rollercoaster.
3 The girl .... her sister about their packing.
4 The woman said she .... sharks.
5 The family couldn't .... what to do for the day.

Read the blog post and decide which answer (A, B, C or D) best fits each gap.

I'm not a tourist. **I live here.**

My family has lived on the coast of Cornwall in south-west England for generations. My grandfather was a fisherman, taking ¹...... out on the sea every day to make a living. Once the main local employer, the fishing industry ²...... problems and has now been partly replaced by tourism. Although not top of the list for many ³...... visitors, Cornwall attracts thousands of UK holidaymakers every year. Of course, they ⁴...... money to the area, but they can also ⁵...... a lot of harm to the local environment. Many people argue that tourism ⁶...... jobs and this is true, up to a point. However, much of the employment lasts only for the main tourist season, not the whole year. For many small communities, a change in population also has a ⁷...... impact on their identity. People from outside Cornwall have bought second homes to stay in over the summer. This affects the locals' quality of ⁸...... – our community is packed with tourists in summer, but like a ghost town in winter.

1	**A** adventures	**B** risks	**C** dangers	**D** problems
2	**A** ran over	**B** ran onto	**C** ran through	**D** ran into
3	**A** foreign	**B** exotic	**C** national	**D** local
4	**A** bring into	**B** bring up	**C** bring in	**D** bring about
5	**A** take	**B** make	**C** get	**D** do
6	**A** provides	**B** employs	**C** contributes	**D** gives
7	**A** wide	**B** huge	**C** large	**D** vast
8	**A** livelihood	**B** life	**C** lifestyle	**D** living

SPEAKING

1 Match the questions (1–8) with the topic areas (A–D). There are two questions for each topic area.

1 What do you usually do at weekends? ......

2 Do you enjoy camping? ......

3 How do you get to school every day? ......

4 Where do you think you will be this time next year? ......

5 Who do you live with? ......

6 Can you play a musical instrument or sing? ......

7 Which country have you visited that you liked most? ......

8 What would your ideal job be? ......

A future plans

B home and daily routine

C free time and entertainment

D holidays and travel

2 🔊 2.7 Listen to four students talking. Which question in Ex 1 do they answer?

3 🔊 2.8 Listen again and match the students (1–4) with the descriptions (A–D).

A gave a good answer with a personal example

B wasn't very polite when asking for clarification

C gave a very short answer with no interesting information

D gave a good answer with a reason for their opinion

1 Student 1 ......

2 Student 2 ......

3 Student 3 ......

4 Student 4 ......

4 Choose the correct words to complete the sentences. Which questions in Ex 1 do the sentences answer?

1 I do something active **like / as** swimming or going for a run **before / because** I don't have much time for sport in the week.

2 I think I'd say Canada. I had a skiing holiday there, which was great for me **that / as** I love winter sports.

3 I cycle most days, but I sometimes get a lift with my friend's mum, **for / by** example when it's raining or when I have a lot to carry.

4 I enjoy working with my hands and I love fashion, **since / so** it would be something that uses those skills, **such as / so as** a clothes designer.

5 Complete the useful phrases with these words. There are three words you do not need.

because   catch   honest   repeating   say   sure (x2)
to repeat   true   used

1 I'm sorry, I didn't quite .... that.

2 Would you mind .... that?

3 Sorry, can you .... that again, please?

4 That's an interesting question. I'm not really .... of the answer, but I think I'd say flying is the best way to travel.

5 To be .... , I've never been abroad, but I'd like to go to New Zealand because my favourite movie was filmed there.

6 I .... to love just playing on the beach, but now I prefer spending time in cities.

7 I'm not really .... which school I'll be at, but I'll still be studying English.

6 🔊 2.9 Listen and mark the main stresses in the sentences in Ex 5.

7 🔊 2.10 Listen and answer the questions. Record and check your answers using the list below. Try again if you need to improve on anything.

Have you:

• used vocabulary that is relevant to each question?

• given interesting answers, but not repeated the whole question?

• given reasons for your answers?

• given examples to support your answers?

WRITING

an article

Do you know how to write a good article?
Try the quiz and find out.

Get writing right!

1   What's the main aim of an article?

inform ☐   entertain ☐   both ☐

**2   Tick ✓ the things you'd expect to find in
a good article.**

very formal or technical language	☐
an eye-catching title	☐
a maximum of two paragraphs	☐
questions that address the reader directly	☐
lively, colourful language	☐
an interesting conclusion	☐
a personal example or anecdote	☐
a new paragraph for each topic / event	☐

Join each pair of sentences using the linker
or time expression. Make any necessary tense
and punctuation changes.

1   We finally found a space on the beach. The
sun went in. (after)

2   I found my ticket. The inspector made me
pay again. (by the time)

3   We reached the coast. We ran into the sea.
(as soon as)

4   I was trying to find my friend. I suddenly
spotted her across the square. (before)

5   We had a few arguments. We still had a
great time. (even though)

6   She didn't get back until late. Her flight was
delayed. (because)

7   My brother wasn't well on the last day. We
cancelled the trip. (so)

8   It was such a fantastic place. We've booked
to go there again. (since)

Look at the titles for articles. Which title
would make you want to read the article?
Why?

A   All about my summer holiday

B   I didn't enjoy myself

C   My dream holiday turned nightmare

Which paragraph makes a more interesting introduction to an article
about a holiday? Why?

A   We were all delighted
when my family won a
road trip across the USA.
I thought it was going to
be a great holiday, but we
had quite a few problems.

B   Have you ever heard the
expression 'the trip of a
lifetime'? That's what I
thought I was getting when
my family won a road trip
across the USA. However,
it didn't quite live up to
expectations. Here's why.

Choose the most interesting language to complete the text.

We were **¹driving / cruising** along the motorway – or freeway
as they call it – in the **²hot / burning** sun when suddenly my
phone **³flew / dropped** out of my hand and **⁴fell / crashed**
onto the road. 'Dad! My phone!' I **⁵said / shouted**. Dad
⁶hit the brakes / stopped and **⁷jumped / got** out of the car. By
the time he got back, we could hear the police car **⁸coming /
speeding** up behind us. 'Sir, do you know it's illegal to stop on
the freeway?' the officer asked.

Which conclusion would finish the article better? Why?

A   Taking everything into
account, it was still an
amazing trip. After all,
you need a few negatives
to help you appreciate the
positives.

B   In my view, the officer wasn't
very nice to us and so I won't
go back to the US.

You have seen this announcement on an English-language website.
Write your article in 140–190 words, using an appropriate style.

Have you been on a memorable journey?

What good or bad things happened to you while you
were travelling?

Send us your article and best will be published on our
website next month.

UNIT CHECK

1 Choose the correct words to complete the conversation.

A: Oh, so you're back then.

B: Yes and I ¹**had / 'd had** a great time in Florida. I ²**was about / 'd wanted** to go there for ages.

A: That's good. But how come you ³**weren't messaging / didn't message** me? I ⁴**saw / was seeing** the pictures you posted, but we ⁵**were going / were thinking** to keep in touch by phone.

B: Yeah, sorry. We ⁶**just did / were just doing** different things all the time. Plus I wasn't allowed to keep texting all the time. I ⁷**was always getting / always got** into trouble for staring at my phone!

A: So ⁸**did you make / had you made** any new friends? I saw some people in your pictures that I didn't recognise.

B: I ⁹**met / 've met** this American kid at one of the theme parks. One day, we ¹⁰**had / were having** lunch at a pizza place when he ¹¹**invited / 'd invited** me to stay at his house – next summer some time. How good is that?

A: What happened to our idea of going to an adventure camp next year? We ¹²**'d been planning / used to plan** that for ages. You ¹³**used to / would** be such a good friend and now it's all about this American kid!

B: We are still friends! I just have one new friend. Why can't you ¹⁴**used to / get used to** that?

2 Complete the sentences with 'a', 'an', 'the' or zero article (–).

1 To help the environment, you should take .... international flight only once .... year.

2 .... most enjoyable holidays are those without .... adults.

3 In general, I think .... boys are better at travelling light than .... girls.

4 If you don't explore .... city on .... foot, you miss .... best parts of .... place.

5 .... destination doesn't become more interesting if .... rich and famous go there.

6 .... dream holiday for me has to include lying on .... beach in .... sunshine.

7 When going abroad, you should try to speak .... little of .... local language.

8 That's .... beach we used to play on when we were .... children.

3 Complete the conversations with an idiom from A and a phrasal verb from B. There is one answer you do not need in each group.

| **A** | blown away by   down in the dumps   high on my list |
| | into the swing of things   over the moon |

| **B** | conjure up   dress up   give up   live up to   think up |

1 A: Have you heard about Lisa? She's really .... about losing the match.

   B: I know. Let's try and .... a way of making her feel better.

2 A: Why didn't you download their latest song?

   B: I really wanted to like it. I was so .... their first song, but this one just didn't .... my expectations.

3 A: Why did you decide to .... the dance class?

   B: Oh, I wasn't making any progress and was starting to feel it was a bit too much.

   A: Oh, please come back. You'll soon get .... again.

4 A: Are you going to Kim's party? She wants everyone to come as their favourite film character.

   B: Oh, do we have to ....? That sort of party isn't very ....

4 Replace the highlighted text with these phrases.

a few everyday words   cause severe damage to   have an impact on
have fun   Keep a record of   run into   tan easily

Travel tips

Follow a few simple rules to help you ¹enjoy yourself and stay healthy and safe.

› ²Write down your passport number and any other important information in a separate file.

› Find out who to contact if you ³have problems – the hotel, your travel agent, a doctor or even the police.

› Be careful in the sun. Prolonged exposure can ⁴badly harm the skin, even if you ⁵go brown quickly.

› Even if you don't speak the local language well, learn ⁶some basic vocabulary so that you can say hello, goodbye and thank you.

› Respect the quality of life of the local people and wildlife. Your actions ⁷affect them.

All in a day's work

READING

Complete the email with these words. There is one word you do not need.

collaboration   distractions   drawback
gearing up   pilot scheme   siblings
support   win-win situation

Dear Parents

We are ¹.. for the new term here at City High and I'm delighted to announce a new ².. for Saturday school. It is open to all years and we hope older ³.. will encourage younger brothers and sisters to attend. Students will be working in small groups for longer study periods, without the ⁴.. of everyday school life. It is an opportunity to get extra help with schoolwork, but also focus on those all-important life skills, such as communication and ⁵.. . I see it as a ⁶.. for both the students and the school. I hope you will give the idea your full ⁷.. .

Read the article about school quickly. Who do you think the writer is?

1 one of the inventors of the gadget
2 a journalist who writes about technology
3 the parent of an ill child

Read the article again and choose the best answer (A, B, C or D).

1 In the first paragraph, what is the writer trying to do?
   A generalise about students not liking going to class
   B explain why some students are off sick for long periods
   C get the reader's interest in a new gadget
   D explain the effects of long-term illness on education

2 What does the writer suggest about the inventors of AV1?
   A They understand the importance of social media for young people.
   B Their company name suits the aim of their invention.
   C They have shown a lot of technical skill in their development.
   D They are interested in how teenagers interact in schools.

3 How does the camera on the avatar work?
   A It lets the ill student see the class without being seen.
   B It is activated by the student who is speaking at any time.
   C It allows just the teacher to see the ill student on screen.
   D It gives visual access to the students in the whole school.

4 What does 'this' in line 23 refer to?
   A the use of the student's voice
   B the contributions to the class
   C the use of the robot
   D the position of the robot

5 The avatar has been designed in such a way as to be
   A the same size as the missing student.
   B easily repaired if knocked off the desk.
   C used only indoors during class time.
   D meaningful to the ill student's classmates.

6 Marthe and one of her classmates agree that
   A the avatar should be available to other groups of students.
   B the benefit is that ill students' education is not interrupted.
   C Marthe's health makes life very challenging for everyone.
   D they miss each other when Marthe is away from class.

Extend

Read the definitions and complete the compound adjectives from the article.

1 lasts a long time (introduction): long-..
2 very necessary (para 1): ....-needed
3 an integral part of a gadget (para 2): ....-in
4 made as they happen, as if face-to-face (para 3): real-..
5 the same size as a person (para 4): ....-size
6 resists water (para 4): water-..
7 that you attend every day (para 6): full-..

Off sick, but still at school

What teenager in the world hasn't thought of staying at home on a schoolday and sending an avatar to class instead? But what about young people who want to go to school, but can't? Students who are missing out on lessons because they are in hospital or have a long-term illness. Meet AV1, the avatar that allows students to attend school even when they are off sick.

AV1 is the brainchild of a Norwegian robotics company appropriately named *No Isolation*. Their aim is to help young people who are hospitalised or going through long-term illness at home to feel less lonely. There is a strong social side to school, with young people making new relationships and interacting with the friends they already have. It is very easy for teenagers with health problems to miss out on this much-needed interaction and so become isolated during a difficult period in their lives.

So how does it work? Inside AV1 is a small computer connected to a control card that powers movement and sound. The robot can move from side to side, to follow who is speaking in class, and also tilt its head. An amplifier connected to the microphone and speaker control the sound. The built-in camera allows the ill student visual access to the activity in the classroom. However, the student is not visible to the rest of the class or the teacher. This is to protect their privacy during the time they are unwell.

AV1 is placed on the desk where the student would normally sit in class. They use an app on their tablet or phone to start the robot up and control its movements. Its eyes light up to show the student is ready to start the class. A light on its head indicates the student wants to speak. Real-time contributions to the class are made through the robot with the student's own voice. This and the slightly humanoid appearance of the robot are important features. In the words of Karen Dolva, co-founder of *No Isolation*, 'This is an avatar, so an extension of yourself.' She describes AV1 as 'the eyes and the ears and the voice' of the ill student at school.

The dimensions of AV1 are also important. Although not life-size, the robot represents the ill child in class. It needs to be portable so that the student's classmates can carry the robot from class to class, and around school during breaks and lunch. AV1 is pretty tough, too. It can survive being knocked off the desk and it's water-resistant in case of showers when taken outside. The students who are in school also need to feel they can relate to the avatar. Karen Dolva explains, 'It can't be just a tiny camera because the other kids can't pick it up and take it with them. This is supposed to be their friend.'

When a high school in Norway got the opportunity to pilot the avatar, they jumped at the chance. AV1 was paired with a student called Marthe, who was unable to attend full-time school. According to Marthe herself, 'It is an amazing opportunity for people with challenges similar to those I face to be able to go to school, attend classes, and still know that they will get the rest they need when they have a bad day.' And in the words of one of her classmates, 'Marthe is a ray of sunshine, so of course we miss her when she's not here in person. But we wave at her and talk to her through the robot. The most important thing is that Marthe gets to attend classes and that she is a part of the group, even though her health challenges this.'

Complete the sentences with the compound adjectives from Ex 4. There is one adjective you do not need.

1 My sister has a .... poster of her favourite footballer on her wall.
2 Your phone is only .... so don't try taking pictures with it when you go diving.
3 I'm still at school so I haven't made any .... plans for the future yet.
4 I'm doing a four-year degree, so I'll be in .... education until I'm twenty-two.
5 Who buys a voice recorder nowadays? Everyone uses the .... function on their phone.
6 After three exhausting weeks of exams, we all got some .... rest.

GRAMMAR

the future

Read the sentences and choose the correct meaning.

1 I'm starting Spanish lessons next term.

This **has already been planned** / **hasn't been planned yet**.

2 I'm sure you'll do well in the exam.

This is a **prediction** / **promise**.

3 When does your next class start?

The speaker wants to know about your **plans** / **timetable**.

4 Lucy is off sick today. I'll text her my lesson notes.

The speaker makes the decision to text the lesson notes **before** / **at** the time of speaking.

5 Vicky is playing really well. She's going to make the first team.

This is **just what I feel** / **based on what I know**.

6 Don't ring at six. We'll be eating dinner.

Dinner **will** / **won't** be finished at six o'clock.

7 Let's meet up on Sunday afternoon. I'll have finished my project by then.

My project will be completed **before** / **on** Sunday.

8 By the time we arrive, we'll have been travelling for a whole day.

This looks forward at an action that will be **finished** / **in progress** until a time in the future. The focus is on the **frequency** / **duration** of the action.

9 I'll message you as soon as class finishes.

The verb 'finishes' refers to the **present** / **future**.

Choose the best option (A or B).

1 You've got a text message.

A I'll read it later.

B I'm reading it later.

2 Can I call round at five thirty?

A Better not. I'll be doing my homework then.

B Better not. I'll have done my homework by then.

3 I can't wait for Friday the 22nd.

A We'll have been finishing our exams by then.

B We'll have finished our exams by then.

4 I'm not very hopeful about this match.

A We're unlikely to win.

B We're due to win.

5 Have you been keen on judo for a long time?

A By this May, I'll be doing judo for three years.

B By this May, I'll have been doing judo for three years.

6 What are your plans for the weekend?

A We'll go to a music festival.

B We're going to a music festival.

Complete the conversations with these verb forms. There is one extra answer in each set you do not need.

> Are you working   'm due to start   'll be hanging out
> 'll have been helping   'll have earned   're going

1 **A:** The end of term at last! This time next week, we **¹**.. at the beach.

B: I won't. I **²**.. my summer job on Monday, don't forget.

A: Oh, yes. **³**.. five days a week?

B: Yes, Monday to Friday. But at least I **⁴**.. some money by the end of the summer.

A: Lucky you! I **⁵**.. my dad in his shop for weeks by the time school starts – unpaid!

> 'll be doing   'll have started   'm unlikely to need
> won't have been studying   you make   you will have

2 **A:** What do you think you **⁶**.. in five years' time?

B: I'm not sure, but I guess I **⁷**.. university or college. What about you?

A: I **⁸**.. on a course, I don't think. I have an idea for a business and I **⁹**.. a university degree for it.

B: Sounds interesting! When **¹⁰**.. your first million, don't forget your old classmates!

Choose the correct words to complete the text.

Andy   Add message | Report

Hi! My mum's just got a new job, so **¹we're moving** / **we'll move** to a new area in a month. This means I'm **²unlikely** / **about** to change schools, which I'm pretty nervous about, to be honest. The new term **³will have been starting** / **will have started** by the time I get there and everyone **⁴is due to know** / **will already know** each other. My parents say **⁵I'll make** / **I'm making** friends quickly, but I keep worrying about the first day when I **⁶walk** / **will walk** in to class. Everyone **⁷will be thinking** / **will have been thinking**, 'Here comes the new kid. What's he **⁸out to be** / **going to be** like?'

Vik   Add message | Report

I did exactly the same last term and I was fine. Don't worry – you **⁹will be** / **are due to be** too. The first day is the worst. After you **¹⁰will get** / **get** through that, **¹¹you're feeling** / **you'll feel** more confident. Just be yourself, find one friendly face and I know **¹²you'll be enjoying** / **you're likely to enjoy** your new school in no time!

VOCABULARY

education and work

3.1 Listen to four short recordings. Complete the sentences with these pairs of words.

attendance/grades	discipline/detention
experiment/handout	syllabus/timetable

1 The teacher was setting up an .... and she had a .... to give to the class.

2 The students were talking about .... in the history class and how three classmates got ....

3 The teachers were discussing adding Mandarin to the school .... The man thought it was a good idea, but was concerned about how it would fit in to the ....

4 The teacher was pleased with her student's .... and she also praised her for an improvement in her ....

Find four words or phrases about work in each spiral. Write them in the correct list.

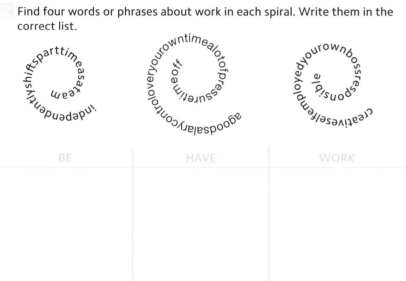

BE	HAVE	WORK

Choose the correct words to complete the text.

Hi, I'm Ali and thanks for inviting me to your careers day. I'm **¹an unemployed / a self-employed** costume designer in the theatre. If you think that sounds like a job with long holidays and lots of time **²down / off**, think again! I'm not only **³responsibility / responsible** for the designs, but also the schedule and budget. I need to work both **⁴independently / independent** and **⁵like / as** a team. People sometimes confuse **⁶being / having** your own boss with working **⁷shifts / part-time**. My job is very much full-time. That means I **⁸have / work** a lot of pressure, but I also have control **⁹over / on** my own time. I can work when I like, provided I get the job done. And I need to do that to have a good **¹⁰money / salary** of course!

Complete the phrasal verbs.

1 It's hard to keep .... hobbies before exam time.

2 I was off school so I need to make .... what I missed.

3 On Saturdays, I catch .... sleep after a week at school.

4 For our class project we came .... the idea of a blog.

5 Karin's new to the club, but she gets .... everyone.

6 I got off my bike on the big hill. I just ran .... energy.

Extend

Match the phrasal verbs with the correct meanings (A–F).

Nobody can **¹measure up to** my sister when it comes to being naughty. She can **²get away with** all sorts of bad behaviour. My little brother adores her and **³goes along with** all of her bad ideas... but of course, he usually gets stuck with the blame.

Me, I don't **⁴go in for** that kind of behaviour at all. I've **⁵given up on** trying to stop them, though, as long as they **⁶keep out of** my private life!

A agree with or support ....

B avoid / stay away from ....

C be as good /skilled as ....

D do often / enjoy ....

E not be punished for ....

F stop hoping for change ....

LISTENING

1 🔊 3.2 Listen to Speaker 1 talking about a scheme for teenagers and their parents. What do you think the name of the scheme is?

A Take time off with your teen
B Take your teen to work
C Take your parent to class
D Take time to go on holiday

2 🔊 3.3 Listen to all five speakers and complete the information.

Speaker	What type of work / job does the relative do?	Where did the speaker spend the day?
1	local government	office
2		
3		
4		
5		

3 🔊 3.4 Listen again. Match the speakers (1–5) with what they say (A–H). There are three extra options you do not need.

A I feel proud that I've taken part in the scheme.
B I was disappointed they didn't know how to treat someone my age.
C I wish my parents had told me what to expect.
D I learned something useful for when I want to get a job.
E I might consider doing the same job as one of my parents.
F I wouldn't recommend the scheme to other teenagers.
G I was surprised by the number of activities in the job.
H I was hoping to learn something new, but didn't.

Speaker 1 ....
Speaker 2 ....
Speaker 3 ....
Speaker 4 ....
Speaker 5 ....

Extend

4 Match the phrases in bold in the sentences (1–8) with the meanings (A–H).

1 It **turned out** a lot better than I expected.
2 I wasn't **stuck with** my dad all the time.
3 Seeing her in her place of work really **opened my eyes**.
4 The team **talked me through** the key stages.
5 My mum **dropped** me **off** at reception.
6 A woman **came over to** me.
7 We did **have a go** at a taste test.
8 She'd like one of us to **follow in her footsteps**.

A do the same (e.g. job) as someone before you did
B have a result that wasn't anticipated
C try / attempt
D take someone to a place by car and leave them there
E have to do something even though you don't want to
F explain in detail
G approach
H make someone realise something

5 Complete the four chats with the correct form of the phrases in Ex 4.

(1)

> Both my parents are surgeons.

Wow! Do you think you
¹ ....
and go into medicine?

> I don't think so.
> I ² .... at
> watching a simple operation
> online and I was nearly sick!

(2)

> What did you think of the careers day?

I enjoyed talking to the people
from the games company. It really
³ .... about
the range of jobs on offer.

> Yes, it was great that they
> ⁴ ....
> all the different possibilities.

(3)

> How was the party?

OK, but I ⁵ ....
with someone I didn't know
very well all evening. She just
⁶ .... me
as soon as I got there.

(4)

> Thanks again for ⁷ ....
> in town yesterday. I thought I was
> going to be late for the match, but it
> all ⁸ .... OK.

No problem. I'm happy to
give you a lift any time.

USE OF ENGLISH 1

1 🔊 3.5 **Listen to six short recordings. Choose the correct countable or uncountable nouns to complete the sentences.**

armchair / furniture	luggage / suitcases	money / pounds
packets / rubbish	skills / training	travel / journey

1 The man says the .... are too heavy to lift.

2 The man isn't happy about the .... that has been left on the bus.

3 The woman is asking if her friend had a good ....

4 The man thinks their pet shouldn't be sitting on an
....

5 The woman can't understand where his .... has gone.

6 The girl is talking about the .... that she thinks are important.

2 **Find the extra word in each sentence.**

1 I haven't given no much thought to future careers.

2 It's a shame that only a few many students attended the course.

3 I'm not very hungry so I only want a little bit pasta.

4 A job in IT gives you plenty of many opportunities.

5 Every few student improved their grades last term.

6 I got up late so I had a little time for breakfast before I left.

3 **Choose the correct words to complete the text.**

What makes a **great job?**

People's opinions vary, of course, but these are
¹plenty / most workers' top 5:

✓ **Recognition:** Almost **²all / every** of us want to be told when
we've done a good job.

✓ **Challenge:** Employees want to develop. A job with **³any / no**
challenge will soon have staff looking for vacancies.

✓ **Flexibility:** This is high on the list for a great **⁴many / several**
people. It shows the employer has a great **⁵plenty / deal** of
confidence in the employee to work independently.

✓ **Variety:** A timetable with **⁶little / a little** variety soon becomes
dull. Even a small change in routine **⁷each / all** week helps
motivation.

✓ **Rewards:** Salary is one reward. But
there are **⁸most / several** other ways of
rewarding staff: good holidays, free
lunches and **⁹a few / few** staff parties.

DREAM JOB

4 **Complete the second sentence so that it has a similar meaning to the first sentence using the word given. Use between two and five words, including the word given.**

1 In my year many students applied to be class representatives.
LARGE
In my year ....
.... students applied to be class representatives.

2 There are few days left for revising before the test.
TIME
There ....
.... left for revising before the test.

3 The school was badly damaged by the storm.
AMOUNT
The storm caused ....
.... to the school.

4 Doing a little revision every day is better than doing twelve hours the night before the test.
BIT
It's better ....
.... revision every day than twelve hours the night before the test.

5 It will be easy for you to pass the test.
PROBLEM
You ....
.... passing the test.

6 You can't deny that all parents want the best education for their children.
EVERY
You can't deny that ....
.... the best education for their children.

5 **Choose the correct words to complete the text.**

The summer means exam time for **¹majority /
most** teenagers. And for a large **²number /
amount** of them that means stress. But what
about the parents? Exams can be stressful for
them, too. **³No / None** parent likes to see their
child anxious, and not **⁴all / every** parents know
how to cope. They want to help and so they jump
in with **⁵lots of / lot of** questions and suggestions.
According to a recent study, this is the last thing
they should do. Instead, parents should make as
⁶few / little interruptions as possible. Bringing in
⁷few / a few snacks is a great idea but without
asking, 'How's it going?' **⁸all / each** time.

USE OF ENGLISH

Match the sentence halves (1–8) with (A–H).

1 I think learning should be free. I don't believe
2 I don't want to be difficult, but if I don't agree
3 You'd be a great school rep. Why not apply
4 Count me out for this film. It doesn't really appeal
5 She's a great player, but you can't always rely
6 I'm so fed up with her. She didn't even apologise
7 Can't we invite both? It's too hard to choose
8 He's fine now, but the accident resulted

A on her to come to practice.
B with you, I'll say so.
C between the two of them.
D for using my racquet without asking.
E for it and see what happens.
F in him being off for a month.
G in private education for anyone.
H to me, but I'll come next time.

Complete the questions with the correct prepositions.

WORK

1 Which job appeals .... you most?

Being a professional musician.

2 If you saw an ad for a job with animals, would you apply .... it?

No way! I'm allergic to animals!

3 If you had to choose .... a huge salary or job satisfaction, what would you go for?

Honestly? I'd choose the money!

RELATIONSHIPS

4 Who do you agree .... most about things?

My sister. She gives good advice.

5 Who outside your family do you rely .... for support?

My music teacher.

6 What was the last thing you had to apologise .... ?

Breaking my mum's shoes.

Read the text and decide which answer (A, B, C or D) best fits each gap.

You're **more skilled** than you think

You need training and experience to succeed **1**........ the world of work. But whatever sector you **2**........ in, there are skills common to most professions. We often refer **3**........ them as 'transferable skills' and here's a list that most employers **4**........ on.

Numeracy

Think of how you cope **5**........ numbers in everyday life – saving for something you want, working out a discount, or getting your fair share of pizza.

IT skills

How might the IT skills you use every day transfer to the world of work?

Communication skills

A project **6**........ from clear communication from people with good listening skills. Think of a time when you got your message across well ... and one when you didn't! What can you learn from this?

Team work

Almost all work depends **7**........ a team effort. What examples of working as a team can you give?

Time management

Good time management **8**........ to success. You'll have shown this every time you've worked out how to get your homework done and play basketball.

1 A from   **B** into   **C** in   **D** on
2 A specialise **B** focus   **C** select   **D** concentrate
3 A to   **B** onto   **C** for   **D** on
4 A insist   **B** demand   **C** ask   **D** require
5 A from   **B** with   **C** for   **D** without
6 A progresses **B** proceeds   **C** improves **D** benefits
7 A from   **B** of   **C** on   **D** by
8 A increases   **B** ends   **C** results   **D** leads

Extend

Write the missing prepositions.

1 apologise for doing something .... a person
2 agree .... a person .... / .... an issue
3 care .... a person who can't look after themselves
4 ask .... an object you want
5 play .... an object

Complete the conversations with the correct prepositions.

1 A: Did you ask your parents .... an electric guitar?
   B: Yes, Dad agreed .... it but Mum said no!
2 A: She never apologises .... being rude.
   B: I know, but she doesn't really care .... other people.
3 A: I'm never picked to play .... the first team. It's not fair!
   B: Why don't you complain .... the coach about it?

SPEAKING

1 Read the speaking task. Match the sentences (1–5) with the points in the task (A–E).

A collecting litter with a group	**How might students benefit from volunteering in these activities?**	**B** being a guide in a local museum
C teaching children to read	**D** helping an elderly person at home	**E** doing a sponsored walk

1 Raising money in this way would give you a sense of achievement and also help you be more active. ....

2 This could improve your communication skills because young people need clear explanations. ....

3 Activities like this improve the area for everyone and working with others teaches you teamwork. ....

4 Going to their house would teach you to be responsible and respectful. ....

5 Dealing with the public would help you become more self-confident and become better at meeting people. ....

2 Write the words in the correct order to make sentences.

1 with / ? / start / we / one / Shall / this

....

2 you / a sponsored walk / think / do / you / ? / helps / How

....

3 think / that / ? / you / What / about / do

....

4 benefit / helping an older person / ? / about / How / the / from

....
....

5 don't / teaches / you / agree / ? / collecting litter / I / think / you / teamwork,

....
....

6 what / one / ? / about / OK, / this

....

3 🔊 3.6 Listen to two students discussing the task in Ex 1. Which two points are they talking about?

4 🔊 3.7 Listen again. Which speaker performs better during the task? Tick the mistakes the other student makes.

deciding about the most important benefit too quickly ☐

not responding fully to the other speaker's comments ☐

not understanding the language in the task ☐

not using a very polite tone ☐

asking the examiner for help ☐

using very direct language ☐

5 Match the sentences that are too direct (1–6) with more appropriate language (A–F).

1 You're wrong about that.

2 Right, this one next.

3 I'm right, aren't I?

4 Tell me what you think.

5 I want to make another point now.

6 We already said that.

A Can I just add something to what you said?

B What do you think about that?

C As we agreed earlier, …

D Shall we move on to this point now?

E Do / Would you agree with that?

F I'm not sure I agree with you.

6 Read the next part of the task and decide if the statements below are true (T) or false (F).

Which activity would students benefit from most?

To answer this question, students would need to:

1 summarise all the ideas they have already discussed. ....

2 come to an agreement if they can. ....

3 give the examiner the answer he / she is expecting. ....

4 suggest several more benefits from volunteering. ....

5 give reasons for the option they choose. ....

7 🔴 Record your answers to the question in Ex 6. Check your answers against the true statements.

WRITING

an essay

Do you know how to write a good essay? Try the quiz and find out.

Get writing right!

1 What style of language is appropriate in an essay?

lively and colourful ☐

formal or semi-formal ☐

2 A good essay includes:

your point of view supported by reasons / evidence. ☐

a list of facts. ☐

complex sentences with appropriate linking words. ☐

a range of different opinions, but not your own. ☐

3 Number the paragraphs (1–5) in the best order for an essay.

a paragraph about the first point in the notes	....
introduction with a general statement about the topic	....
a paragraph about your own idea	....
a conclusion with a summary of your ideas.	....
a paragraph about the second point in the notes	....

Link the ideas using 'both … and', 'neither … nor', or 'either … or'.

1 My mum didn't do IT at school. And my dad didn't do it.
.... IT at school.

2 I'm learning Spanish at school and also German.
I'm learning ....

3 We could walk to school. Or we could wait for the bus.
We could ....

Rewrite the examples using 's or s'.

1 the grades of all the students
the students' grades

2 the performance of an individual school
the ....

3 the handouts produced by one teacher
the ....

4 the involvement of several parents
the ....

Read the essay quickly. What is the topic? Decide which line (A–F) best fits each gap (1–6).

A Likewise, people say there are differences

B It is often said that young people

C Moreover, being in a mixed class

D However, this is not always about gender

E As a teenager at a mixed school

F To sum up, I can't say

Although most students go to mixed schools, a number of people feel that boys and girls benefit from single-sex education. ¹......, I feel this topic is important.

Some people believe that teenage boys and girls have different skills. These are typically science-based subjects for boys and language-based subjects for girls. ²...... in how the two genders behave in class.

Another important point is achievement. ³...... in single-sex classes get better grades. This is because people believe that students of the same gender work more efficiently together.

From my own experience, I can see that there are differences in how my classmates cope with school. ⁴....... Each student is an individual and therefore it is important not to generalise.

⁵...... I agree with the statement. I think it's important for both boys and girls to learn from each other in school. ⁶...... is much closer to what happens in the workplace and in life in general.

Read the task. Write your essay in 140–190 words, using an appropriate style.

Students can learn better in mixed-age classes. Do you agree?

Notes

Write about:

1 learning being based on ability not age

2 older students helping younger ones

3 … (your own idea)

UNIT CHECK

1 Decide which answer (A, B or C) best fits each gap.

1 Don't worry if you haven't got the handout. I .... mine for you.

    A 'll copy   **B** copy   **C** 'm copying

2 I think I .... my project by the weekend.

    A 'm finishing   **B** 'll have finished   **C** finish

3 What .... after school? Would you like to watch a film?

    A do you do   **B** are you doing   **C** will you do

4 By the time we land, we .... in this plane for nine hours.

    A 'll sit   **B** 'll have sat   **C** 'll have been sitting

5 When there .... a vacancy where I work, I'll let you know.

    A is going to be   **B** will be   **C** is

6 I can't get this app to work. .... me?

    A Will you help   **B** Do you help   **C** Are you helping

7 When you're in bed on Saturday morning, I .... hard.

    A work   **B** 'll work   **C** 'll be working

8 When I'm sixteen, I .... the piano for eleven years.

    A 'll have been playing   **B** 'll be playing   **C** 'm playing

2 Choose the correct words to complete the conversation.

A: Did you see that documentary about the perfect school?

B: **¹Nor / No** school is perfect – you do exams there!

A: No seriously, it was asking why **²all / every** schools look the same. **³Lots / Lot** of school buildings are like brick boxes.

B: I guess you're right. **⁴Few / A few** teenagers would choose to design our school the way it is.

A: So that's why they asked a large **⁵number / amount** of people 'What makes the perfect school?' And not just for **⁶teacher's and student's / teachers' and students'** opinions, they asked **⁷plenty / several** architects and psychologists, too. What they came up with was amazing – a place that **⁸both / either** encouraged learning and looked good.

3 Complete the sentences with linking words.

1 .... my school nor my language club teaches Russian.

2 We can .... go out for pizza or get a takeaway.

3 .... my brother and sister are really good at athletics.

4 Read the definitions and complete the words.

1 your teacher might give you this after a lesson: h _ _ _ _ _ _

2 behave or you might end up in this: d _ _ _ _ _ _ _ _

3 the marks you get for schoolwork / in exams: g _ _ _ _ _

4 the act of going regularly to school: a _ _ _ _ _ _ _ _ _

5 you might do this in chemistry: e _ _ _ _ _ _ _ _

5 Choose the word or phrase in each group (1–6) that doesn't go with the verb.

1	work	shifts / a job / part- / full-time / as a team
2	have	a good salary / off sick / a lot of pressure / time off
3	keep up with	an activity / your progress / a hobby / a course
4	run out of	ideas / energy / money / drawbacks
5	come up with	a solution / a skill / an idea / a plan
6	catch up on	your friends / work / revision / sleep

6 🔊 3.8 Listen to six short recordings. Complete the sentences with a verb from A in the correct form and a preposition from B.

| **A** | apologise   believe   benefit   choose depend   succeed |
| **B** | between   for   from   in   in   on |

1 He wants his friend to .... being unkind.

2 She's finding it hard to .... two possible jobs.

3 He says his plans for the future .... his exam results.

4 She .... revision rituals and superstitions.

5 He thinks he's .... going to a revision day.

6 She's .... getting some coding to work.

7 Which preposition can complete the questions or sentences in each pair?

1 **A** Just ask .... help if you don't understand.

    B Which part-time job have you applied .... ?

2 **A** I cope .... exam pressure better now.

    B My parents usually agree .... each other.

3 **A** The new design resulted .... bigger sales.

    B I'm not sure what subject to specialise .... at college.

4 **A** Which sites do you refer .... most for homework?

    B Their behaviour lead .... them being in detention.

PART 1

Read the text and decide which answer (A, B, C or D) best fits each gap.

Are you sure you're not a nervous flyer?

In today's world, we've all got used to affordable air ⁰ <u>travel</u> to exotic destinations. This **1** .... on access to secure airports, and the skills of the pilot and flight crew. But would you be willing to take the **2** .... of flying into either of these airports?

Princess Juliana is an international airport in the Caribbean. The landing approach is over the water and pilots have to make constant checks to avoid ending **3** .... in the sea. Huge mountains at the end of the runway make take-off just as difficult to **4** .... with.

Getting to Paro in the beautiful country of Bhutan by air also takes a **5** .... of adventure. You would want a pilot who had **6** .... in negotiating very tight spaces. In fact, only a few pilots in the world currently have a licence to land there due to its secluded location deep in the Himalayas.

If you're a nervous flyer and going to one of these places isn't **7** .... on your list, then there's no need to worry. **8** .... tourism offers a huge range of destinations to choose from. And if you fly, you can always check the length of the runway first …

0	**A** journey	**B** travel	**C** excursion	**D** flight
1	**A** consists	**B** applies	**C** requires	**D** relies
2	**A** risk	**B** danger	**C** fear	**D** threat
3	**A** across	**B** up	**C** over	**D** above
4	**A** handle	**B** manage	**C** succeed	**D** cope
5	**A** sense	**B** feeling	**C** sensation	**D** perception
6	**A** dedicated	**B** devoted	**C** specialised	**D** concentrated
7	**A** strong	**B** high	**C** tall	**D** great
8	**A** Large	**B** Big	**C** Mass	**D** Huge

PART 2

For questions 9–16, complete the text with one word in each gap.

I'll start revising in a minute …

The exam season is due ⁰ .... <u>to</u> .... start and this means anxious teenagers across the country will **9** .... revising like mad. So you would think they'd be far **10** .... busy for social media. Think again. Most teens with an exam timetable **11** .... stop nor reduce their social media use. In fact, a study shows that during a six-week revision period, teenagers spend **12** .... additional forty-three hours keeping up with their friends online.

Apps like Snapchat work in two ways: they prevent teens from starting their revision and distract them if they **13** .... already been working for a while. And no one loses concentration **14** .... easily than exam-stressed teens! On average, they spend little more than half an hour revising before they get distracted – thirty-eight minutes to be precise. They also have a number **15** .... creative ways to avoid studying – reorganising their books, cleaning the house, even dressing **16** .... their pets!

PART 3

For questions 17–24, read the text. Use the word given at the end of some of the lines to form a word that fits in the gap in the same line.

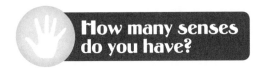

How many senses do you have?

The usual answer is five:
0 ....sight............... , hearing, touch, taste and smell. But a more **SEE**
17 .... look at how the **SCIENCE**
body works suggests there are a lot more.
So why the 18 .... **DIFFER**
in number? It's all to do with sensors.
These are what make the world
19 .... to us. Sensors **ACCESS**
in the eye don't just make us see what's
20 .... They detect **VISION**
light and dark, and colour. There are
skin sensors that help to keep us
21 .... by detecting **COMFORT**
hot, cold, itch and pressure, as well as
touch. One of the most important types
of skin sensors tells us when something
is 22 .... How else **PAIN**
would we keep ourselves safe?

If damage is caused to the sensors
in the ear, it might not result in
23 .... , but your **DEAF**
balance may be affected. Other senses
include hunger, thirst, knowing where
your body parts are in relation to
each other, and a sense of time.
So if anyone asks you, 'How many
senses are there?' remember not to
sound 24 .... by **FOOL**
answering 'five'.

PART 4

For questions 25–30, complete the second sentence so that it has a similar meaning to the first sentence, using the word given. Do not change the word given. Use between two and five words, including the word given.

0 I went abroad for the first time last year.
NEVER
I ....had never been............... abroad before last year.

25 Playing music and singing are equally enjoyable in a group.
AS
Playing music .... in a group.

26 We'd never walked so far before.
EVER
That's .... walked.

27 The security officer checked our passport and then she let us through.
HAD
The security officer let us through ....
.... at our passports.

28 We took off an hour ago and it will take three hours to complete the flight.
FLYING
By the time we land, we ....
.... for four hours.

29 I enjoy writing my blog a lot.
DEAL
I get ....
enjoyment from writing my blog.

30 There aren't many good clothes shops near here.
ONLY
There ....
good clothes shops near here.

4 The heart of the city

READING

1 Complete the words in the sentences.

1 We hardly recognised the area – the streets once d _ f _ _ _ d by graffiti had been replaced with huge i _ p _ _ _ _ g houses and fashionable shops.

2 The complicated i _ _ u _ s of housing, transport and air quality face many cities, but each place has to come up with its own solution.

3 My brother's student accommodation is in an area that's quite cheap, but there aren't many a _ _ n _ _ _ _ s like good shops nearby.

4 Cities are finding it i _ _ _ _ a _ _ _ _ _ y difficult to meet the wide-ranging needs of their population.

5 It's important to people who have emigrated to keep in touch with their a _ _ e _ _ _ _ l homeland.

6 Soon you may not need to go into town at all. Sit in your cosy, i _ _ _ l _ _ _ d flat and experience the s _ _ u _ _ _ _ d city of your dreams, all through virtual reality.

2 Read the text quickly. Which description A–C best describes the article?

A the use of the city for different forms of entertainment

B profiles of different street performers

C the best cities to see street art

3 Read the article again. Match the questions (1–10) with the paragraphs (A–D). Each paragraph may be chosen more than once.

Which paragraph mentions that …

1 the audience feels a performance is specially for them?

2 the public can see part of the city in a completely new way?

3 a performer is unlikely to remain in the same part of the city?

4 the audience were important or influential people?

5 the audience influences what the performer does?

6 the public didn't always believe in a group of performers?

7 this group's work was considered to be damaging city life?

8 this group is required to have official permission to work?

9 this group has been in evidence in cities for centuries?

10 a performer may make a career of their talent?

Extend

4 Find the words or phrases in the article that mean the following.

1 interrupting and trying to embarrass a performer (A)
....

2 short of money due to bad fortune (A)
....

3 became very good at a particular skill (A)
....

4 think about someone who is in a difficult situation (A)
....

5 actions that are both dangerous and thrilling (B)
....

6 be caused by (C) ....

7 get you to look at something (C) ....

8 having an important effect on something (D)
....

9 got through a difficult period earlier in life (D)
....

10 pointless, without result (D) ....

5 Complete what this slackliner street performer says with the correct form of the words or phrases from Ex 4.

" I've heard people say some strange things about street performers. That they must be
¹... , even homeless. Or that working on the street must be ²... a lack of education. It's true that some of us have
³... , but many are graduates with a good lifestyle. In my case, I need to earn enough to eat well and to take care of myself. To do
⁴... for different crowds in the same day takes strength and stamina. And a lot of practice. It's quite easy to ⁵... people's
.... , but to get the crowd to really appreciate you, you have to give them something extraordinary. I need to go higher, faster, further … or go home! All street performers want to
⁶... on a city, to see it come to life with sound, colour and movement. And each of us has
⁷... in our own way to become as good as we are. So check us out as you walk by. All we ask is a few minutes of your time … and a little of your money. "

Street stories

City life is not all about great shopping or hanging out at the coffee shop. How about when the streets offer you ... ?

A concert

Buskers are part of the city soundscape as much as traffic, sirens and mobiles. Covering everything from opera to folk, musicians and singers are perhaps the most common form of street performer. For singers, no equipment is needed and many musicians limit themselves to just a guitar or small keyboard. Keeping your equipment light is important. Moving on when the crowd starts heckling with insults or the weather turns bad is all part of the job – as is being moved on by the authorities. Buskers often want to perform in the same places and there can be fierce competition for each site. But you'd be wrong to assume that all buskers are down on their luck. It's possible to earn a reasonable living and some even turn professional having learned their craft on the streets. However well they perform, they keep the city vibrant, so next time you hear a street musician, spare a thought for them and maybe a few coins.

A circus

Acrobats, clowns and high-wire walkers have abandoned tents and theatres in favour of the open air and a spontaneous crowd. New forms of spectacle have also been created. Slacklining is one: a combination of balance and acrobatics on a line of woven material that can be fixed between two objects. A skilled slackliner can perform incredible jumps and stunts. But why do them in the street? For many performers it's about the unpredictability of the crowd. Each audience is unique, making the artist change their performance to suit the likes of the crowd. However, this form of work isn't trouble-free. As well as the obvious physical demands, there are restrictions. Performing without a permit is often illegal and crowds may be limited to as few as eight people in some areas. But street circus is here to stay. You don't need to wait for the circus to come to town, now the circus comes to you.

A conjurer

Magicians have kept audiences guessing for centuries. Medieval kings and queens often employed a magician as an entertainer or healer. However, it wasn't until the nineteenth century that the form of stage magic that we know today was developed. Theatres and later TV shows were the magician's workplace, often attracting huge audiences. But viewers weren't always convinced by TV magic, suspecting that it may all be down to camera work. Magicians then moved into what is called 'close-up magic', letting the audience see the trick at first hand, literally. This ultimate test of a magician's talent is now out on the streets. Performing right next to a spectator, right in the middle of their hometown makes the magic somehow personal. And for the spectator, seeing their watch or coin disappear right in front of their eyes makes the question 'How did they do that?' all the more intriguing. Why not take a closer look if a street magician tries to attract your attention? After all, you'll always get your watch back.

A canvas

Artists have a long and proud history of making their mark on a city. Some argue that street art has its roots in prehistoric cave paintings, developing over time from the examples of graffiti found in ancient Greece and Rome. The birth of modern street art is widely thought to have been in Philadelphia in the 1960s. But one thing is certain – street art has survived a troubled past. The artists' names or 'tags' that covered urban settings in the 1970s were seen as pure vandalism. But attempts to clean up these areas and clear away the artists have been in vain. There are few cities in the world without some form of street art. And now it's become a form of entertainment in its own right. 3-D chalk artists across the world are creating visual extravaganzas that trick the passerby into seeing fully three-dimensional scenes on a completely flat pavement. So take a walk through the city and you might be thrown into a whole new dimension.

GRAMMAR

conditionals

Match the sentences (1–5) with the explanations (A–F). One sentence needs two explanations.

1 If I walk in the country, I feel relaxed. ....
2 If parking isn't free, people won't visit. ....
3 If I could design my own house, it would have a huge games room. ....
4 If you hadn't kicked the ball so hard, the window wouldn't have broken. ....
5 If we'd grown up on the same street, we might have gone to the same school. ....

A This refers to the possible result of an unreal or imagined past situation.
B This refers to a possible result in the future.
C This refers to an unreal or imagined past situation or event.
D When can replace If in this sentence.
E This refers to the present or future, but isn't likely to happen.
F This happens every time.

Choose the correct words to complete the sentences.

1 If you **need / will need** to find a particular place, **you'll check / check** out the plan on the interactive screens.
2 When I **will walk / walk** into that part of town, I **always get / 'll always get** a bit scared.
3 If you **don't / not** come with me to the festival, I'**ll / 'd** never speak to you again.
4 If I **could / could have** do any job in the future, I'**d have been / I'd be** an architect.
5 If you hadn't **been staring / stared** at your phone, you **didn't walk / wouldn't have walked** into me.
6 The trains get really packed so I'**d set / I'll set** off early if I **weren't / were** you.
7 We'll always be friends. Even if you'**ll move / move** a long way away, I'**ll visit / I visit** you at weekends.
8 If you **didn't tell / hadn't told** me about the strike, I **would wait / might have been waiting** for the bus until now.

Which sentence in Ex 2 includes:

A a threat? ....
B some advice? ....
C an instruction? ....
D a promise? ....
E a criticism? ....

4.1 Listen to the beginning of six conditional sentences. Choose the correct ending (A or B).

1 A ... the ticket will come out.
  B ... the ticket comes out.
2 A ... we'd lose a lot of money.
  B ... we'll lose a lot of money.
3 A ... if you don't sit down.
  B ... if you wouldn't sit down.
4 A ... if I'd been you.
  B ... if I were you.
5 A ... if you'd missed the flight?
  B ... if you missed the flight?
6 A ... you might hear me.
  B ... you might have heard me.

Complete the article with the correct form of the verbs. Use short forms where possible.

Could you be a placemaker?

How ¹ .... (you / feel) if you look around where you live? Safe or vulnerable, inspired or bored? Or maybe you think, 'Why worry? I couldn't have a say about my city even if I ² .... (want) to.' Now an organisation called the Project for Public Places wants to change that. They transform public spaces and build strong communities. They call this 'placemaking' and they involve young people in the process.

If you ³ .... (be born) in Fremantle, Australia, you could have helped to create a skatepark with a difference. When kids turn up there now, they ⁴ .... just .... (not / skate). There's a parkour park, climbing wall, table tennis and a stage.

If you ⁵ .... (be) a street artist in your town, where would you paint – and stay legal? The Alley Project in Detroit, USA, has put professional artists together with 120 young people to showcase local talent.

So what ⁶ .... (you / create) if you could be a placemaker? And if you'd been the head of planning, how ⁷ .... (you / do) things differently?

Read the responses to the article in Ex 5. Cross out two extra words in each response.

1 JJ16   Add message | Report

I'd have pull down the old shopping mall and build a new market place if I could to.

2 Teena   Add message | Report

Cool idea, but how do you get everyone to agree? If you were asked my class 'What does the town need?', you'd have get thirty different answers!

3 eco-kid   Add message | Report

Why didn't anyone tell us about placemaking? If we'd hadn't known about it, we might not would have been living in such a boring place for all this time!

VOCABULARY

town and country

1 Complete the sentences with these pairs of adjectives.

> express + winding   handy + overcrowded
> inner-city + well-connected   remote + secure

Are you happier
out on the town **or** down in the country?

Tim

It's town for me – not right in the .... areas, but out in the suburbs. There's plenty to do and you're .... by public transport.

Lin

I live in a small town with a lot of local amenities. It's .... because you can walk everywhere and it isn't so .... as in a big city.

Mel

I could never leave the city for a .... country village. It might be more .... because of less crime, but what do people do all day?

Eddie

We have decent transport systems here including trains. You can get an .... service to London, but enjoy bike rides along peaceful .... lanes, too.

2 Find six nouns in each puzzle. Make six compound nouns from these words and complete the conversation.

leisurepowerpublicapartment countytourist

blockstationtransportcottage complexspots

....
....
....

....
....
....

A: So what's it like living out of town now? Are you surrounded by cows?

B: I'm not living in a **1** ...., you know. We're in a modern **2** .... It's just smaller than the ones you get in the centre.

A: But I guess it's prettier than round here. Are you living near some nice **3** .... ?

B: Yes, in one direction, but if you go the other way, there's the **4** .... !

A: That doesn't sound very attractive! And do you need to get lifts everywhere?

B: No, the **5** .... is pretty reliable, if you don't want to go anywhere on a Sunday. But the one thing I really miss is the big **6** .... I have to come back into town for my diving classes.

3 🔊 4.2 Listen to six short recordings. Match the words in A and B to make compound nouns and answer the question.

A city   market   road   sales   weather   window

B conditions   department   markings   shopping   square   walls

What is each recording about?
1 bad ....
2 a meeting about the ....
3 the view from the ....
4 a special event in the ....
5 an opinion about ....
6 a problem with the ....

Extend

4 Write the definitions as compound nouns. (Clues! Two of the compounds are written as one word. Watch out for an irregular plural.)

1 the quality of the air: ....
2 life in the city: ....
3 lighting in the streets: ....
4 water from the rain: ....
5 steps you take with your feet:
....
6 temperature of the air: ....

5 Complete the article with some of the compound nouns from Ex 4.

Eco-friendly is fun!

Sustainable doesn't have to be serious. We look at new ways of going green and improving **1** ....

Supertrees
A Dutch designer has mixed the DNA of luminescent marine bacteria with plant cells. He plans to produce trees that glow in the dark that may eventually replace traditional **2** .... Singapore already has man-made metal trees which can take in and give out heat and so regulate **3** .... They are also designed to collect **4** .... in wet weather.

LISTENING

🔊 4.3 Listen to eight people talking in different situations. Choose the correct words to complete the sentences.

1 The man is on his way **home** / **to his son's school.**

2 Their friend's new house is **a long distance away** / **very impressive.**

3 The student is **at the start** / **near the end** of his course.

4 The boy is finding it **easy** / **difficult** to attract people's attention.

5 The woman lives in a **small rural** / **large urban** community.

6 The girl stayed with her aunt for **twenty-four hours** / **on Saturday and Sunday.**

7 The farm has a **modern** / **old-fashioned** information centre.

8 The film isn't **very popular at school** / **on the next day.**

🔊 4.4 Listen again and choose the correct answer (A, B or C).

1 You hear a man leaving a message for his son. What does the boy need to do?

A get the next bus

B not move from where he is

C start walking home

2 You overhear a brother and sister talking. What are they looking at?

A a map

B a celebrity magazine

C a social media site

3 You hear part of an interview with a student. Where is he living?

A at home with his parents

B in a room on the university site

C in a flatshare with friends

4 You hear two teenagers talking in the street. What is the boy doing?

A interviewing a games designer

B going with a friend to a games event

C helping to promote a games event

5 You hear an announcement. What is the speaker doing?

A getting support for a campaign

B warning people about new building plans

C asking people to sign a petition

6 You hear a girl talking about a trip to her aunt's. What was the girl's problem?

A She didn't enjoy horse-riding.

B She felt tired.

C She was bored a lot of the time.

7 You hear two friends talking about an urban farm. Which feature of the farm did the boy like best?

A being able to leave his little brother in the play area

B finding out information about food production

C tasting different foods produced on the farm

8 You hear part of a phone conversation between two friends. What do they agree about?

A how to get to town

B where to meet in town

C what to do in town

Extend

Complete the sentences with these words or phrases.

> Don't bother going   Do you fancy coming
> have you found   I'd better be
> I don't suppose you would   just off the main square
> remember   more or less what I expected

1 .... to the bus stop because the buses are in the same traffic jam as me.

2 **A:** So, tell us Ryan, how .... your first month?

B: The course is ....

3 I thought .... near college, you know, closer to all the amenities.

4 .... like a leaflet about a games fair?

5 It's on in town, in the town hall ....

7 .... to that urban farm near here? It's all up and running now.

8 The bus drivers are on strike today, ... ?

Complete the conversations with the words or phrases from Ex 3.

1 **A:** [1] .... going to the new sports shop after school?

B: I didn't know there was one.

A: Yes, I told you about it, [2] .... ? It's [3] .... the high street near Starbucks.

B: Oh, yes, that's right. I'd like to go, but [4] .... back by six because I've got football practice later.

2 **A:** Hi, how's it going? How [5] .... the first few days working here?

B: It's OK. The job is [6] .... , but it's quite hard to make friends. [7] .... introduce me to the other Saturday staff?

A: Sure, most of them are really nice. But [8] .... talking to Tom. He's always in a bad mood.

USE OF ENGLISH 1

1 Match the sentence halves (1–6) with (A–F).

1 I've saved you some pizza in
2 We'll stay living in the country unless
3 It'll be easier to get around when
4 You can use the local amenities as
5 I'll come and pick you up later on
6 It's fine to have a barbecue on the beach provided

A long as you are resident in the area.
B condition that it isn't after midnight.
C that you clean up afterwards.
D case you're hungry when you get in.
E the village school closes.
F the roadworks are completed.

2 Find and correct four mistakes in these sentences.

1 You can borrow my bike provided that you will take good care of it.
2 When the water level in the river rises, the village always floods.
3 I wouldn't want to live in the capital unless I had a lot of money.
4 I'll let you have the bigger bedroom on a condition that you would keep it tidy.
5 Take a jumper in case of it gets cold on the way back from town.
6 The phone reception is good as long as you're not in the middle of nowhere.
7 The city will have a housing crisis if it builds more affordable homes.
8 We bought some snacks in case we got hungry on the journey home.

3 🔊 4.5 Listen and complete what each person thinks about their situation with the correct form of these verbs.

| can | live | not talk | not be | not come |
| not show | not wear | train |

1 If only we .... in a quieter area.
2 I wish the chemistry teacher .... so strict.
3 If only my sister .... off all the time.
4 I wish I .... go home for lunch.
5 If only we .... camping.
6 I wish our neighbour .... to me like I'm a child.
7 If only I .... a bit harder.
8 I wish I .... these shoes.

4 What might you say in these situations? Complete the sentences with the pairs of verbs.

> be more careful + forgive me
> have a room of my own + leave her stuff everywhere
> not go red + leave me alone

1 You have to share with your sister who's very untidy.
If only I ....
I wish she ....
2 Someone in your class made fun of you in front of your friends.
If only I ....
I wish she ....
3 You tore your brother's favourite top.
If only I ....
I wish he ....

5 🔵 Complete the article with one word in each gap.

The **house** of the **future**

Anyone can build their own home ¹ .... that they have land and money. But that might all change – with printable houses. In ² .... this sounds like science fiction, it's already fact thanks to 3D printing. A company in Russia has already built – or should I say printed – a house in less than a day.

This isn't just clever technology, it's a way of addressing the housing crisis. ³ .... we find more sustainable ways of building homes, the crisis will only get worse. As ⁴ .... as people continue to move to urban areas, land will become increasingly limited.

What about ⁵ .... you already have a house and you want to move? That's easy enough now, but only ⁶ .... condition that you find the right house. In the future, you may just take your house with you. Several companies are looking into the idea of movable houses, some that are also drones. Why drive to a new city when you could fly your old house there?

So future families who say, 'I wish I ⁷ .... build my own house.' or 'If only we ⁸ .... not come here, I want to move.' won't need a builder, just a printer.

USE OF ENGLISH 2

Choose the correct words to complete the sentences.

1 What's the new music shop **like / as**?

2 He's got a part-time job **as / like** a waiter.

3 I wish we had more places to hang out **like / as** a youth club or skatepark.

4 The design of the gallery is amazing. It looks **as / like** a ship.

5 Please tidy up. It's **like / as** a tip in there.

6 I go to the same school **like / as** him.

Complete the pairs of sentences with the correct prepositions.

in + out of (x2)   on + in (x2)

1 **A** The bus arrived at 11.15, exactly .... time.

 B There was a huge queue at the security desk, but we still got to the plane .... good time for take-off.

2 **A** Only one more exam to do. The end is .... sight!

 B Don't let Annie see her present. Please put it .... sight.

3 **A** Call the fire service – the house next door is .... fire!

 B We walked into the garden to see the barbecue .... flames and Dad with the fire extinguisher.

4 **A** Never put yourself .... danger online. Always know who you are talking to.

 B Everyone had left their homes before the floods and so they were .... danger.

Complete the sentences with the correct prepositions.

1 It's important to be .... control of your pace when you go running. Set off too fast and you'll get .... breath.

2 .... the whole, I don't mind spending time .... myself at weekends.

3 It was .... least an hour before the traffic was .... the move again after the accident.

4 Receiving a card written .... hand really took me .... surprise. I usually get texts and tweets.

5 .... all means listen to music, but don't sing along to every song .... the top of your voice!

4.6 Choose the correct words to complete the conversations. Then listen and check your answers.

1 **A:** You're very quiet. Have you got something on your **¹mind / memory**?

 B: Well, for **²one / a** thing I'm worried about playing the concert solo. The composer is going to be there in **³show / person**. I'm OK in rehearsal, but it's different doing it for **⁴true / real**. What if I drop the music and all the pages land out of **⁵practice / order** on the floor?

 A: That won't happen. You'll be fine!

2 **A:** How was your weekend at your cousins' place?

 B: It was OK for the most **⁶bit / part**, but I felt a bit out of **⁷space / place**, because they both have the latest clothes and trainers.

 A: But your clothes aren't out of **⁸time / date**. You always look in fashion.

 B: No, I know, but they dress like models. And then my aunt complained we'd left the house all untidy. She likes everything to be in perfect **⁹position / order**.

 A: Are you seeing them again?

 B: Yes, next weekend, but I want to try to put the visit on **¹⁰wait / hold**.

Read the article and decide which answer (A, B, C or D) best fits each gap.

A new meaning to going by tube

There have been many suggestions for solving urban traffic congestion, but the strangest is the CarTube. This aims to take traffic off London's streets and put it in underground tunnels. The organisation behind CarTube describes it **¹** .... 'the future of urban mass transport'. Using automated electric cars in a new network of tunnels, the system hopes to get people to their destination in good **²** .... and at no **³** .... Fantastic in theory, not so great in practice. **⁴** .... a start, London already has a huge network of tunnels and pipes in **⁵** .... for existing trains, water and waste. So would there be space? Another key issue is the use of fully automated cars. Although these are becoming more accepted as an idea for the future, they are not yet **⁶** .... reach of the average city commuter. And a further objection has been raised: why hide cars out of **⁷** .... underground? Wouldn't it be better to do away with the private car **⁸** .... good in favour of truly public transport?

1	**A** as	**B** like	**C** as if	**D** as much
2	**A** case	**B** fact	**C** hour	**D** time
3	**A** danger	**B** risk	**C** harm	**D** hurt
4	**A** From	**B** Out of	**C** With	**D** For
5	**A** place	**B** person	**C** case	**D** sight
6	**A** by	**B** on	**C** in	**D** out of
7	**A** date	**B** sight	**C** order	**D** place
8	**A** by	**B** out of	**C** at	**D** for

SPEAKING

1 Read the questions (1–6). Find two phrases (A–L) you could use to answer each one.

1 What do you think makes someone a good neighbour? Why?

2 What kind of things can help people be proud of the place they live in? Why?

3 Some people say it's difficult to live in a city. What do you think? Why?

4 Do you think living in a capital city is special? Why?

5 Is it important to know the language of the country you are visiting? Why?

6 Do you think it's better for children to grow up in the country? Why?

A air pollution from urban traffic ....

B be quiet and respectful ....

C communicate with local people ....

D famous people in your hometown ....

E more contact with nature ....

F national cultural events ....

G higher crime levels than rural areas ....

H care about shared areas ....

I understand a different culture ....

J clean and attractive public spaces ....

K more freedom to explore ....

L home of the country's leaders ....

2 Choose the correct words to complete the opinions. Which questions in Ex 1 are the students answering?

1 I haven't got much **experiment / experience** of this, because I've never lived in Moscow, but I don't think it would necessarily be better than another big city. I **dream / imagine** that it could be quite stressful with the number of tourists there all the time.

2 **Like / As** I see it, people feel good about their hometown if there are different activities to take part in. Things like good sports facilities and leisure centres are important, but **truly / frankly**, I think that a lot of places don't provide enough for teenagers.

3 **By / In** my opinion, it's all about having respect for people and places. I **believe / I'm believing** that you shouldn't always complain about people around you, but think about what you can do to make relationships better.

3 Read the responses to some of the questions in Ex 1. Find the extra word in each sentence.

1 If you would ask me, young kids have more opportunities if they are brought up in a city.

2 I'd have definitely say that the capital city of any country has a special attraction.

3 To be honest you, I don't understand why people say living in a city is challenging.

4 I'm pretty sure of that you can learn a lot by chatting with local people about their town.

5 I'm absolutely too convinced that being a good neighbour is about respecting people's privacy.

6 This is just own my opinion, but people often enjoy talking about someone from their town who has achieved something important.

4 🔊 4.7 Listen to six students answering the questions in Ex 1. Which two students do not give full enough answers?

5 🔊 4.8 Listen to the questions and record your answers. Listen to your answers and check them using the list below. Try again if you need to improve on anything.

Have you:

• used different expressions for giving your opinion?

• used a wide range of language to answer each question?

• given full answers with reasons and examples?

• paraphrased any words that you don't know?

WRITING

an email

Do you know how to write a good email? Try the quiz and find out.

Get writing right!

1 Which four statements are not true?

An email can be formal or informal.	☐
You don't need to write an email in paragraphs.	☐
Avoid giving your own opinion.	☐
An email should be written in shorter sentences without linkers.	☐
You need to include a greeting and closing expression.	☐
Spelling, grammar and punctuation aren't so important.	☐

Complete the sentences with a verb from A and a noun/phrase from B. Which opinions are positive and which are negative?

A catch losing made make makes takes tell

B a difference a train excuses sleep the difference your breath away your day

1 Public transport used to be awful, but now you can .... to town every fifteen minutes.

2 The design of the new town hall is stunning. It really .... every time you look at it.

3 No one trusts the council. They've been promising to build a new leisure complex for years, but then they just ....

4 The noise from the roadworks starts early in the morning. Local people have been complaining of ....

5 If only they'd cleared up the main square before. It's .... such .... to people's impression of the town.

6 Volunteers planted trees and flowers on some waste ground. Just walking past it ....

7 The food in the café was changed to organic, but to me it just tasted the same. I couldn't .... from the old menu.

Replace the highlighted parts of these messages with these phrases.

be honest with you   lost patience   lost track of   made a fuss   made such a mess of   make the most   took control

I wish I'd gone to the science centre before. I had so much fun there that I **¹forgot all about time**. If you go, spend the whole day and **²take full advantage of** the interactive displays.

To **³tell you the truth**, we've given up waiting for the council to install fast broadband. The village has **⁴got fed up with waiting** and is raising the money itself.

No one really **⁵was in charge of** the project. The planners **⁶made so many mistakes with** the design that the skatepark was really dull. We **⁷complained** and so they closed it. If only we'd seen the plans earlier.

Tick (✓) the greetings you can use in an informal email.

1 Dear Best friend ☐   3 Dear (Ewa) ☐
2 Hi (Miguel) ☐   4 Dear Sir or Madam ☐

Choose one extra word in each sentence or phrase. Which one can you use for the first paragraph? Where do you use the others?

1 Thanks much again.
2 All the best you.
3 It was great to hear of about your holiday.
4 Hope that can helps.
5 I've just read about your a good news.
6 Take you care!
7 Thanks you for your message.
8 Bye soon for now!

Read the task. Write your email in 140–190 words, using an appropriate style.

Thanks for your message. I'm glad I was able to help with your homework. Can I ask you a favour in return? In my geography class, we're doing a project about how cities change. What about where you live? How has it changed and what is it like now? What has been positive and what do you wish they'd done differently? If you could email your answers to me, I'd be really grateful. Thanks!
Piotr

UNIT CHECK

1 Match the sentence beginnings (1–7) and endings (A–G).

1 When you press the button,
2 If people leave their car at home just one day a week,
3 We'd love to live right in the city centre
4 If we hadn't fought against the new development,
5 I would have found you earlier
6 If you can create a house with a 3D-printer,
7 We might never have met

A if the housing was more affordable.
B if you'd been waiting in the right place.
C the sensor recognises your fingerprint.
D will they make whole cities in the same way?
E if we hadn't been living in the same street.
F all the town's green spaces would have been lost.
G air pollution will improve over time.

2 Choose the correct words to complete the sentences.

1 The project will be put on hold **if / unless** more funds can be found.
2 My sister is about to go travelling for a year so I'll have a room of my own **if / when** she leaves.
3 Bring some sun cream **in case / in case of** it's hot later.
4 I'll come on condition **as / that** we're back by seven.
5 I wish I **could / can** go to the beach later.
6 If only they **hadn't built / didn't build** the shopping complex so far away. It takes ages to get there.

3 Complete the article with one word in each gap.

COME AND HANG OUT ROUND MY PLACE

If you've ever thought of a skyscraper **1**.................. a building rooted in the ground, think again. Architects in New York have come up with a skyscraper that hangs down from an asteroid. If I **2**.................. not seen it reported in several places, I might have thought it was a joke!

Named Analemma, if it **3**.................. ever constructed, it would be the tallest building ever made. And it would travel thousands of miles a day, passing over cities **4**.................. New York, Havana and Panama City. In **5**.................. you were wondering about scale, the tower is intended to be the size of a floating city, with a large residential section, offices and commercial spaces.

So, as **6**.................. as we all have a head for heights, could this be the housing of the future? Part of me thinks it sounds amazing and I wish they **7**.................. build it soon. But the rest of me wants to keep my feet on planet Earth.

4 Read the definitions and complete the adjectives.

1 with good transport links: w _ _ l-c _ _ _ _ _ _ _ d
2 safe: s _ _ _ _ e
3 with too many people: o _ _ _ _ _ _ _ _ _ d
4 fast: e _ _ _ _ _ s
5 from the heart of an urban area: i _ _ _ r-c _ _ y
6 not straight: w _ _ _ _ _ g
7 far away: r _ _ _ _ e
8 local and convenient: h _ _ _ y

5 Complete the sentences with a word from A and a word from B in each gap.

A entrance housing play traffic water weather

B area conditions crisis gates level sign

1 It's dangerous to climb over the .... to the park.
2 Remember to check the .... in the pool. It may be too deep.
3 The .... was full of children every day of the summer.
4 The match was cancelled due to the icy ....
5 Affordable apartments are what we need to beat the ....
6 We didn't see the .... for the speed limit.

6 Complete the sentences with the correct prepositions.

1 I was .... breath .... the time I'd climbed the steep hill so I waited before I was .... the move again.
2 I ate a yoghurt that wasn't .... date, but I don't think I was .... risk. .... the whole, if it smells OK, it's fine to eat.
3 When I'm .... myself, I love singing .... the top of my voice. It really helps me destress when I have a lot .... my mind.
4 Seeing my favourite star .... person took me .... surprise. In fact, she looked a little .... place wearing ordinary clothes and walking round town.
5 The pan was .... fire, but the chef was .... control of the situation and no one was .... danger.

7 Choose one word or phrase in each set that isn't possible.

1 catch: a train / a cold / the light / on board
2 lose: interest / a flight / patience / your temper
3 make: a difference / the right thing / a fuss / a mess
4 take: charge / control / arrangements / your breath away
5 tell: a joke / a lie / something funny / the difference

5 A good sport

READING

1 Complete the conversations with these words.

> boast   jinx   nil   relieve   rivals   rooting for
> superior   yelling

A: Good shot, well played!

B: Who are you ¹... ?

A: Jo Richards. He's sure to win. He's by far the
² .... player.

A: Do you mind not ³... in my
ear?

B: Sorry, it's just I'm so anxious about the final score.

A: Take a few deep breaths. That's meant to
⁴... stress.

A: I wouldn't normally ⁵... , but
we played brilliantly.

B: What was the score?

A: Eight– ⁶... to us.

A: How come you always wear that hat to
competitions?

B: I first wore my lucky cap when I wasn't
doing well and then my luck changed. It's
always with me at competitions so as not to
⁷... my performance.

A: You don't need a cap to help you beat your
⁸... .

B: Possibly, but I'm still going to wear the cap!

2 Read the first paragraph of the blog. Choose the
picture that best illustrates who the blogger is.

3 Read the blog post and choose the correct answer (A, B, C or D).

1 What is the main purpose of the introduction?

  A to illustrate the difference between live sports and games on TV

  B to ask the reader about their experience of being a sports fan

  C to highlight the role of relatives in becoming a sports fan

  D to tell an interesting story about a family who likes football

2 What does the writer say about being a fan of a local team or player?

  A The sportspeople don't have to play brilliantly to get huge support from the fans.

  B Fans from the same area are more likely to know about the history of their club.

  C It's cheaper to get to matches if you live in the same geographical area as your team.

  D If you can't get to a stadium to see a game, it's easy to follow it on the news.

3 According to the writer, what might make a person become a sports fan?

  A being influenced by a particular brand of sports clothes

  B developing an interest in a sport you have never tried before

  C travelling to another country and seeing the international importance of sport

  D witnessing outstanding sporting performance by a team or player

4 What does the writer mean when she uses the phrase 'jump on the bandwagon' in line 32?

  A shout very loudly at matches, but not really understand the game

  B withdraw support when a team stops being successful

  C not consider yourself a true supporter of a team

  D annoy people by talking about nothing else, but your team

5 In the fourth paragraph, the writer suggests that you can't be a true fan if you

  A ever find your team's performance boring.

  B don't listen to others who have more knowledge than you.

  C haven't made the choice of team voluntarily.

  D don't have friends who are as enthusiastic as you.

6 In the final paragraph, how does the writer summarise the importance of family and sport?

  A Being under pressure from her family shows she's a true fan.

  B Being fans of the same team brings the family closer together.

  C Having to devote time to sport is just part of family life.

  D Having the same interests as older generations is something to be proud of.

Team talk

HOME | **BLOG** | GALLERY | ABOUT | CONTACT

I'm on my feet, team scarf raised above my head, yelling at the TV as our top scorer touches down in the closing seconds of the game. I look around at my grandpa, dad and uncle and tears sting my eyes. It's an emotional moment. Three generations of the same family united in their love for their team. I was raised on a diet of live and TV games, and team stats. Even my first party dress had the Chicago Bears logo all over it. So I can't say that I really chose the team, it chose me. But if a team or sport isn't in your family DNA, how do you know who to root for?

The most obvious route to becoming a sports fan is geographical. If there's a team or player who competes for your hometown, it creates an almost automatic affinity. You share the same space, the same history, maybe even the same accent. Local sportspeople are a source of civic pride and provoke fierce loyalty in their fans, even when the sporting performance is less than perfect. There's also a practical consideration: living in the same area as your team or homegrown hero means you actually get to see live games and follow their progress in local news.

Another reason is style. On occasions, a person can be simply so impressed by an individual sportsperson that they adopt the sport. Seeing Angelique Kerber return a seemingly impossible shot can turn a non-sports fan tennis crazy. Likewise, Usain Bolt powering along the track has made athletics fans of us all. Dream teams can also have the same effect. Now you don't need to be from the city of Barcelona to back Barca football club. Like many other soccer teams, they have developed into a brand that stands for style and success, with huge international appeal.

Some say that sport shouldn't be about style at all, but about a gut feeling that you will support players through thick and thin. Which brings me to the possibly less noble reasons for choosing a team. For any 'true' supporter, the worst kind of fans are those who jump on the bandwagon. They shout their support loudest when times are good and the top trophies are being won, but are nowhere to be seen when the bad times hit. These fairweather fans follow a team or player through the glory days only to switch allegiance at the first sign of trouble. And they really annoy the fans who remain loyal through the inevitable highs and lows of sporting life.

If team-switching makes you a fake fan, so does peer pressure. No one should support a team or player because they are told to. Of course, if you spend time with a diehard fan of any sport, the enthusiasm starts to rub off on you. So you may find yourself developing a genuine interest and benefiting from that person's knowledge. But to be told you have to offer your support because your dad / mom / boyfriend / girlfriend does is the road to boredom and resentment. And by the way, it's always clear when a person is at a game who doesn't really want to be there.

So what about my own case? Do I consider myself a 'true' fan? Of course. Hasn't there been pressure from my family to do what they do? Well, I don't see it that way. I don't have to devote myself to their team or to sport at all. I enjoy the tight connection that being in a fan family offers me. The support we show our team is an extension of the support we show for each other. It's a kind of inheritance, as much as having my dad's nose, being good at music like my mom, or owning a ring that was my grandma's. Who wouldn't want to root for that?

Extend

4 Find the words or phrases in the blog post that match the definitions.

1 a strong connection (para 1) ....

2 a very strong feeling of support (para 1)

   ....

3 to support (para 2) ....

4 through good and bad times (para 3) ....

5 a supporter who is loyal and refuses to change (para 4)

   ....

6 to be passed on to you (para 4) ....

32

GRAMMAR

infinitive and verb + -ing

1 Choose the correct words to complete the rules.

1 **Running** is my favourite form of exercise.
The -ing form here is **an adjective / a noun**.

2 You can't **make** people **enjoy** sport.
Another verb that follows this pattern is **allow / let**.

3 It can be **challenging / difficult / fun / interesting** …
The **to-infinitive / -ing form** follows words like this.

4 You can download the fitness app **in order to monitor** your progress.
You **can / can't** use the -ing form after certain phrases that express purpose.

5 I didn't **expect to enjoy** the match as much as I did.
Another verb that follows this pattern is **admit / promise**.

6 I've never been very **keen on playing** team sports.
The -ing form is used here because **it comes after a preposition / it's talking about the present**.

2 Choose the correct verb in each pair to complete the sentences.

1 managed / succeeded
  A I just .... to beat my personal best in the race.
  B She .... in completing the race in record time.

2 allow me / let me
  A My coach wouldn't .... try the 1500-metre race.
  B My parents don't .... to go running after dark.

3 offered / suggested
  A Dad .... teaching Mum golf.
  B The PE teacher .... to give us extra training.

4 make / force
  A You'll never .... me to enjoy football the way you do.
  B You can't .... me support the same team as you.

5 able / capable
  A I've never been .... of throwing a ball very far.
  B I'd love to be .... to serve really well in tennis.

6 feel like / want
  A Do you .... coming to the gym with me?
  B Why don't you .... to try a new sport?

3 Choose the correct words to complete the conversation.

A: Selfies at the gym? Why can't people work out without **[1]telling / to tell** everyone on social media?

B: Some people can't help **[2]to share / sharing** everything online. It's just a habit.

A: Can you imagine **[3]to run / running** a marathon in just over two hours? How would you prepare your body **[4]to do / doing** that?

B: It involves **[5]training / to train** for hours of course but they also say, that top runners are born, not made. They have a special capacity that permits **[6]to take / them to take** in more oxygen when they run.

4 Complete the article with the correct form of the verbs.

Making the most of
music

Music has always played a large part in
[1] .... (motivate) athletes to perform well. Research by Dr Karagorrghis, a psychologist at Brunel University, suggests that [2] .... (listen) to music while exercising moderately can make you feel like you aren't working as hard. Hearing music you associate with memories of high performance can also help you feel inspired [3] .... (push) yourself harder while working out.

But can music really make you better at sports? This research shows it can help [4] .... (encourage) you to exercise as you begin a routine, making you feel motivated and eager to reach your goals. Once you start working really hard music won't help you [5] .... (sustain) your exercise efforts. However, it can help you cool down again and relax as your heart rate is [6] .... (return) to a normal level, particularly if you listen to tracks with a simple, slower beat. So basically, music can be most helpful at the beginning and end of a workout!

Health professionals do advise athletes [7] .... (not/listen) to loud music through headphones on a regular basis. They recommend [8] .... (follow) the 'eighty for ninety' rule: limiting the volume to eighty percent of the maximum for no more than ninety minutes a day. And never wear headphones when exercising outdoors. You need to be able to hear what's going on around you in order to stay safe.

VOCABULARY

sport

1 🔊 5.1 Listen to three people talking about sport. What is each person talking about? Listen and choose the correct answer.

1	spectators	opponents	teammates
2	coordination	teamwork	training
3	a championship	a trophy	a title

2 Match two of these nouns with each of the verbs (1–5).

a championship   an opponent   a silver medal   a tournament   coordination
fans   prize money   spectators   the rival team   training

1 take part in / enter / qualify for / win: ..../...................

2 attract / delight / disappoint: ..../...................

3 require / involve / demand: ..../...................

4 compete for / win: ..../...................

5 defeat / beat: ..../...................

3 Read the blog post and decide which answer (A, B, C or D) best fits each gap.

Training in a **team of one**

I have a confession to make – I don't play team sports. I know that they ¹.......................... fans all over the world, but they're just not for me. I used to play hockey, but was never good enough to ².......................... for school competitions. Maybe I just didn't have the coordination you ³.......................... for hitting the ball. Whatever the reason, it doesn't mean that I'm a couch potato now. I run and cycle four to five times a week, so I'm pretty fit. I'm not part of any club, but I sometimes ⁴.......................... part in events to support local charities. Although I don't enter ⁵.......................... or ever compete for ⁶.......................... , I am competitive – with myself. I may never ⁷.......................... an opponent, but for me that is not what exercise is about. I love the personal challenge of improving. That may not involve ⁸.......................... , but it does take determination.

1	**A** demand	**B** delight	**C** depend	**D** defend
2	**A** win	**B** succeed	**C** enter	**D** qualify
3	**A** require	**B** involve	**C** demand	**D** apply
4	**A** have	**B** do	**C** take	**D** make
5	**A** medals	**B** performances	**C** trophies	**D** championships
6	**A** events	**B** titles	**C** competitions	**D** races
7	**A** defeat	**B** win	**C** compete	**D** qualify
8	**A** team	**B** teammate	**C** teamwork	**D** team player

4 Complete the sentences with the missing words.

1 Nick is so reliable. I can always count .... him to score.

2 Despite not being favourites, we took .... the rival team and won four to three.

3 Olga shows .... all the time. She never stops talking about all her trophies.

4 The hockey team were knocked .... in the last round by older players.

5 I hate working .... at the gym. I'd much rather go swimming.

Extend

5 Match the examples (1–5) with the types of phrasal verbs (A–E).

1 I **ran out of energy**.

2 Please **pick up the ball**. / Please **pick the ball up**.

3 Very few fans **turned up**.

4 Please **pick it up**.

5 Tell the crowd to **get off the pitch**.

A two-part; doesn't have an object; not separable

B two-part; must have an object; separable

C two-part, separable; must be separated when the object is a pronoun

D two-part; must have an object; not separable

E three-part; must have an object; not separable

6 Match the highlighted phrasal verbs in the sentences (1–6) with the meanings (A–F). Which verbs are separable in these contexts?

1 It's essential to warm up before you start the race.

2 What time does the match kick off?

3 After a lot of bad behaviour, the referee had to send off two players.

4 What made you get into horse-riding?

5 If you come down with a cold, you can still do some light exercise.

6 We'll need to put off the final until the track is repaired.

A become interested in

B start

C ask to leave the game

D postpone

E start to suffer from

F get the body ready for exercise

49

LISTENING

🔊 **5.2** Listen to an interview with a boy about his favourite sport. Why has he been invited on the radio programme?

A to say how he became champion

B to talk about why some sports are more popular

C to introduce people to a sport they may not know about

🔊 **5.3** Listen again and choose the correct answer (A, B or C).

1 How do people react when Nathan first talks about floorball?

    A People say they already know a lot about it.

    B People misunderstand what he's referring to.

    C People think it sounds a funny sport to play.

2 How is floorball different from other similar sports?

    A It's played both indoors and outdoors.

    B It's played in teams of five.

    C It's never played in the open air.

3 Why in Nathan's opinion is floorball exciting?

    A Competing for just twenty minutes forces players to score quickly.

    B Replacing players at any point alters what happens in the game.

    C Playing for more than ninety minutes means you require a lot of skills.

4 According to Nathan, what's important to be able to play floorball well?

    A having the correct weight of equipment

    B competing with people of a similar age

    C being skilled, but not necessarily strong

5 What made Nathan first try floorball?

    A His youth club didn't have football or basketball on offer.

    B He was curious to try a sport with both genders in a team.

    C He became bored of playing old-fashioned team sports.

6 How does Nathan feel if people call floorball uncool?

    A He doesn't care as he's happy to play a sport that is different.

    B He doesn't agree because he says floorball will be as popular as football one day.

    C He doesn't understand why his sport is less popular than he would like.

7 In Nathan's opinion, what is the future for floorball?

    A It will become more popular in places where it is already played.

    B It is becoming more popular now that it's an Olympic sport.

    C It needs to become an international sport to grow in popularity.

Extend

Choose the correct words to complete the sentences.

1 I must admit, that's a **new one on / news to** me.

2 They **throw / launch** into a long description of Liverpool's latest match.

3 You won't find us freezing to **death / die** on an outdoor hockey pitch.

4 A successful player relies more on tactics than strength in floorball. A good **job / work** because I'm not exactly Superman!

5 To be honest, it doesn't really **mind / bother** me what other people say.

6 It suits me to **do / make** my own thing and not to play the same old games as everyone else.

7 **Since when / For how long** do we need a popularity contest for sport?

8 There are sixty member associations from all continents, so it's pretty **many / much** international.

Complete the chatroom posts with the correct form of the phrases from Ex 3. There is one phrase you do not need.

● ● ●

Can a sport be *cool?*

I was just flipping through a magazine and I came across a questionnaire: Is your sport in or out of fashion? Apparently, judo is cool and trendy, but poor netball is just the opposite. This idea of a sport being in fashion is a ¹.............................. . What do you think?

K8   Add message | Report

Sounds a bit silly to me. Though it's a ²..........................
that I don't play netball. 🙂 Give me athletics any day!

Ayjay   Add message | Report

³.......................... has netball become uncool? It's a great
game – ⁴.......................... the best sport I've ever played.

JoJo   Add message | Report

Don't let it ⁵.......................... you, just
⁶.......................... and play whatever you like.

GameBoy   Add message | Report

Only one true cool sport, I'm afraid, and that's gaming.
Much better than ⁷..........................
on some muddy
pitch somewhere.

USE OF ENGLISH 1

1 Choose the correct words to complete the sentences.

1 I think it's time we **bring / brought** on a substitute.

2 Three players are ill. **Would / Had** we better cancel the game?

3 I'd rather you **didn't / wouldn't** spend all day out.

4 You'd better **leaving / leave** the game. You're injured.

5 I'm exhausted! Is it time we **go / to go** home now?

6 I'd rather **going / go** for a run than play handball.

2 Complete the sentences with the correct form of the verbs. In which two sentences are two forms possible?

1 I regret ever .... (become) a fan of this team. They're hopeless.

2 If those weights are too much, try .... (start) with something lighter.

3 Can we take a break? I need to stop .... (catch) my breath.

4 The crowd started .... (cheer) as soon as the star player came on.

5 Did you remember .... (book) the gym? It gets really busy at weekends.

6 Although my team wasn't playing well, I continued .... (support) them.

7 Sorry, I forgot .... (mention) that we had training yesterday.

8 Ignore the rain. Let's go on .... (play) for the full eighty minutes.

3 🔊 5.4 **Listen to five questions or statements from different conversations and choose the correct next line (A or B).**

1 A Don't forget to get tickets for the live basketball match.

 B I'll never forget getting tickets to my first live basketball match.

2 A Sorry. I meant to phone to let you know.

 B That means phoning to let you know.

3 A Thanks, but I stopped eating sugar a couple of weeks ago.

 B Thanks, but I stopped to eat sugar a couple of weeks ago.

4 A Sure, I remember giving it back to you before the weekend.

 B Sure, but remember to give it back to me before the weekend.

5 A I know. I regret saying that now. I'm sorry.

 B I know. I regret to say I'm sorry.

4 Complete the article with the correct form of the verbs.

●●●

Time for talent

Would you rather [1] .... (play) in a team of just boys, just girls, or in a team of the best players? I've always wanted the challenge of competing with – and against – the best. I remember [2] .... (ask) if I could join the boys' basketball team. The manager said, 'You'd better [3] .... (stay) with the girls. It'll be easier for you.' Of course, I didn't stop [4] .... (practise). If anything, it made me more determined.

But now some people in sport are trying [5] .... (change) things. They realise that sport isn't all about strength. Performing well means [6] .... (develop) techniques and skills – for both genders. And remembering [7] .... (focus) on talent and not gender benefits sport at all levels.

So what about the future? It's strange that one of the newest sports is leading the way. E-sports have been looking at ways of promoting mixed teams on their tournaments. But whether you're a gamer or a golfer, it's time we [8] .... (see) past gender in favour of talent and skill.

5 Complete the second sentence so that it has a similar meaning to the first sentence using the word given. Use between two and five words, including the word given.

1 I am sorry, but we have been knocked out of the tournament.
 REGRET
 I .... you that we have been knocked out of the tournament.

2 These trainers are worn out. I should get a new pair.
 GOT
 These trainers are worn out. It's .... a new pair.

3 I'm not keen on playing football, but I love basketball.
 WOULD
 I .... than football.

4 The manager ought to buy some new players before next season.
 HAD
 The manager .... some new players before next season.

5 The teams continued to play into injury time.
 WENT
 The teams .... into injury time.

6 You must make an effort to attend every practice session.
 TRY
 It's important to .... every practice session.

51

USE OF ENGLISH 2

Form nouns from the verbs. Which is the odd one out in each group?

1 exhaust, expect, connect ....

2 differ, embarrass, amuse ....

3 assist, appear, achieve ....

4 behave, frustrate, motivate ....

5 question, decide, trade ....

Complete the conversations with the correct form of the words. Which two words do not need to change?

A: Have you seen much **1** .... (improve) in your tennis?

B: Not much, to be honest. I think I need more **2** .... (guide), you know, proper training.

A: There's a good coach at my club. She's very experienced and she's got a lot of **3** .... (qualify).

A: What do you think of the new sports kit?

B: The **4** .... (design) and **5** .... (comfort) are great, but I can't say I like the colour.

A: Sorry, but all the kits are already in **6** .... (produce).

A: That new striker must be the **7** .... (discover) of the century. He's amazing!

B: Yes, we're delighted about the **8** .... (decide) to sign him up. Let's hope he can live up to our **9** .... (expect).

Complete the sentences with the correct prefixes.

1 Don't ....behave or be ....polite in class.

2 ....payment of bike loan due today.

3 Can we ....arrange the match? My cousin has arrived ....expectedly.

4 ....honest or ....moral behaviour will not be tolerated.

5 I think you ....understood the question. Sections of the essay are ....relevant.

6 ....visible drones made ....legal.

Complete the sentences with the correct form of the words in brackets in the correct order, using negative prefixes.

1 It's .... to think that something is good value just because it's .... (logic, expense)

2 If you .... of the way someone behaves because they are always talking .... you should tell them. (sense, approve)

3 Be careful with gestures and other .... responses if you are .... with the local culture. (verbal, familiar)

4 Giving away your password was the most .... thing you've ever done, but I guess it's .... now you have changed it. (responsible, relevant)

Read the article and complete it with the correct form of the word in capitals.

Fitness needn't cost a fortune

I never go to the gym. Don't
1 .... me, a gym is a great place to get fit and it isn't that I lack **2** .... It's just that for me membership at a well-run centre is completely
3 .... Plus there's the problem of the contract. If you decide not to go, it works out very expensive because the fee is usually not
4 .... So how do you get fit on a budget? The answer is **5** .... simple: use what you have around you. There's an almost ready-made gym in and around your home. No, I'm not talking **6** .... ! Water bottles or tins can be used as weights, stairs provide great aerobic exercise, and push-ups can be done against any wall or floor. Work in your own time and at your own pace, without the **7** .... of having to sign up for a class. But also be prepared to explain the **8** .... of the tins from the kitchen cupboard! 😊
Have fun!

UNDERSTAND

COMMIT

AFFORD

FUND

CREDIBLE

SENSE

CONVENIENT

APPEAR

SPEAKING

1 Which of these words can be used to describe photo A, photo B or both?

coach   competitive   equipment   everyday clothes   fresh air
friendships   indoors   outdoors   physical exercise
pre-match talk   relaxed   sociable   team kit   teamwork

2 Put the words in the correct order to make sentences. Which photo does each sentence refer to?

1 of / a / it's / the / Perhaps / final / tournament.

....

2 park. / of / looks / a / It / like / kind

....

3 out / school. / they're / Maybe / after / hanging / just

....

4 match / of / be / beginning / may / not / It / the / the

....

3 Choose the correct words to complete the sentences.

1 From their body language, the boys appear tense, so the coach **may / can** not be very happy with them.

2 It **looks / looks like** relaxed and informal.

3 They've **probable / probably** known each other for quite a long time.

4 The other team **couldn't / might** not be an easy opponent to beat.

5 It **looks like / looks** he's feeling tired.

6 I **get / take** the impression that they're playing just for fun.

7 They may **had / have** already lost to the other team before.

4 5.5 Listen to six students talking about the photos and complete the sentences. Then listen again and mark the main stresses.

1 .... the friends, who are not competing with each other, the team are .... thinking about the score.

2 .... groups may spend a lot of time together, but for .... reasons.

3 The team .... be worried about making mistakes in front of spectators .... for the friends it doesn't matter if they do something wrong.

4 As they're playing to win, the team .... not enjoy the activity as .... as the group of friends.

5 In the first picture, the friends are .... using the equipment, but in the first it .... be half-time or during a pre-match talk.

6 .... the friends don't need to think about motivation whereas for the team that's an .... part of the activity.

5 Complete a student's answer with these words.

appear   background   beat   benefit   definitely   equipment
getting   good   hand   looks   main   notice

Well, the first thing to **1**........................ is that it **2**........................ like the same activity of basketball, although you can't see any **3**........................ in the first picture, so it could be a different sport. Unlike the second picture, the team are playing indoors and you can see the rival team in the **4**........................ . The group of friends seem to be enjoying being outdoors in the fresh air. The **5**........................ difference between the two groups is the reason for playing. In the first picture, it's **6**........................ a competitive situation, but in the second the group are playing just for fun. For the friends, the biggest **7**........................ is just being in each other's company and **8**........................ some exercise. It probably doesn't matter who wins. On the other **9**........................, for the team the score is likely to be the most important thing. From their body language, they **10**........................ to be listening to the coach very carefully. Maybe he is giving advice on how to **11**........................ their opponents. Playing in a competitive way like this is **12**........................ for increasing your motivation and possibly your fitness too. It's also very important for team-building.

6 What question was the student asked?

Compare the pictures and say ...

A how you think these different groups of people are feeling.

B what you think the advantages are of doing sport in these different ways.

C why these people have chosen these places to spend time together.

7 Record your answers to the questions in Ex 6. Listen and think about how you could improve them.

WRITING

an article

1 Read the task and underline the key words.

You have seen this post on an English-language website.

Do you feel stressed?

We want articles on how people deal with stress. Tell us what things you do to beat stress and how they make you feel better.

The best articles will appear on our site next month.

2 Choose the correct words to complete the sentences.

1 Life today can be **stressful / stressed** for young people.

2 **Stress / The stress** is part of everyday life and can be a good thing.

3 It's normal to get **stressed / stressing** at exam time.

4 When you're stressed **over / out**, do something active.

5 No one should live **below / under** stress for long periods.

3 Match the sentence beginnings (1–6) and endings (A–F).

1 A long walk always clears

2 It's good to try and look

3 Try to eat food that's good for

4 Exam nerves always get me

5 The thing that puts me

6 Don't forget to make

A my head when I'm busy.

B time for seeing friends.

C down so I need advice then.

D in a good mood is music.

E your overall health.

F on the bright side and be positive.

4 Complete the sentences with the correct form of the verbs.

1 When you feel like .... (take) a break, have one.

2 All in all, there's no such thing as a stress-free life, but I recommend you .... (try) these tips and see what works for you.

3 Are you fed up with .... (get) stressed out?

4 There's no point .... (worry) about what you can't change.

5 Try to avoid .... (stare) at a screen late at night.

6 What's the one thing that makes us all .... (feel) low sometimes? Stress.

7 So to sum up, stress can make us perform better, but when things get too much, it's always possible .... (make) positive changes.

8 If you're organised, you won't let yourself .... (get) too stressed out at exam times.

5 Match the sentences in Ex 4 (1–8) with these sections of an article.

Introduction	....	....
Main paragraphs	....	....
	....	....
Conclusion	....	....

6 Complete the sentences with these phrasal verbs. Then match the sentences (1–6) with the topics (A–E). There is one topic that matches two sentences.

get back to   get down   get round to   get through   get together   get up

1 A short sleep can help your concentration, but not for too long – .... after about twenty minutes.

2 Don't let arguments .... you .... They're part of everyday life.

3 If you can't .... having a proper meal, eat fruit rather than sweets.

4 Have a break from Instagram. The world won't have changed when you .... it.

5 This is a stressful period to .... , so a revision plan is essential.

6 Enjoy your days off. .... with friends and do what makes you happy.

A free time ....   D relationships ....

B social media ....   E diet ....

C studying / exams ....

7 Look at the writing task in Ex 1 again. Which two titles are better for this article?

A From stressed to best   C Top tips for tackling stress

B My ways of beating stress   D Stress isn't good

8 Write your article in 140–190 words, using an appropriate style.

UNIT CHECK

1 Complete the conversation with the correct form of the verbs.

A: Have you seen that new ballet for fitness class? It says it's open to guys as well as girls.

B: Yes, I was quite tempted ¹... (sign up).

A: You're joking! Will they make you ²... (wear) a tutu?

B: Oh, there's no point ³... (talk) to you. I can expect you ⁴... (make) a joke of everything.

A: It's just a bit surprising ⁵... (think) of you doing ballet.

B: It's ballet training, not dancing! And my coach advised me ⁶... (consider) it, for flexibility and strength – exactly what I need for athletics.

A: OK, sorry. Are you likely ⁷... (join) the class?

B: Yes, I think so. Do you feel like ⁸... (come) too?

A: I think I'll carry on ⁹... (do) weights at the gym.

2 Complete the sentences with the correct form of these words.

'd better + see 'd rather + not tell 'd rather + ride it's time + blow
it's time + finish

1 It's late. I think .... we .... our run.

2 I'm not in the cycling club. I .... on my own.

3 Your wrist is swollen. You .... the nurse.

4 I .... you .... me how to play. That's not your job.

5 The ninety minutes are over. .... the final whistle.

3 Complete the article with one word in each gap.

Give pushy parents the red card!

I'll never ¹... being at my first school sports day and winning a race. It's one of my clearest memories. The teachers ²... time congratulating all the kids so that no one felt left out. It was a nice introduction to sport and now ³... rugby is part of my life. I would look forward to ⁴... some exercise every weekend. That was until the pushy parents turned up. They shout insults if a player makes a mistake, even at their own kids! I think they do it ⁵... as to make the children more competitive, but it's awful. Last week, one woman wouldn't stop yelling at her son. The referee said she ⁶... better calm down or he wouldn't ⁷... her to attend another match. It's time she and parents like her ⁸... how to behave.

4 Replace the hightlighted text with these phrasal verbs.

count on get back to gets me down get through
get together get up showing off taken on
worked out

1 A: I offered this gym pass to my sister, but she turned it down. Would you like it?

B: Yes, please! It's been ages since I did some exercise at the gym.

2 A: He's always trying to be the centre of attention on the court.

B: I know. It's just a pity you can't rely on him to score!

3 A: Playing in the winter always makes me miserable.

B: I know, but let's warm up and we'll survive the session.

4 A: How's your ankle? Are you able to stand up and walk on it?

B: Yes, but only slowly. I can't return to playing sport yet.

5 A: Do you want to meet up this weekend?

B: Sorry I can't. I've accepted the job of coaching the swimming team.

5 Complete the sentences with the correct form of these pairs of words.

amuse + sense apply + relevant approve + logical
behave + embarrass expensive + responsible

1 Most of the equipment was ...., but it was still .... to leave it lying all over the field.

2 Two parents had to leave the match when their .... became an .... to the whole school.

3 How can playing computer games for .... be called a sport? That sounds like .... to me.

4 Why do people .... of mixed teams? It seems .... to me when there are so many good female players.

5 I had to fill in a huge .... form at the gym and most of the questions were .... to someone my age.

55

READING

1 Complete the movie review with these words.

blur   exploits   miniature   narrative   sequence

Attack of the No-bots

⭐⭐⭐⭐⭐

You don't often get science fiction and comedy in one movie, but *Attack of the No-bots* offers just that. It's about the ¹ .... of an army of ² .... robots sent to attack Earth. The problem is they have been badly programmed and do the exact opposite of what they are supposed to! The film starts with the population of a town trying to make out what the ³ .... of activity in the skies is. They realise thousands of bots are descending and expect an attack with killer lasers, but instead they get a shower of flowers! The ⁴ .... of the rest of the film is just as silly, but great fun. It's basically a ⁵ .... of events in which the bots do all they can to make friends and live like humans.

2 Read the article about dyslexia quickly. Tick (✓) the sentences that best describe the article.

A The writer talks about dyslexia from a personal point of view. ☐

B The article is written for a general, non-scientific reader. ☐

C The article offers hints and tips for people experiencing reading difficulties. ☐

D The writer's aim is to help the reader understand problems faced by dyslexics. ☐

E The style used is mainly factual and neutral. ☐

F The writer suggests ways that the reader could find out more about the topic. ☐

3 Read the article again and choose which sentence (A–G) fits each gap (1–6). You do not need one of the sentences.

A In this way, it's possible to get an insight into the time and effort required for a dyslexic to process text.

B Sensing movement in completely static text is a common in many dyslexics.

C And because no two dyslexics experience the condition in the same way, understanding an individual's frustration with reading is even more challenging.

D Instead, they often have high levels of creativity and develop strong problem-solving skills in many areas.

E However, it isn't a perfect experiment as dyslexia takes many forms.

F This amounts to about 700 million children and adults, although the figure could be higher as it is often undiagnosed.

G Equally important is education of the general public to improve the understanding of people with reading difficulties.

Extend

4 Read the definitions. Find words in the article to complete the phrases.

1 be common to people who are related (para 1): .... families

2 understand more fully (para 2): get a .... of something

3 decreases the speed or rate (para 3): .... down

4 in the incorrect position / order (para 4): the .... way ....

5 begin again (para 5): .... to the ....

6 not appreciate fully (para 5): .... for ....

7 succeed in dealing with problems (para 6): .... their challenges

8 people who are very successful (para 6): high-.............................

5 Complete the sentences with the correct forms of some of the words or phrases from Ex 4.

1 We started the race well, but then we took the wrong route and had to .... We weren't last, but that mistake really .... us ....

2 Never .... people .... Always say thank you when they help you .... a .... or a difficulty.

Try being me for a day: dyslexia

In the next in our series of articles on viewpoints and understanding how others live, we look at what it's like to be dyslexic. Although a very common condition, dyslexia is not easily understood. It is generally defined as a permanent learning difficulty that affects reading and spelling despite normal intelligence levels and eyesight.

It is estimated that at least one in ten people worldwide has the condition. [1].. . Dyslexia runs in families and it can affect co-ordination, short-term memory and the ability to recall names, as well as the problems of understanding written language. Lack of fluency in reading not only has a negative effect on progress at school, but it also lowers confidence and self-esteem.

For those of us with no experience of dyslexia, it's hard to imagine being unable to work out letters on a screen or page easily and quickly. [2].. . That's why a graphic designer, himself dyslexic, has created a typeface that aims to help people get a better appreciation of the condition.

Daniel Britton broke down the alphabet in the Helvetica typeface, taking away forty percent of the lines to produce a skeleton of each letter. Although this doesn't necessarily imitate what a dyslexic person sees, it slows down a non-dyslexic's reading. [3].. . In Daniel's own words, 'I need the viewer to have to work to read something so simple as a poster.'

In today's world where we read so much on screen, how does a dyslexic deal with the internet? A Swedish developer and blogger called Victor Widell was inspired by a dyslexic friend to find out just that. He took her words and turned them into a simulation that shows non-dyslexics how unstable the text is on screen. Part of his friend's original words were, 'A friend who has dyslexia described to me how she experiences reading. She can read, but it takes a lot of concentration and the letters seem to 'jump around'.' [4].. . A further characteristic is seeing the letters d, and b, and p and q the wrong way round, which makes it impossible to distinguish one from another.

As a result of the coding used for the simulation, Widell was able to make the letters constantly change position so that they appear to bounce on the screen. When you think you've worked out a word, the letters become mixed up again and you have to go back to the start. Widell's clever use of coding gives us a clear example of the challenges of dyslexia with something that we all take for granted. [5].. . Some people with the condition said the simulation represented what they experienced while others said it was easier or just different.

What is clear is the need for further research into the condition so it is diagnosed early. Improved teacher training is also necessary to help dyslexics overcome their challenges. [6].. . In recent times, a number of high-achievers in different fields have revealed that they are dyslexic, not least the billionaire entrepreneurs Bill Gates and Richard Branson. A surprisingly large number of actors have also overcome dyslexia to follow their chosen career, including Tom Cruise, Orlando Bloom and Keira Knightley.

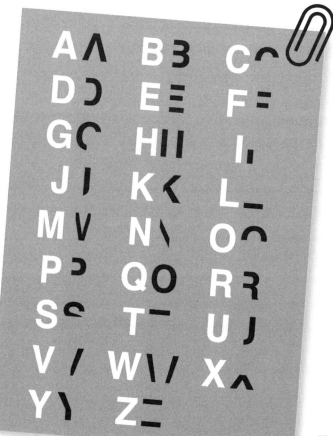

GRAMMAR

the passive

Read the statements about filming wildlife and decide if they are true (T) or false (F)?

1 The wildlife is being filmed in its natural habitat.

In this sentence, the focus is on the camera operators, not on the animals. ....

2 **A** You should respect other people's opinions.

B Other people's opinions should be respected.

Sentence B is more formal than A. ....

3 The footage of the eagle was filmed on location in Spain.

This sentence needs 'by the camera crew' to be complete. ....

4 I stepped on a snake and nearly got bitten.

This sentence is more likely to appear in conversation than formal writing. ....

5 She was awarded first prize for her film on local wildlife.

You wouldn't normally use *got* instead of *was* in this sentence. ....

6 **A** It is said that cats are more independent than dogs.

B Cats are said to be more independent than dogs.

Sentences A and B don't mean the same thing. ....

Complete the sentences with one missing word.

1 She was really upset about .... dropped from the basketball team.

2 We were disappointed because the film we wanted to see .... being shown.

3 The lift is out of order. It .... be repaired as soon as possible.

4 Keep your ticket because you might .... asked to show it at any time.

5 Our online magazine .... published once a month.

6 The castle was .... out of stone in the tenth century.

7 We couldn't cross over the water because the bridge .... been completed.

8 Factories across the region are .... closed due to the economic crisis.

9 The theft is still under investigation and the thief .... not yet been found.

10 Mum is working just now so she doesn't want to .... disturbed.

Complete the second sentence so that it has a similar meaning to the first sentence. Give two answers for number 6.

1 People say she's the best singer of her generation.
She ....

2 People claim that the result of the election was unfair.
It ....

3 The papers report that the celebrities got married in secret.
The celebrities ....

4 Millions of people all over the world shared the online video.
The online video ....

5 They made us wait for hours before they let us into the stadium.
We ....
before we ....

6 They showed the visitors the most interesting parts of the city.
The most interesting parts of the city ....
The visitors ....

Complete the article with a suitable form of the verbs in passive form. Use short forms where possible.

Dare to step into the darkness

Have you ever walked around your town after dark? Darkness [1] .... always .... (associate) with crime. It [2] .... also .... (think) to be the time for ghosts and monsters, so why go out after midnight? Simply to get a new perspective on where you live. Walks in the hours of darkness [3] .... now .... (offer) by a group called NightOwls.

I was nervous about trying a nightwalk, but I [4] .... (persuade) to give it a go and I'm glad I did. At 2 a.m. last Sunday, as the group [5] .... (guide) away from the streetlights, the town felt like a film set. And after my eyes had adjusted to the darkness, I felt surprisingly at home. My hearing [6] .... (allow) to take over. Car horns and mobiles [7] .... (replace) by the sounds of wildlife and the area [8] .... (light) by a million stars.

In our hi-tech world, we [9] .... so easily .... (get/distract) by gadgets. On a nightwalk, smartphones [10] .... (not have/leave) at home, but they [11] .... (must/keep) turned off. NightOwls want walkers to [12] .... (integrate) into the experience as fully as possible.

VOCABULARY

time and place

1 🔊 6.1 **Listen and choose the correct options (A, B or C) to complete the sentences.**

1 The ball is being kicked .... the wall.
   A across   **B** against   **C** towards

2 The girl is standing .... the house.
   A out   **B** out of   **C** outside

3 The friends are walking .... the forest.
   A through   **B** towards   **C** around

4 The woman is stuck .... the lift.
   A inside   **B** into   **C** to

5 The cars are speeding .... the race track.
   A above   **B** among   **C** round

6 The boy wasn't allowed .... the bus.
   A out of   **B** into   **C** onto

7 He challenged us to run .... the field.
   A round   **B** across   **C** into

8 The boy spilled a drink .... his phone.
   A above   **B** upon   **C** over

2 **Complete the conversations with these pairs of prepositions.**

across + opposite   among + between   into + inside   outside + out of
next to + near   under + below   up + above

1 **A:** It had better be worth walking .... this hill.
   B: We'll get great views from .... !

2 **A:** What's the matter with Jack? He's standing .... the club looking fed up.
   B: He just walked right .... the place without saying anything.

3 **A:** I wouldn't like to live just .... the road.
   B: I don't mind being just .... my college. It means I'm never late!

4 **A:** How are we going to find Lisa .... all these hundreds of people?
   B: She's just texted to say she's standing .... the burger van and the clothes stall.

5 **A:** The record shop used to be here, right .... the sandwich shop.
   B: Well, it looks like it closed down. Let's see if there are any other music shops .... here.

6 **A:** It's a really old trick. The magician climbs .... the box and it's sealed with chains and …
   B: They drop the curtain and then open the box and there's no one .... it! That's ancient!

7 **A:** Did you hear about that kid who found all those gold coins .... a tree?
   B: Apparently, they were buried a long way .... the surface of the soil.

3 **Replace the highlighted words or phrases with these prepositions.**

above   beneath   beside   by   round   towards

1 Keep going in the direction of the station and you'll find the car park on the left. ....

2 In the event of an emergency, life jackets are located underneath your seat. ....

3 We sat next to the river just enjoying the peace and quiet. ....

4 You can't miss the turning. It's just near the bank. ....

5 My dream is to sail around the world before I'm thirty. ....

6 You could see every detail of the glider as it flew just over our heads. ....

4 **Choose the correct words to complete the text.**

Moving forward **with music**

Learning to play an instrument can be frustrating. Sometimes you feel you're really doing well and your progress feels ¹**accelerated / speeded** up.
At other times, you can feel a bit stuck at the same level and ²**occasional / occasionally** you might even feel you're going backwards! If that happens, just ³**stick at / in** it and don't give up. It's worth trying some new techniques to help keep up the ⁴**moment / momentum**. For example, if you practise on a ⁵**daily / day** basis, change your start time or choice of music. And remember that you're learning ⁶**throughout / whenever** the time you're practising, although that feeling of progress may come and go.

5 🔊 **Complete the sentences with one word in each gap.**

1 Don't start your revision at the .... minute. Prepare in .... time for your first exam.

2 Hurry up! We're running .... The bus leaves at 8.15 and it's usually .... time.

3 I can't come out. I'm in the .... of my revision and it'll be too late .... the time I've finished.

4 I was on the .... of panicking because I didn't think we'd be in .... for the start of the concert.

5 Everyone finds controlling the bike difficult to begin .... You'll get used to it in .... time.

6 We used to meet up .... other weekend, but not recently. I guess we'll catch up .... or later.

LISTENING

6.2 **Listen to a young person talking about sound maps. Tick (✓) the topics he mentions.**

A how he became interested in sound maps ☐

B the equipment he has bought ☐

C the benefits of sound maps ☐

D how to become an expert mapper ☐

E suggestions for making your first sound map ☐

F how to produce good interviews ☐

G a different way of producing a local map ☐

H the life of a professional sound recordist ☐

6.3 **Listen again and complete the sentences with a word or short phrase.**

Mapping with s⦿und

♫ Adam first became interested in sound maps when he was studying ¹ .... at school.

♫ Adam says he is pleased that ² .... has improved to make sound mapping easier.

♫ The fact that sound can create clearer ³ .... than images really interests Adam.

♫ Nowadays, Adam says it's possible to create sound maps without expensive ⁴ ....

♫ As a simple tip, Adam reminds listeners to add a short ⁵ .... each time a recording is made.

♫ Map Maker is recommended by Adam as one of the simplest ⁶ .... to use.

♫ Adam states that most fans of sound mapping start their hobby with a map of their ⁷ ....

♫ According to Adam, when making a sound walk, local people provide the most useful facts in ⁸ ....

♫ Adam uses the word ⁹ .... to describe how many global sound maps are easily available on the internet.

♫ Adam's favourite site is ¹⁰ .... because of the variety of recordings on offer.

Extend

Match the phrases from the recording (1–8) with the definitions (A–H).

1 the technology has really moved on

2 the key thing is to include a brief description for every audio file

3 I would start simple and work your way up to something more sophisticated.

4 They know their region better than anyone and so can really bring the place to life.

5 take you off the beaten track to hidden spots.

6 But you don't have to keep it local.

7 I can't get over the number of maps that offer a global sound tour.

8 What's to stop you having a go?

A am surprised, shocked or amused by

B the most important consideration

C far from places that people normally visit

D trying something

E make somewhere interesting or exciting

F improved / become more sophisticated

G focus on just things that are near to you

H make progress in a slow and controlled way

Find and correct seven mistakes in the conversation.

A: So what are we going to do for this project? We need ideas that will increase tourism.

B: People expect clear information with one tap of a screen. Things have moved up from the days of paper maps and leaflets.

A: You're right. I can't go over the number of sites that have too much information. People can't choose what to do so they don't make a go at anything at all.

B: So maybe we should focus on a smaller area, you know, just keep it close.

A: Wouldn't that be a bit boring? The most key thing is to get people interested in this area. We'd need something that would really bring the place to live for them.

B: How about creating a top ten list of things to do in and around the city? Some could be right in the centre and others more of the beaten track. With just ten, we focus on fewer activities, but in more detail.

A: Nice! Let's get started.

USE OF ENGLISH 1

1 🔊 6.4 **Listen to six short recordings. Match the speakers (1–6) with the sentences (A–F) you think they say next.**

A Why don't we have a special cake made?

B I'm having my braces removed tomorrow. I can't wait to have straight teeth!

C It would be my dream to get some boots made to fit me exactly.

D I'd better go and get my eyes tested.

E So there wouldn't be any point in getting nail art done.

F If not, find the fastest way of having that tattoo removed.

Speaker 1 ....
Speaker 2 ....
Speaker 3 ....
Speaker 4 ....
Speaker 5 ....
Speaker 6 ....

2 **Choose the correct ending to complete the sentences (A or B).**

1 I broke my wrist, but I'll be having the plaster
   A taking off soon.
   B taken off soon.

2 On the first day of the school trip, I had
   A my phone taken from my bag.
   B someone to take my phone from my bag.

3 It's time they grew up. They can't have
   A everyone do everything for them all the time.
   B everyone did everything for them all the time.

4 He cheated. He got his friend
   A writing all his essays for him.
   B to write all his essays for him.

5 It's popular for parties so the hall needs
   A booking a long time in advance.
   B to book a long time in advance.

3 **Complete the chatroom posts with the correct form of these verbs.**

---
get + build   get + understand   have + steal   have + take out
---

Make one change

What one thing would make your life better?

K8ty — Add message | Report

I share a room with my noisy sister. If I could, I ¹... my own private space .... on top of our flat.

StarGirl — Add message | Report

My friend's stopped speaking to me. If I could, I'd go back in time and ²... her .... I didn't mean to hurt her.

LH@16 — Add message | Report

To be a million miles from here. I ³... a tooth .... and I'm petrified. 😬

4 **Choose the correct words to complete the post.**

● ● ●

Too busy?
Online services are happy to help

People complain they don't have time to run everyday errands – things like picking up an order from a shop, or getting shoes ¹**to be repaired / repaired**. Now you can ²**have / need** jobs like these done for you.

If your computer needs ³**be updated / updating**, don't waste time staying in for the technician. Having someone else ⁴**done / do** it frees up your time for something more interesting. And more and more people are ⁵**making / getting** others to queue for them – for the latest iPhone, concert tickets or even a visa.

5 **Complete the second sentence so that it has a similar meaning to the first sentence, using the word given. Use between two and five words, including the word given.**

1 There's a place in town where they unlock your phone really quickly.
   CAN
   There's a place in town where you .... really quickly.

2 I was twelve when they took out my appendix in an emergency operation.
   HAD
   I was twelve when I .... in an emergency operation.

3 You have to pay extra if they send the tickets to your home address.
   GET
   You have to pay extra .... to your home address.

4 Little children love it when you tell them stories.
   HAVING
   Little children love .... to them.

5 I'd like to pay someone to make my clothes rather than buy them from a shop.
   MADE
   I like to .... rather than buy them from a shop.

USE OF ENGLISH 2

Make new words from the highlighted words in the clues. Find the mystery word.

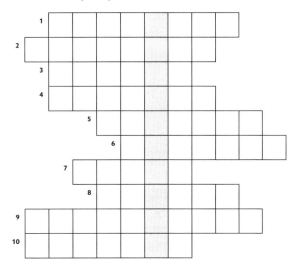

1 you have this when you're strong
2 the result of being accurate
3 how long something is
4 you might feel like this if you fail
5 the time you arrive
6 you act this way when you're happy
7 happening every day
8 how much you weigh is this
9 you have this when you feel enthusiastic
10 you get this when things are varied

Mystery word: ....

Complete the headlines with the correct form of these words.

confidence   drama   industry   long   poison   strong

1 **Man bitten by .... spider**

2 **Chaos on trains after day of .... action**

3 **Talks .... Anglo-American agreement**

4 **Teenager cycles .... of Britain for charity**

5 **City manager .... of trophy**

6 **Price of gold rises ....**

Complete the sentences with the correct form of the words in brackets.

1 I think I'm about the right .... (weigh) for my .... (high).
2 Seeing a live band is really .... (excite), but I can only afford to do it .... (occasion).
3 You need to dig a hole that's the correct .... (deep) and .... (wide) before you plant a tree.
4 Due to the .... (environment) damage from the oil spill, the island's .... (inhabit) were forced to abandon their homes.
5 Social media helps you .... (wide) your network of friends, but it doesn't do much to .... (deep) relationships.

Extend

Read the article and complete it with the correct form of the word in capitals.

The human Swan

If you want to know what it's like to be a bird, ask [1] .... Sacha Dench. In December 2016, she flew 7,000 kilometres by motorised paraglider to accompany a group of Bewick's swans on their migration.   **CONSERVE**

Sacha's aim was to find out more about this [2] .... endangered species. In fifteen years, the number of Bewick's surviving migration fell from 29,000 to just 18,000, so it was essential to find out if there were any [3] .... patterns that would explain this decline. It was already known that hunters posed a [4] .... threat to the birds during migration, so part of Sacha's role was also as [5] .... She spent time with hunters trying to [6] .... their awareness of the importance of this species.   **CRITIC**   **BEHAVIOUR**   **DEAD**   **EDUCATE**   **HEIGHT**

As you might imagine, there was no [7] .... of publicity for this expedition. The scale of the journey and Sacha's [8] .... support for these iconic birds caught the public's imagination.   **SHORT**   **PASSION**

SPEAKING

1 Read the discussion task. Tick (✓) the correct answers in the list.

Discuss with a partner:

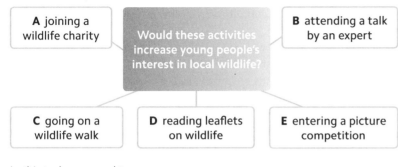

A joining a wildlife charity

Would these activities increase young people's interest in local wildlife?

B attending a talk by an expert

C going on a wildlife walk

D reading leaflets on wildlife

E entering a picture competition

In this task, you need to:

1 put the activities in order of personal preference ☐

2 discuss the benefits of the different activities ☐

3 discuss all five activities in detail ☐

4 suggest the best activity for your partner ☐

5 give reasons for your opinions ☐

6 agree on everything with your partner ☐

7 listen and respond to your partner's opinions ☐

8 find the one right answer to the question in the task ☐

9 ask your partner questions to clarify their opinion ☐

2 Read the conversations. Which activities (A–E) in the task in Ex 1 are the students discussing?

1 A: I don't think that would be a very motivating idea. You can't get much information on just bits of paper.

B: I agree. That option seems a bit old-fashioned when people are used to getting information interactively.

2 A: That seems quite appealing. I mean, getting the information from someone with a lot of local knowledge could be interesting.

B: Yes, and if it could be linked to other subjects, maybe geography or biology, that would make it really relevant.

3 A: I'm not sure about this one. It would depend on the type of work the organisation does. And if you had to pay a lot to join, that would put young people off.

B: I see what you mean, but I think it could be a good way of getting young people involved. They could see directly how their work was helping wildlife.

4 A: I like the suggestion in this option. It could involve big groups and being in direct contact with the birds and animals would be more motivating than just researching them inside.

B: Yes, definitely. The idea of an outside classroom is fun. If there was a worksheet to complete, you could learn a lot. It could even be made into a project.

5 A: That sounds fun. Anything where you work as a team for a prize is motivating. And you'd need to research local animals to be able to take part.

B: That's a good point, but it might appeal more to people who are creative and taking pictures. For that reason, it might not be the best option to motivate a lot of young people.

3 Choose the correct words to complete the sentences.

1 I wouldn't really sign up for a charity **if / because** you needed to pay something every month.

2 I think the talk is **definitely / definite** less interesting than the walk because it could be more like a normal lesson.

3 I don't think leaflets are **such / so** great, do you?

4 **To / In** my opinion, making a poster is more motivating than just reading leaflets.

5 I think the competition would create **most / more** interest than the talk, especially if the prize was beneficial to the whole community.

6 The talk and the walk would be more effective than a competition because we can't **do / make** without local knowledge.

4 🔊 6.5 Read the next part of the task. Listen to two students discussing their answers. Which two options do they choose?

Now you have a minute to decide which two activities would increase young people's interest in local wildlife the most.

5 🔊 6.6 Listen again and complete the sentences the students use to come to an agreement.

1 ...., which two options do you think are best?

2 What .... ?

3 So, ... the talk, the walk and the competition. Let's .... about this.

4 .... of the walk and the competition?

5 OK, so .... the walk and the competition as the best two options.

6 Complete the sentences with these question tags.

aren't there   does it   do they   isn't it

1 There are better ways of creating interest in wildlife, ... ?

2 Learning in an interactive way is a lot more motivating, ... ?

3 Having a speaker in school doesn't seem very different from a class, ... ?

4 Most young people don't have much time to do charity work, ... ?

7 🔴 Now record your answer to the task in Ex 1 and then the task in Ex 4. Listen to your recording and check if you included all the important points from the checklist in Ex 1.

WRITING

an essay

Read the task and choose the correct answer.

What is the main topic of the essay?

A the amount of information available today

B the accuracy of information available today

In your English class, you have been talking about the importance of getting reliable information in everyday life. Your English teacher has asked you to write an essay.

Write your essay using all the notes and giving reasons for your point of view.

Can we rely on the information we get every day? What do you think?

Notes

Write about:

1 articles

2 advertisements

3 .... (your own idea)

Which topics could be used for the third point in the essay? Tick (✓) the correct options.

1 Wikipedia ☐

2 life before smartphones ☐

3 social media ☐

4 product reviews ☐

5 privacy online ☐

6 being honest with your friends ☐

Add one missing word to each example in the correct place.

1 In first place, it's important to know why this information was sent to you.

2 Texts are not always what they seem – instance, some adverts look like information documents, but they are actually selling a product.

3 On whole, I'd say that you can trust what you read, but you still need to be careful.

4 With reference Wikipedia, it's clear when the information is not accurate or complete.

5 As far I'm concerned, it's getting harder to know which information is reliable.

6 People need to know who produced the information. What more, they need to understand why.

Read the sentences and link them using the words in brackets. Add any extra words if necessary.

1 You need to know if the reviewer really tried the product. It's important to check if they were paid to write the review. (well / that)

You need to know if the reviewer really tried the product. As well as that, it's important to check if they were paid to write the review.

2 There are a number of things you need to check. It's important to know if the text is written in a neutral way. (First / all)

3 Some documents are full of mistakes. We're only allowed to use reliable sites for homework. (For / reason)

4 There is so much news on social media. It's important to be selective. (In / view)

5 On the one hand we are fortunate to have information at our fingertips. We need to be cautious. (but / hand)

6 There are different ways of checking information. Comparing against two or three other documents is a good technique. (example)

Write the words in the correct order to make sentences.

1 people / Generally / ignore / speaking, / online advertising. / I think

....

2 getting / In / my / is best. / opinion, / advice / from someone I know

....

3 important / Regarding / it's / check / to / different sources. / the news,

....

4 an important skill. / conclusion, / manage information / to / learning / is / In

....

5 different / are / Articles / from / points of view. / written / many

....

Replace the highlighted text with these more formal phrases.

access   bear in mind   huge variety   it is said   on an hourly basis   sole
tend to   widen your range of

1 It has never been easier to get information. ....

2 People say that material on the internet is unreliable. ....

3 News needs to be updated every hour. ....

4 It's advisable to read a lot of different sources. ....

5 People often read just one newspaper. ....

6 There are a lot of different types of information. ....

7 Remember that celebrities are paid to promote a product or service. ....

8 The only aim of adverts is to get you to spend money. ....

Write your answer to the question in Ex 1. Write your essay in 140–190 words, using an appropriate style.

UNIT CHECK

1 Complete the sentences with the correct passive form of the verbs.

1 Spanish classes .... (hold) three times a week in the language centre.

2 The city centre is closed because a movie .... (film) there at the moment.

3 How many tickets for the school party .... (already / sell)?

4 The archaeologists found that the entire village .... (destroy) by fire.

5 I don't think the network .... (update) before the end of next week.

6 My brother might .... (promote) to captain of the first team.

7 I don't remember .... (invite) to her party. Are you sure I was on the list?

8 He .... (say) to be the best young chess player in the world right now.

2 Complete the chatroom posts with the correct form of the verbs.

School makeovers

I was reading about this competition in New Zealand to give schools a makeover. Staff and students describe what work needs to **1** .... (do) or what facilities they would like to have. The school that wins **2** .... all the work .... (get/complete) free.

They had some really creative ideas. One place came up with the idea of outdoor classrooms. They **3** .... a pond .... (have/build) and **4** .... some trees .... (get/plant) so that students could do environmental projects.

So, how would you **5** .... your school .... (have/make) over?

| Dani | Add message | Report |

I like the idea of outdoor classrooms. Sadly, our indoor classrooms **6** .... (need/paint) a nice bright colour, so that would be my priority.

| Maura | Add message | Report |

Actually, we're **7** .... a new sports hall .... (have/construct) right now. I can't wait to see it complete.

| Nik | Add message | Report |

My school needs a complete makeover, starting with the student lockers. They aren't secure, so I **8** .... some stuff .... (get/take) out of mine last week. It's such a pain.

3 Read the information and complete the seating plan with the correct names.

....	....	....	......Jake......
....	....	....	....

Vicky sat at the corner of the table, but not opposite Jake.

Misha refused to sit next to Ali, but ended up across the table from him.

Rani insisted on being between her two best friends, Claire and Misha.

Ali spent the evening beside Jake.

Su had to shout to be heard by Vicky from right across the other side of the table.

Kyle hates sitting on the end and he wanted to be on the same side as Ali and Jake.

Vicky didn't say much to Kyle although she was by him all evening.

4 Complete the conversations with the correct form of the words.

1 **A:** What's the best way to .... (strong) your online security?

B: Keep changing your password and update your .... (private) settings.

2 **A:** They say that yoga is a good way to help with .... (anxious).

B: Yes, I've heard that it can be .... (benefit) too.

3 **A:** I'm so sorry. I .... (accident) tore your jacket when I borrowed it.

B: Oh, don't feel too .... (guilt). I'm sure it can be repaired.

4 **A:** There's been no .... (short) of interest in the idea of a class rep.

B: Great. I wonder how many .... (apply) there will be.

5 **A:** Why would anyone want to be a .... (collect) of old mobile phones?

B: I know. Some people get .... (please) from the strangest things.

6 **A:** I really like your dad. He's much more .... (tolerate) than mine!

B: Yes, I'm .... (fortune) that he doesn't often lose his temper.

PART 1

Read the text and decide which answer (A, B, C or D) best fits each gap.

It's not mess, Mum, it's art

Do your parents complain **0** _about_ the mess in your bedroom **1**....... other day? Are they always asking when you're going to **2**....... round to putting everything away? Well, next time they're in the **3**....... of telling you to tidy up, you can inform them it isn't mess, but art!

An exhibition at a London museum has put together a series of pictures of the private space of twenty-six teenagers. A number of objects collected from their lives have also been put on **4**....... – everything from party pictures to chocolate wrappers.

The collected items have allowed these young people to **5**....... a record of important moments in their life. Things like toys that a teenager may have **6**....... interest in appear in the pictures alongside more recent items. This provides a link between the young person's past and their current identity.

In fact, the exhibition is all about identity. These young people are **7**....... the point of finding out who they are and their room reflects what's going on in their lives. One important theme is the use of social media. A recurring image is of a phone or laptop left on the bed, but always in easy **8**....... , showing that the bedroom is a place of comfort, but also communication.

0	**A** for	**B** around	**C** on	**D** about
1	**A** every	**B** each	**C** both	**D** all
2	**A** get	**B** go	**C** move	**D** carry
3	**A** centre	**B** middle	**C** place	**D** heart
4	**A** proof	**B** sign	**C** exhibit	**D** show
5	**A** hold	**B** take	**C** keep	**D** do
6	**A** lost	**B** hidden	**C** disappeared	**D** wasted
7	**A** onto	**B** on	**C** in	**D** into
8	**A** distance	**B** hand	**C** reach	**D** touch

PART 2

For questions 9–16, complete the text with one word in each gap.

Never too late to say sorry

Have you 0 .... _ever_ .... **come across a news story that makes you feel good? Here's one from Canada.** Residents of the city of Vancouver **9** .... a motorbike stolen from outside their apartment complex. Mel Flesher, the owner's girlfriend, put out an immediate appeal on Facebook for help in **10** .... anyone saw the bike. Her message must have **11** .... read by people in the local area, including the thieves themselves! A short time later the bike was returned along with a note written **12** .... hand. It was clear from the note that the thieves regretted **13** .... the bike and that they wanted to apologise to the owners. The thieves even advised **14** .... on how to protect it from theft in the future. If **15** .... more people did the right thing like this! And it really shows you the power of social media. If Mel hadn't gone online to tell people what had happened, she might never **16** .... got the bike back.

PART 3

For questions 17–24, read the text below. Use the word given at the end of some of the lines to form a word that fits in the gap in the same line.

 ## *Never take another bad selfie*

An **0** _____unbelievably_____ large
number of selfies are taken every
day, but have you ever taken one and
got an **17** ....
result? Well, now a computer
scientist, Andrej Kaparthy, is here to
help. He has shown there's nothing
18 .... about the
perfect selfie. He's actually come
up with a formula that gives you
complete **19** ....
in every picture and takes the
20 .... out of
the process.

Kaparthy created an artificial
intelligence network that can categorise
images. Working from pictures that had
the most online 'likes', followers and
tags, the system was given data about
what makes an image a success or a
21 .... The final
best 100 selfies were analysed to create
a set of tips.

For women and girls, the face should
take up one third of the image and
it's best to take the picture at an
angle. Style of hair is important:
wear it down, the longer the better.
22 .... is important
for men and boys too. They should
style their hair up, and take the shot
straight on.

Shooting in black and white can
23 .... the impact
of an image. And despite the worldwide
24 .... for group
selfies, these are best avoided if you
want a successful picture.

BELIEVE

EXPECT

ACCIDENT

CONFIDENT

FRUSTRATE

FAIL

APPEAR

STRONG

ENTHUSIASTIC

PART 4

For questions 25–30, complete the second sentence so that it has a similar meaning to the first sentence, using the word given. Do not change the word given. Use between two and five words, including the word given.

0 We think that Class 9 will win the tournament.
EXPECT
We ....expect Class 9 to win................ the tournament.

25 I've lost touch with my friends since we moved to the country.
WOULD
I .... lost touch
with my friends if we hadn't moved to the country.

26 Maxine has decided not to play the guitar any more.
GIVE
Maxine has decided ....
the guitar.

27 It wouldn't be wise for you to carry on working.
HAD
You .... carry
on working.

28 I tore your jacket by accident.
MEAN
I .... your
jacket.

29 People believe he escaped with all the money.
RUN
He .... away
with all the money.

30 At sixteen, I'm too young to vote.
ENOUGH
At sixteen, I'm ....
to vote.

7 The full story

READING

Complete the blog post with these words.

> appeal   daydream   deliver   genuinely
> make-believe   memorable   realised   spooky

Get your head in the clouds

The other afternoon, I was sitting by the window in class. My mind floated away from the topic of history and it was a while before I [1] .... my teacher was standing next to me saying, 'Stop looking out of the window and concentrate!' I know that the middle of a history lesson isn't the best place to [2] .... , but it seems that we all step into a [3] .... world from time to time. So why? What's the [4] .... and is there any benefit? Well, as well as being enjoyable, it seems that letting your mind wander is [5] .... good for you. It can help build creativity and may even [6] .... the solution to a problem. Although the thoughts you have during the day may be less [7] .... than a [8] .... nightmare that wakes you up in the night, perhaps we should all spend a little more time with our head in the clouds.

Read the article about fanfiction quickly and answer the questions.

1 Which of the four people have written fanfiction?
2 Which two people write for a living?
3 Who has the most negative opinion of fanfiction?
4 What type of company does Nicole work for?

Read the article again. Match the questions (1–10) with the people (A–D).

Which person …

1 wasn't immediately popular with readers?
2 says that fanfiction can't be justified by the number of readers?
3 uses fanfiction sites as a way of finding what readers like?
4 involves their fans in the writing process?
5 doesn't agree that fanfiction writers are inferior?
6 believes that a story belongs to a global audience?
7 points out that many fanfiction writers don't use their own name?
8 had the same level of disappointment in a story as other readers?
9 hasn't lost out financially because of fanfiction?
10 tried to remove access to fanfiction material based on their work?

Extend

Match the highlighted phrases in the sentences (1–8) with the definitions (A–H).

1 We asked four people for their take on this growing form of storytelling.
2 I set about writing my own ending.
3 Having their comments keeps me going.
4 I was by no means an overnight success.
5 We keep a close eye on the main fanfiction sites.
6 We want to see who are the up-and-coming writers.
7 Fanfiction is often seen as second best.
8 I've made a name for myself as a successful science fiction writer.

A observe carefully
B likely to succeed
C become well known and popular
D thought of as less good
E opinion of
F achievement didn't come quickly or easily
G helps me continue
H started

Complete the online posts on a debate about fanfiction, with the correct form of the highlighted phrases from Ex 4.

Fanfiction: fun for readers or unfair to original writers?

In fanfiction, also known as fanfic, writers borrow characters and concepts from books, films, and TV shows, and write alternative storylines. We asked four people for their take on this growing form of storytelling.

Lin

People are often curious about how I got started, but it was really quite simple. I read the last chapter of a novel and I hated the ending! Not only was it a bad ending to the story, the characters seemed to have lost their original personality. So I set about writing my own ending, just for fun. It was when I found that other fans were as dissatisfied as me with the same book, that I decided to make my version available online. It was an instant hit, with some fans saying my work was more credible and enjoyable. Now I'm a regular fanfic writer with thousands of readers worldwide. Having their comments helps me shape what happens next and keeps me going. It's that ongoing interaction that distinguishes fanfiction from other forms of writing.

Nicole

Personally, fanfiction wouldn't be my reading of choice, but I don't have any moral problem with it. If it keeps people reading and brings them enjoyment, so much the better. Professionally, it isn't something we have as part of our list, but we do keep a close eye on the main fanfiction sites, just to see which genre is most popular and who are the up-and-coming writers. There's a surprising amount of talent out there, although some professionals prefer not to admit it. Fanfiction is often seen as second best, as if the writers are just imitators of 'real' authors. I don't see it like that. They may not have invented the characters, but the narratives are all their own work. The fans also take the writing very seriously and give brutally honest feedback. So fanfiction can be an excellent training ground.

Jake

I started out of love for the characters in my favourite books. It wasn't because I thought I could do better than the original author; I just wanted to see what would happen to their characters in different situations. I was by no means an overnight success, but over time my fan base grew. What I didn't realise was that I was developing as a writer and growing in confidence. Then a publisher got in touch to see if I had any ideas for an original work. I did and I'm now in my fifth year as a professional writer. Many professional writers query the fairness of their work being copied. All I can say is, my sales haven't suffered. And once a story is out in the world, it's really owned by the readers, so I can't control it.

Simon

Having made a name for myself as a successful science fiction writer, I was horrified when my characters started appearing all over the online story site Wattpad. I contacted my publisher to see if we could get all the stories related to my work taken down. They can't take any action unless the writers receive an income from their stories. Some say I should be flattered, but my objection is about who owns the work. Writers need to have professional respect for each other and not just take what they want from another person's creativity. Just because fanfiction has a huge audience doesn't make it right. Most of these writers remain anonymous on Wattpad, which seems to indicate they're less than proud of what they do.

The big debate: fanfiction

✔ **FOR:** My [1] .... fanfiction is that it's pure escapism. The genre I like is band fanfic, so I get to read about the imaginary antics of my favourite group. It's been said that it invades the bands' privacy, but they have chosen to [2] .... in the music world, so why should they complain? You could argue that fanfic [3] .... people's interest in the musicians .... And the writers work just as hard as professional authors. It can take years to build up a lot of readers – no one is an [4] .... on these sites. In the world of fiction, there's something for everyone. If you don't like fanfic, don't read it!

✖ **AGAINST:** The reason that fanfic is [5] .... is because it is! The stories can never be as good as the ones written by the original author. It was their idea in the first place. And to [6] .... a career in writing only to have someone copy your work must be so annoying. Why should professional writers have to [7] .... on the fanfiction sites to check how their ideas are being used? For me, the only way for [8] .... storytellers to stand out is to be original. Use your own ideas, not someone else's!

GRAMMAR

reported speech

Choose the correct words to complete the rules.

1 'I'm watching my favourite soap now.'

To report this sentence in the past, you need the **present / past** continuous. 'Now' **needs / doesn't need** to change.

2 'Most people nowadays choose to watch movies on Netflix.'

'Choose' **can / can't** stay the same when you report this sentence.

3 'I would love to be an actress if I could, but it might not be a secure career.'

The modals 'would', 'could' and 'might' **change / don't change** when you report this sentence.

4 'I had seen the film before.'

To report this sentence about another person, you change the **pronoun / tense**, not the **tense / pronoun**.

5 'Have you ever appeared on TV or radio?'

You report this question with **a question word / if or whether**.

6 'What was the last movie you saw at the cinema?'

You report this question with **a question word / if or whether**.

Choose one word in each reported statement that is extra.

1 The survey asked how often did we read classic literature.

2 She said we could have download the book for free.

3 The journalist asked if that he had always been keen on writing.

4 I explained that I'd had already seen that episode the day before.

5 My classmate refused to tell to me the answer.

6 The tutor wanted to know what if genre we were interested in.

7 The writer said us it was going to be his last book for teenagers.

8 The students wanted to know how many stories he does writes a year.

Complete the reported sentences.

1 'I'll see you both later at the leisure complex.'
My sister said ....

2 'This is the worst TV programme I've ever seen.'
Mum said ....

3 'We're reading a great new story at our book club at the moment.'
My friend said ....

4 'I left my Kindle on the sofa here, but now I can't find it.'
My brother said ....

5 'You must all write a paragraph plan before you start this task.'
The teacher said ....

6 'I was watching a film when you texted last night.'
Dad said ....

7 'I'm going to publish my first book of short stories next year.'
She told us ....

8 'We might go to the book festival tomorrow.'
My friends told me ....

🔊 7.1 **Listen to young people talking to a writer at a booktalk. Complete the sentences to report what they asked her.**

1 The first person wanted to know .... graphic novels.

2 A boy asked .... that Gina illustrated the books ....

3 A girl asked Gina .... novels.

4 The same fan wanted to know .... to finish each book.

5 A boy asked .... different types of novels.

6 In the last question, a girl wanted to know .... into films.

Complete the article with one word in each gap.

Why I'm an ex-fan of teen fiction

I recently told my friends that I [1].. given up reading teenage fiction. [2].. couldn't quite believe it and asked me [3].. I was abandoning the genre after being such a big fan. In a word, clichés – all those stereotypical plots and characters that fill the world of teen fiction. I explained that the books I had read in the [4].. month were all full of clichés. There's the character that's anxious and always asking [5].. people like them or not. And the nasty one – usually a girl – who turns out to be really lovely underneath. It's just that her problematic parents have [6].. her she was horrid as a child. Not forgetting the heroin who is beautiful although she doesn't realise it. And then there are the names. I asked my friends how many people they know who [7].. called Katniss, Effie, or Echo. And the answer, of course, is none. But silly names are everywhere in teen fiction. So I'm keeping away until someone tells [8].. they've found a readable novel with a main character called Chris.

VOCABULARY

storytelling: literature, film and TV

1 Read the questions and fill in the missing words.

Which word beginning with:

e
is read on screen? **1** _ _ _ _ _
is the last part of a story? **2** _ _ _ _ _ _

i
refers to pictures that go with text?
3 _ _ _ _ _ _ _ _ _ _ _ _

n
is a long imaginary story? **4** _ _ _ _ _

p
is a book with a flexible card cover?
5 _ _ _ _ _ _ _ _ _

is a short part of a book or poem?
6 _ _ _ _ _ _

means to produce a book, magazine, etc. in large quantities? **7** _ _ _ _ _

is a person or company that manages the production and sale of reading material? **8** _ _ _ _ _ _ _ _ _

s
means several books, films or TV programmes about the same characters and subjects **9** _ _ _ _ _ _

2 Match the sentence halves (1–8) with (A–H).

1 I've no idea why the series got such rave
2 It had such a complicated
3 That's so frustrating! I hate it when the final
4 It made a refreshing change for the main
5 It was too dull to finish. It had such a weak
6 My mum cries at movies. Even with a happy
7 My dad says action movies are all just special
8 No one predicted that! It was a real unexpected

A twist when the boys turned out to be brothers.
B effects and computer-generated images.
C storyline that I got bored.
D character to be someone quite ordinary.
E plot that I couldn't understand any of it.
F ending, she's always in tears.
G scene leaves you guessing what happened.
H reviews. I thought it was all a bit dull.

3 Complete the article with these phrasal verbs.

cheer up   fall for   figure out   give in   go for   leave out   look up   take in

How not to *make a hero*

There's nothing like a good movie to **1** .... you .... after a hard week. And for excitement and escapism, a lot of people **2** .... an action movie. But all action heroes seem the same. I just can't **3** .... why movies all follow the same formula:

The more times the hero fights the bad guy, the better

In classical stories, the hero only battles against the villain once. So why repeat the fight in movies? Why not **4** .... the repetition and have one memorable battle scene?

Heroes can't be hurt

The average hero experiences explosions, crashes, and attacks from every angle. They keep fighting and never **5** .... and survive without a scratch. Of course, it's just a movie, but who's going to **6** .... that?

Heroes are male

It's hard to **7** .... how few female action heroes there are. Why can't an action hero be a heroine? Let's hope movie makers realise that heroes come in all shapes and sizes. Then things might start to **8** .... and we'll get heroes we can really believe in.

Extend

4 Replace the hightlighted words with these phrasal verbs.

bring in   join in   live for   stand for   make up   use up   point out   read out

1 I don't think I have a very vivid imagination. I find it hard to **invent** stories.
....

2 The teacher told us to come prepared to **tell** our story to the class.
....

3 Plan your writing. Don't **exploit** all your good ideas at the start or you'll be left with nothing to say at the end. ....

4 Don't you hate it when writers **include** new characters to replace your favourites? ....

5 What do the letters J.R.R. **represent** in Tolkien's name?
....

6 Why do you **direct my attention to** all the mistakes in a plot? It really spoils the film. ....

7 She **looks forward to** watching that TV programme all week. She talks about nothing else! ....

8 If we did a group storywriting activity, would you **participate**?
....

71

LISTENING

🔊 7.2 **Listen to eight people talking in eight different situations. What are the people talking about? Number the list (A–H) in the same order as the recordings.**

A making a request by phone ....

B different ways of enjoying movies ....

C a frustrating ending ....

D feeling nervous ....

E how to be a writer ....

F advice on writing better stories ....

G a contest for young storytellers ....

H a change in attitude ....

🔊 7.3 **Listen again and choose the correct answer (A, B or C).**

1 You hear a father and son talking. What do they disagree about?

  A which film to download and watch at the weekend

  B where is the best place to see an action film

  C what annoys them about the cinema

2 You hear a girl talking about a book review. How did she feel after reading it?

  A upset   **B** delighted   **C** confused

3 You overhear a boy talking on the phone to his friend. What is he going to do?

  A sing in a musical performance

  B audition for a play

  C play in a band on stage

4 You hear part of an interview with an author. What advice does she give to new writers?

  A have your own identity

  B write for different audiences

  C be better than average

5 You hear a tutor in a storywriting class. Which aspect of the students' writing does he say needs improving?

  A the beginning

  B the dialogues

  C the characters and plot

6 You hear two friends talking about a TV programme. Why isn't the girl happy?

  A The story was a waste of time.

  B The story was on social media.

  C The story hasn't been concluded.

7 You hear some information about a story competition. Which new rule has been introduced?

  A You have to write more than 1,000 words.

  B You can't have taken part in a previous year.

  C You have to be younger than thirteen or older than eighteen.

8 You hear a boy phoning a helpline. What is the boy doing?

  A booking an extra ticket

  B checking the location of the seats

  C asking for a refund

Extend

Choose the correct words to complete the different conversations.

1 **A:** Do you ¹**feel / fancy** like going to the cinema later?

  B: No, not really. Why ²**worry / bother** travelling all the way into town when we have Netflix? Let's have a ³**see / look** at what's on. How about a vampire story?

  A: You're ⁴**laughing / kidding**! I'm not sitting through another one of those!

2 **A:** How was the audition?

  B: Not great. I ⁵**messed / mixed** up and had to repeat the lines three times.

  A: Well, there's no ⁶**such / sort** thing as a perfect reading.

  B: Yes, but I really ⁷**made / got** it all wrong – the character, the voice, the timing, everything.

  A: Could you try for another part?

  B: I doubt it. I think the director ⁸**took / gave** an instant dislike to me right ⁹**for / from** the start.

🔊 7.4 **Listen and check your answers to Ex 3.**

USE OF ENGLISH 1

1 Match these reporting verbs with phrases and questions in direct speech.

admit   agree   boast   congratulate   deny
encourage   suggest   threaten

1 'Go on! Enter the competition and you'll win!'
....

2 'OK, I'll pay for the cinema tickets.'
....

3 'I did not write all these negative reviews.'
....

4 'How about watching that horror movie?'
....

5 'Well done on getting your book published!'
....

6 'I'll call the manager if you don't turn off your phone!'
....

7 'Yes, it's true that this is my last film.'
....

8 'We had the very best seats in the theatre!'
....

2 Match the sentence halves (1–8) with (A–H).

1 My friend's dad offered
2 The writer strongly denied
3 We finally persuaded
4 The reviewer apologised
5 Our drama tutor recommended
6 The novelist didn't agree
7 Andy and his friends boasted
8 I wish you'd warned

A stealing the plot from another author.
B with the publisher on having his book televised.
C for including incorrect information on the website.
D me against watching that series. It's addictive.
E to give us a lift to the cinema.
F that we saw the play performed by professionals.
G my sister to watch a horror movie.
H about meeting all the actors after the show.

3 Report the sentences with these verbs. There are two verbs you do not need.

boast   complain   congratulate   insist   invite
promise   recommend   threaten   warn

The things people say

When I won Young Playwright of the Year, I got the opportunity to have my play performed by professional actors. These were people's reactions …

1 My parents said, 'That's fantastic! You deserved to win.'
2 'Don't sign a contract until I've checked it', my brother said.
3 My best friend said, 'I'll read everything you ever write.'
4 A girl I'd never met said, 'We must do a selfie together.'
5 'You'd better get a good agent,' my tutor said.
6 'Would you like to go on local radio?' a journalist asked.
7 'I should have won. That's really unfair!' the other finalist said.

1 My parents .... the competition.
2 My brother .... the contract until he'd checked it.
3 My best friend .... everything I ever wrote.
4 A girl I'd never met .... a selfie together.
5 My tutor .... a good agent.
6 A journalist .... on local radio.
7 The other finalist ....

4 Complete the second sentence so that it has a similar meaning to the first sentence using the word given. Use between two and five words, including the word given.

1 'It was me who borrowed the DVD without asking,' my sister said.
ADMITTED
My sister .... the DVD without asking.

2 'We'll sign copies of the book after the reading,' the writers said.
PROMISED
The writers .... copies of the book after the reading.

3 'I won't take the smallest part in the play,' Nick said.
REFUSED
Nick .... the smallest part in the play.

4 'I wrote the best story on the website.' my brother said.
BOASTED
My brother .... the best story on the website.

5 'Don't use your phones during the play,' the teacher said to us.
TOLD
The teacher .... our phones during the play.

6 'I'm so happy that you got the main part in the play, Eddie,' Helen said.
CONGRATULATED
Helen .... the main part in the play.

USE OF ENGLISH 2

Complete the texts with the correct prepositions.

Quiet please!

Exam .... progress.

Please apply .... email to the address below.

Please choose the relevant option .... screen.

YES   NO

Ghost Tours

Explore the city .... night

.... *Second Thoughts*

A guide to decision-making

.... conclusion, I think that ...

Complete the conversations with these prepositions.

at (x2)   for (x2)   in

A: So, Elizabeth, do you get called Lizzie ¹....... short?

B: Yes, ²....... general my family call me Liz or Lizzie. But it's funny ³....... times in class because there are five girls all called Elizabeth.

A: That must be fun at registration!

B: Well, it was difficult ⁴....... first, ⁵....... sure. But now we get called different names.

at   by   on

A: That course was hopeless!

B: I know. All the tutor did was talk ⁶....... length about himself. We didn't learn anything! ⁷....... rights, we should get our money back.

A: Shall we ask for a refund?

B: He's ⁸....... his way home now so there's nothing we can do for the moment.

Choose the correct words to complete the sentences.

1 That's typical **of / from** my sister. She never tidies up, but she's **surprising / surprised** at how messy her room is.

2 I'm similar **as / to** my mum in looks, but I take after my dad too. We're both **interested / clever** at making things.

3 It's common to be slow **for / at** picking up a new skill. Once you get **dedicated / involved** in the activity, it gets easier.

4 Being aware **to / of** other people's needs makes you **good / successful** in relationships.

5 I was **horrified / ashamed** at the nasty comments. Why aren't writers more respectful **from / of** each other?

6 The staff are **experienced / capable** in looking after wildlife and they are dedicated **to / for** the animals.

7 I'm not sure what to study. I'm **brilliant / interested** in design, but I don't want to be limited **at / to** just one area.

Read the article and choose the best answer (A, B, C or D).

Too much TV?

Once people might have been ¹.............. of spending the whole weekend in front the TV. Now, thanks to Netflix and TV ².............. demand, that has all changed. Fans can 'binge watch' a whole series and watch it all at once. During one of these sessions, people are ³.............. of consuming a month's viewing in a weekend.

According ⁴.............. a survey by Netflix, sixty-one percent of a sample of viewers regularly binge watch. But why? Are we really staying up later to watch TV by ⁵.............. ? Well, the programme makers don't make it easy for us. Scriptwriters are ⁶.............. at creating tension at the end of each episode so we want to find out what happens next.

Should we be concerned that people get so ⁷.............. to a TV series? Well, a night binge will make you tired, but even ⁸.............. day, it can be problematic. Sitting for hours slows your metabolism, leaving you with low energy levels.

1	**A** surprised	**B** dedicated	**C** interested	**D** ashamed
2	**A** on	**B** in	**C** by	**D** at
3	**A** clever	**B** experienced	**C** capable	**D** able
4	**A** to	**B** for	**C** by	**D** on
5	**A** ease	**B** choice	**C** need	**D** reason
6	**A** obsessed	**B** brilliant	**C** dedicated	**D** experienced
7	**A** involved	**B** respectful	**C** similar	**D** attached
8	**A** for	**B** at	**C** by	**D** on

SPEAKING

1 Match the questions (1–6) with the answers (A–F).

1 Why do you think young people spend more time looking at screens than reading printed books?

2 Do you think young people spend too much time watching TV? Why / why not?

3 Which films have you seen or books have you read more than once?

4 Do you think that watching TV or films in English improves language skills?

5 Is it easier to read a story in a book or watch it as a film? Why?

6 Is TV becoming less popular as a form of family entertainment?

A There's a series of cartoons for Spanish teenagers that I've enjoyed over and over again.

B Yes, I'd say so because everyone now has access to programmes on their own laptop or phone, so people don't watch them together.

C That could be true, but it would depend on your level. For instance, it might be very difficult for beginners to follow complicated dialogue.

D Well, in a printed story you don't usually have pictures, of course, so you have to use your imagination more than with a movie.

E I'd say that it's because we all have phones or tablets with us all the time. It's easier to download a story than carry a novel around.

F I'm not sure about that. Some young people are interested in soaps and dramas, but they enjoy doing other things too.

2 🔊 7.5 Listen to two pairs of students. Which question in Ex 1 is each pair discussing?

3 🔊 7.6 Listen again and complete the phrases.

1 Yes, I .... that.

2 I agree with you ....

3 I have to admit, ...

4 Yes, I ....

5 No, I ....

6 I couldn't ....

7 Yes, you're ....

8 I know ....

4 Complete the conversations with these pairs of words.

don't + that   isn't + true   perhaps + about
really + think   sure + agree   wouldn't + agree

1 Which films have you seen or books have you read more than once?

A: I'm a sci-fi fan so I've seen the *Star Wars* series several times. Any film or book with a strong storyline like that is worth repeating.

B: I'm not **1** .... I **2** .... I don't really enjoy seeing or reading the same thing more than once. Once I know the story, I can't see the point of going over it again.

A: But **3** .... you think **4** .... you pick up on different things each time? The first time, you get the story, but there's a lot more in the language and the effects.

B: Maybe, but **5** .... it **6** .... that you miss out on other stories if you read or watch the same thing?

A: Possibly, but I'm still a *Star Wars* fan.

2 Is it easier to read a story in a book or watch it as a film? Why?

A: I'd say that in general a film is easier to follow because you can understand a lot from the images.

B: But do you **7** .... **8** .... that films are always easier? I mean, in some films they change the plot so the story isn't as clear as in the book..

A: **9** .... , but what **10** .... films that aren't written from books? I still think special effects and music make a film more enjoyable than a book.

B: Yes, but **11** .... you **12** .... that for some stories it's better to use your imagination when reading rather than just watching?

5 🔊 7.7 Listen and answer the questions. Record and check your answers using the list below. Try again if you need to improve on anything.

Have you:
- used different expressions for giving your opinion?
- used a wide range of language to answer each question?
- given full answers with reasons and examples?
- paraphrased any words that you don't know?

7 The full story

WRITING

a story

Choose the correct answer for each question.

1 Which style is appropriate for a story?
  A lively and descriptive
  B neutral or impersonal
  C formal and factual

2 Which one of these would not make a good story?
  A adjectives and adverbs
  B short sentences for dramatic effect
  C a clear narrative
  D a list of actions without any linkers
  E direct speech
  F starting sentences in different ways

Read the task. Number the paragraph plan (A–D) in the correct order.

Are you an up-and-coming writer?

We're looking for short stories for our website.
Your story must begin with this sentence:

As soon as I posted the comment, I wished I hadn't.

Your story must include:
• a secret
• an apology

A give the background to the situation ....
B introduce the situation and main characters ....
C bring events to a conclusion ....
D build the tension before the climax to the story ....

Complete part of a story with the correct form of the verbs.

As soon as I posted the comment, I wished I hadn't. As quick as a flash, replies ¹............................ (appear) all over social media. It was as if the whole world ²............................ (see) it. What ³............................ I .... (go) to do? My best friend, Vicky, ⁴............................ (make) me promise not to give away her secret. And I had just broken that promise.

The week before, we ⁵............................ (chat) about the end-of-term party. Vicky whispered, 'I ⁶............................ (go / invite) Max to come with me.' She smiled shyly, her cheeks turning a little red. 'But you must promise faithfully not to tell anyone,' she added. I ⁷............................ (nod) quickly in agreement.

Now Vicky ⁸............................ (stand) there, her phone in her hand. Our eyes ⁹............................ (meet). She was close to tears. I was overwhelmed with guilt. 'How could you?' she demanded, her voice shaking with emotion.

Find descriptive words or phrases in the story in Ex 3 for the following.

1 immediately ....
2 said in a low voice ....
3 nearly crying ....

Choose the correct words to complete the sentences.

1 It all went **terribly / beautifully** from the start.
2 I panicked. I was **totally / partly** lost.
3 With no shade, the whole square became **pleasantly / unbearably** hot.
4 Despite the age and condition of the bus, it was **completely / surprisingly** comfortable.
5 At the end of our **happily / incredibly** challenging journey, we had become friends.

Complete the sentences with the adjectives given in the correct order.

1 At the top of the mountain, a .... castle came into view. (stone / ancient / spooky)
2 Resting my head on the .... pillow, I was soon fast asleep. (white / cool / cotton)
3 The object that glittered in the sunlight turned out to be a .... coin. (round / gold / beautiful)
4 The last space in the compartment was taken by a .... man. (Spanish / young / shy)

Read the advertisement from an international magazine. Write your story in 120–190 words, in an appropriate style.

Calling teen storytellers!

We are looking for writers for the short story section of our magazine.

Your story must begin with this sentence:

As soon as I found the old letter, I knew what I had to do.

Your story must include:
• a stranger
• a journey

UNIT CHECK

1 Write the statements and questions in reported speech.

1 'I'm going to drama school next year,' Emily said.

Emily said ....

2 'We haven't caught up on the first episode yet,' my friends said.

My friends said ....

3 'I won't bother finishing this story,' my sister said.

My sister said ....

4 'What's the worst programme on TV at the moment?' the girl asked us.

The girl asked us ....

5 'Who won best actress at the award ceremony last night?' dad asked.

Dad asked ....

6 'Does it take a long time to learn your lines?' the boy wanted to know.

The boy wanted to know ....

2 🔊 7.8 Listen and complete the sentences with these verbs.

admit + drop   advise + pay   congratulate + get
invite + come along   promise + come and see

1 My tutor .... into drama school.
2 My grandmother .... me on stage.
3 My sister .... my book in the bath.
4 Kelly .... to the story group after school.
5 My friend .... to see that film at the cinema.

3 Complete the second sentence so that it has a similar meaning to the first sentence using the word given. Use between two and five words, including the word given.

1 'Katy, don't forget to take the library books back,' Dad said.

REMINDED

Dad .... the library books back.

2 'I'm sorry I missed your performance in the play,' my aunt said.

APOLOGISED

My aunt .... performance in the play

3 'I did not borrow your DVD without asking,' my sister said.

DENIED

My sister .... DVD without asking.

4 'Don't expect a very satisfying ending to the film,' Kim said to us.

WARNED

Kim .... a very satisfying ending to the film.

4 Complete the words in the text.

Matt is the **1**m _ _ n c _ _ _ _ _ _ _ r of the crime thriller *Late Shift*. It's well acted with good **2**s _ _ _ _ _ l e _ _ _ _ _ _ s. But here's the difference. *Late Shift* is interactive. It's the audience who create the **3**u _ _ _ _ _ _ _ _ d t _ _ _ _ _ s in the story by responding to prompts on their smartphone. So, if you've ever been disappointed by a film that had **4**r _ _ e r _ _ _ _ _ s because of a **5**w _ _ k s _ _ _ _ _ _ _ e or a too **6**c _ _ _ _ _ _ _ _ _ d p _ _ t, perhaps interactive cinema is the future. Imagine you decide if a movie has a **7**h _ _ _ y e _ _ _ _ g or not. And just by watching again you could change the **8**f _ _ _ l s _ _ _ e altogether.

5 Choose the correct words to complete the sentences.

1 Why did you **figure out** / **fall for** her story?
2 **Cheer up** / **Look up**! Life isn't that bad.
3 Which film would you **take in** / **go for**?
4 They **left out** / **gave in** key parts of the plot.

6 Complete the article with a preposition in each gap.

The wonderful world of cinema snacks

Popcorn is typical **1**....... what's available at cinemas, but why be limited **2**....... just that? You might be surprised **3**....... what movie-goers munch. The Japanese, **4**....... instance, go for tiny dried crabs covered in salt or sugar when watching the action **5**....... screen. In a Cambodian cinema you might be offered insect snacks, **6**....... particular roasted ants covered in chocolate. China's favourite snack is called 'umeboshi' – dried and salted plums. According **7**....... the locals, they help prevent ageing, so **8**....... theory you could leave the cinema looking younger than when you arrived!

In it together

READING

Complete the sentences with these words.

crash course dribbling heading lunatic
make allowances muttered slouching streaming

1 It was a cold wet weekend so I spent the whole time .... at home.

2 If you've been ill, I'm sure the teacher will .... for you and extend the deadline.

3 She spent too long .... the ball and then lost it. She should have tried a shot at the goal.

4 We started .... towards the coast, but ran into a roadblock, so we had to turn back.

5 I saw an advert for intensive tuition that made me laugh – a .... in driving!

6 We lost sight of each other in the crowd as people were .... past us.

7 Camping out in winter seemed like a fun thing to do, but it turned out to be a .... idea – we ended up with ice on the inside of the tent.

8 The student .... a reason for being late and sat down at the back of the class.

Read the article about social media sharing quickly. Tick (✓) the sentences which describe it.

1 The article is written from a teenager's point of view. ☐

2 The writer seems extremely angry with a parent. ☐

3 The main aim is to highlight a problem in family life. ☐

4 The writer has done some research for the article. ☐

Read the article again and choose the correct answer (A, B, C or D).

1 In the first paragraph we learn that the writer has just
   A posted a comment about a picture.
   B eaten a sandwich after a football match.
   C come across an image of himself.
   D taken and uploaded a picture online.

2 What does the writer want his mother to do?
   A Think before taking a picture.
   B Be more proud of him and his success.
   C Remind him what he was like when younger.
   D Have as much fun as he does at matches.

3 The writer is surprised by the amount of 'sharenting'
   A because it starts when children are very young.
   B although parents don't start until their child is five.
   C because it makes young people feel anxious.
   D although he's been brought up with technology.

4 By the age he is now, the writer had expected to
   A be more in control of his own life.
   B have fewer images shared by his parents.
   C be able to remove images he doesn't like.
   D not see any images of him from the past.

5 In the fifth paragraph, the writer suggests that
   A rules set for children are not always followed by parents.
   B the family of the writer's friend doesn't post images of her.
   C parents need to monitor their children more closely online.
   D online safety is more important than control and privacy.

6 What does the writer mean by the phrase 'stay behind the times' (line 51)?
   A not follow your child at all on social media
   B not keep up with technological development
   C limit the number of times posts are uploaded
   D stay out of someone's private life altogether

Extend

Find the words or phrases in the article for the definitions.

1 continued with an action (para 1) ....

2 sweet and attractive (para 2) ....

3 choose the best time to do something (para 2) ....

4 not at all fashionable (para 4) ....

5 annoys me (para 5) ....

6 everything their children do (para 5) ....

7 acting immediately (para 5) ....

8 give my opinion (para 6) ....

When sharing
isn't such fun

Glancing down at the screen, I see that yet again my face is all over social media. This time eating a sandwich. In fact, wolfing down a sandwich as I'm starving after a football match. It's at that moment when I'm hot, sweaty and with mayonnaise all round my mouth that my mum takes a picture and posts it. Comments flood in about how I look, how greedy I must be, and even how I'm showing off. Me showing off? I wasn't ready for the picture, didn't ask for it and the last thing I wanted was for it to go online. But my mum went ahead anyway.

To be fair to her, we had in fact just won the match, so she wanted to spread the news of our success. Capturing some post-match action was in her mind just a bit of fun. And me with food round my mouth just reminded her of how cute I was as a little kid. A picture of a five-year-old relishing food is one thing, but when you're fifteen, it's not a great look. I know I should be happy that she felt proud of me, but I just wish she would pick her moments with the camera.

And it seems I'm not the only one. More and more young people are expressing anxiety at the amount their parents share about them online. There's even a word for it: 'sharenting': the constant posting by parents of content related to their children. And even for someone born into the so-called digital age, I was amazed by the facts and figures. The average child will have had a digital identity created by the age of six months, many from the day they are born. A study found that typical parents will have done 1,500 picture shares by the time their child is five. This amounts to an average number of 300 online images a year.

I have to admit I don't look at my own digital picture history if I can avoid it. The one of me on the first day of school was enough. Skinny in an oversized uniform and with a haircut that was anything but trendy. But I had reckoned on a bit less sharenting now I'm in my teens. My online space is important to me. I want to be the one in control of my digital footprint, especially as content related to me is going to be around forever. If that post-match image makes me groan now, what's it going to be like when I'm twenty-five? Or if a girlfriend sees it?

This is what gets me about the whole sharenting question. In a world where adults are telling us to respect others and think before we act, how does that fit with them taking pictures of their kids' every move? One of my friends has her social media accounts monitored twenty-four seven by her parents, but her family posts images of her online without a second thought. She doesn't seem to mind too much, but I can't help thinking that the relationship is a little one-sided. Of course, we all need to stay safe online, but we also want some control and privacy.

It might seem strange to talk about privacy in relation to global communication, but for some teenagers the internet is their personal space, the one opportunity to be themselves away from the boundaries of school and home life. No one's asking parents to stay behind the times and pretend the digital revolution never *line 51* happened. But it really is a question of consent. If I'm not happy about a picture or other content related to me, I should have my say on whether it gets uploaded or not. If family life is about respecting each other, then on behalf of teenagers everywhere, parents please, no posts without permission. (And, mum, I really hope you're reading this …)

---

6 Complete the comment about the article with the correct form of the words or phrases from Ex 4.

User 1	Add message	Report

Great article! Thanks for letting us ¹.. about sharenting. I agree with the 'ask before you post' idea. In my family, it was my grandparents who just used to ².. and post stuff all the time ³.. . I was into ballet for a while and they were so impressed that they really did share ⁴.. ! A traditional ballet dress is ⁵.. and I did get a few nasty comments back. But what ⁶.. about images of girls is that we have to be seen as pretty or ⁷.. . That's partly why I gave up ballet in favour of street dance. My grandparents are still proud, but they ⁸.. to take pictures – I'm not sure that jeans and a baggy top is their favourite look!

GRAMMAR

modal verbs

Choose the correct description (A or B) to match each sentence (1–6).

1 You ought to have said sorry.

   A advice for the future   **B** criticism of the past

2 She can't have phoned. I haven't had any missed calls.

   A I'm sure she did.   **B** I'm sure she didn't.

3 You must have been delighted to get first prize.

   A I'm sure you were.   **B** I'm not sure you were.

4 The parcel might have got lost.

   A I'm certain.   **B** It's possible.

5 He needn't have waited.

   A It wasn't necessary, but he did.   **B** It wasn't necessary so he didn't.

6 He didn't need to wait.

   A He definitely waited.   **B** We don't know if he waited.

Choose the correct words to complete the sentences.

1 We **were able to / could** chat for a couple of minutes.

2 Siblings should **have educated / be educated** at the same school.

3 We **should have been / should be** told the truth weeks ago.

4 It **can't / must** have been a very good party. Hardly anyone went.

5 I **may / can** have left my sweater on the school bus.

6 You needn't **have walked / walk** the dog. I'd already done it.

7 I **may not have gone / wasn't allowed to go** out with my friends.

8 He **could / can** have been in the first team, but he lost interest in rugby.

Complete the second sentence so that it has a similar meaning to the first sentence using the word given. Use between two and five words, including the word given.

1 It was a shame that we couldn't go out at the weekend.

   ABLE

   It was a shame that we .... go out at the weekend.

2 I'm sure I didn't meet her at the party because I wasn't there.

   MET

   I .... her at the party because I wasn't there.

3 It was a waste of money to buy a new racquet because I found my old one.

   HAVE

   I .... a new racquet because I found my old one.

4 Why didn't you look where you were going?

   OUGHT

   You .... where you were going.

5 You can stay in bed if you want to.

   GET

   You .... up if you don't want to.

6 You have to turn off the lights when you leave.

   MUST

   The lights .... off when you leave.

Complete the article with these modal forms.

can be interpreted   can make   can't have been
Could I have been   have to be   may have been
might be able   might be unfriended
might have gone   might lose
must have done   ought not to have posted

I've been unfollowed!

In today's world, we [1].. or break a relationship with one tap of the screen. We all know we [2].. on social media at any time. But when it happens, it hurts. Our first reaction is to think, 'I [3].. something wrong. Maybe I [4].. that last picture. [5].. more exciting, more amusing or just better in some way?

According to a psychology researcher, being unfollowed [6].. as a sign of exclusion – you feel you have been left out of the group. And while you [7].. touch with someone in a real-world relationship, an unfollow hurts more because it was done on purpose.' And, of course, we immediately unfollow the person back.

But does it [8].. like this? If we see social media as a way of sharing content as much as making friends, we [9].. to take a more logical view when things go wrong. After all, the decision might not have been personal. You [10].. unfollowed for a whole range of reasons. So the next time it happens, maybe think, 'Our interests [11].. in different directions.' rather than 'I [12].. much good at making friends.'

VOCABULARY

personality

1 Write words in the chart that fit each definition.

behaving in a way that shows you're happy	....
behaving in a way that is unusual	....
behaving in a way that shows you think you are being criticised	....
behaving in a way that makes people notice you	....
doing careless things without thinking	....
brave	....
behaving in an unpleasant or rude way because you think you are better than others	....
willing to help others	....

2 Complete the conversations with these pairs of words.

anti-social + courteous   possessive + demanding
talkative + immature   thoughtful + stubborn

1 A: What do you think is your best and worst quality?

B: I'd say I'm quite ....
I like doing little things to make people happy. Although once I've made a decision, I'm really
....

2 A: That new girl at school never talks to anyone. She doesn't even say 'hi'. Why is she so .... ?

B: She was rude to one of the teachers. She'll never settle in if she isn't
.... to the staff.

3 A: Have you fallen out with Angela?

B: Not really, but she was getting a bit
.... – she didn't want me to spend time with my other friends.

A: I knew someone like that. He was really
.... , too. Everything had to be done the way he liked.

4 A: Do you think it's good to be chatty?

B: It depends.

A: A .... person can be good in a group, but not if they take over the conversation. If you never listen, you could come across as a bit childish or
....

3 Complete the text with the correct form of the words. Which word doesn't need to change?

Who are your role models?

The people I have the most **1** .... (admire) for are my parents. They taught me the importance of **2** .... (honest) and **3** .... (loyal). Their example has always been to show **4** .... (sympathise) when people are in trouble, so I think I developed a **5** .... (willing) to help others.

My singing teacher has also been an important influence. She taught me the importance of **6** .... (discipline), but also **7** .... (flexible).

4 Complete the sentences with the correct form of 'have' or 'keep'.

1 I .... a lot in common with my cousins, but I'm happy .... a chat with them on social media.

2 When I give my presentation, I .... in mind what you said about speaking clearly.

3 I'm so sorry .... you waiting all this time.

4 My parents .... a word with the neighbour about the noise last weekend, but it hasn't stopped.

5 If you .... your desk tidy, you'd find your stuff!

5 Complete the blog post with a verb from A and a phrase from B in each gap.

A 're having   'm beginning to have   couldn't keep
have   keeps   keep   started having

B a bad day   a secret   difficulty   her mouth shut
in touch   nothing to do   serious doubts

Putting the END in friENDship

I like to think of myself as loyal, so ending a friendship would be hard. But I **1** .... about one friend in particular. He's been really two-faced and sneaky. What do you think? What would make you end a friendship?

Andrea
For me it's all about trust. A friend is someone who can **2** .... I shared my most private thoughts with someone, but she **3** .... I **4** ....
with that person now.

Tom
What I can't stand are fairweather friends. You know the type, you **5** .... , and they are nowhere to be seen. My ex-best friend was just like that. I **6** .... with things and she dropped me immediately. If you know someone who only **7** .... when times are good, you might be better off without them.

LISTENING

🔊 8.1 **Listen to a girl talking about a group activity. Which topic does she talk about?**

A joining a quiz club

B starting a games club

C getting involved in a drama club

D having fun in a team

E working hard to be accepted into a team

🔊 8.2 **Listen again. Match the speakers (1–5) with what they say about their group (A–H). There are three extra letters.**

A My role has changed from when I first joined the group.

B Being in the group has helped me decide my future career.

C The group didn't immediately accept me because I lacked the skills they had.

D It didn't take me long to get to know the members of the group.

E I set up the group to give people my age a new way of enjoying themselves.

F Because of my age, I'm sometimes excluded from the group.

G The more experienced members of the group support me.

H I had to be persuaded to join the group, but then I really got into it.

Speaker 1	....
Speaker 2	....
Speaker 3	....
Speaker 4	....
Speaker 5	....

Extend

Match the highlighted phrases in the sentences (1–8) with the meanings (A–H).

1 The oldest member of our group is in her fifties.

2 The whole team took me under their wing.

3 We won our first tournament by miles.

4 Since our first win, we haven't looked back.

5 I saw this group perform live.

6 I was desperate to be allowed in.

7 I used to spend the day glued to my screen.

8 I'm a regular at the group meetings.

A looked after and protected me

B I often go to

C wanted very much

D do a show in front of an audience

E not paying attention to anything else

F very easily, by a large number or amount

G aged between fifty and fifty-nine

H have continued to be successful

Complete the four conversations with the correct form of the phrases from Ex 3.

1 A: I'm ¹.. get a place in the school band.

B: Don't worry. You're the best drummer ².. .

2 A: Thanks, but I don't have much experience ³.. on stage.

B: Just go to the audition. Once you've got over your nerves, you won't ⁴.. .

3 A: What got you into martial arts?

B: My sister took up judo ⁵.. twenties. At that time you'd have found me ⁶.. a TV screen, but over time her enthusiasm rubbed off on me.

4 A: So did you join a club for teenagers?

B: Actually, there wasn't one, but the older people at my sister's club ⁷.. . I've been ⁸.. there ever since.

USE OF ENGLISH

Choose the extra word in each sentence.

1 We lost touch when I changed schools despite of being very close for years.

2 The festival will always be one of my happiest memories in spite of have the awful weather.

3 Despite the even fact that we argue all the time, my twin is my best friend.

4 I don't think I'm spoiled in spite of I'm being the youngest.

5 Not only were we born on the same day, but we too also have the same middle name.

6 Not only did she was unfriend me, but she also talked behind my back.

Choose the correct ending (A or B).

1 I stayed up to watch the end of the movie despite
   A being tired.
   B I was tired.

2 I get on well with my brother, in spite
   A the age difference.
   B of the age difference.

3 She managed to continue despite
   A her injured hand.
   B have an injured hand.

4 We've been best friends for ages in spite
   A of having the fact that we're very different.
   B of the fact that we're very different.

Join the sentences using 'not only … but also'.

1 She talks behind your back. She tells lies.
   Not ....
   ....

2 He ignored my messages. He unfollowed me.
   Not ....
   ....

3 She's fun to be with. She's a loyal friend.
   Not ....
   ....

4 I'd given her advice. I'd lent her some money.
   Not ....
   ....

5 You've been late every day this week. You've missed three deadlines.
   Not ....
   ....

6 They were playing loud music. They were shouting at the top of their voices.
   Not ....
   ....

Complete the blog post with these phrases. There are two answers that you do not need.

but I also   despite confusing   despite the confusion   despite the fact that
did I forget   I forgot   spite of being   was I messaging

I won't win any **best friend** awards

I am a rubbish friend. There, I've said it! I know what I should do to be better, but I just don't. I bought my best friend some birthday chocolates. Not only ¹................................. to give them to her, ²................................. ate them myself. And believe it or not, I actually have quite a lot of friends in ³................................. so hopeless. And they're loyal to me, ⁴................................. I'm always late, never remember people's names and take ages to make a decision. I don't mean to be a pain in the neck, I just get distracted. Yesterday, not only ⁵................................. the wrong Helen (there are two in our group), but I also managed to unfollow them both by mistake. Luckily, they're still speaking to me, ⁶................................. . 😷

Complete the second sentence so that it has a similar meaning to the first sentence using the word given. Use between two and five words, including the word given.

1 I had to apologise even though I hadn't done anything wrong.
   DESPITE
   I had to apologise .... anything wrong.

2 He behaved badly and he blamed everyone else.
   ONLY
   Not .... badly, but he also blamed everyone else.

3 The party was great fun although the music wasn't brilliant.
   BEING
   The party was great fun .... brilliant.

4 Although she was ill, she came to school as often as she could.
   SPITE
   In .... , she came to school as often as she could.

5 My sister is away at college, but I still chat with her every day.
   FACT
   I still chat with my sister every day .... she is away at college.

83

USE OF ENGLISH 2

Complete the sentences with these phrasal verbs and two or three prepositions. Use the same phrasal verb in A and B for each question.

come across (+ as)   fill in (+ on)
get along (+ with)   hang out (+ with)

1 A The plot's quite complicated so do you want me .... you .... before the next episode?

B When I see you later, I .... you .... all the latest news.

2 A You used to be best friends with Jack. Why .... you .... well recently?

B I'm lucky because I .... always .... my siblings really well.

3 A The skatepark is a popular place for local kids ....

B We were friends for ages until she started .... a different crowd.

4 A The day I met him, he .... a bit of a know-all, but he's actually good fun.

B If you feel nervous before speaking in public, good preparation will help you .... well.

Replace the highlighted words with these phrasal verbs. Add a pronoun where necessary.

carry on   clear up   get over   put off   speak up

A: Hi, I haven't seen you at the match on your own before. You're usually here with Paul.

B: We haven't seen each other in a while. His recent behaviour has **1**made me not want to.

A: But you're still going to **2**continue being mates?

B: I'm not sure. He's been talking behind my back and said some nasty things. It's hard to **3**recover from the shock of that.

A: Sure, but have you asked him why?

B: No, I'm just keeping out of his way for now.

A: Listen, he's in the wrong, so you should **4**give your opinion and tell him how you feel. That's the only way you're going to **5**solve the problem.

1 ....
2 ....
3 ....
4 ....
5 ....

8.3 **Complete the text with one word in each gap. Then listen and check your answers.**

Only a true friend will speak **1**........................... and tell you when you're being an idiot. After being best friends with Ellen for years, I **2**........................... up with a really bad crowd of people. Everyone I knew had to put up **3**........................... my terrible antics. But not Ellen. She was completely honest with me about how stupid I was being. After I was excluded from school, Ellen reached out **4**........................... me and offered support. Over time, I was able to **5**........................... over all my problems and carry **6**........................... with my education. If Ellen hadn't **7**........................... up for our friendship, I couldn't have done that. Now she's one of the people I **8**........................... up to and admire most.

Choose the correct words to complete the sentences.

1 A bad day can **have / make** a negative effect on your week, but don't **miss / waste** time looking back; look forward.

2 I asked the tutor to **bear / accept** me in mind for the main part in the play. I **get / have** nothing to lose by asking.

3 After being ill, pay **attention / application** to your diet and take some exercise to build up your **strength / strong**.

4 It's never easy to **put / pick** yourself up off the floor after a disappointment, but take a **wide / deep** breath and try again.

5 When setting yourself a **score / goal**, there's no point **in / on** making it so difficult that you can never achieve it.

Read the article and choose the best answer (A, B, C or D).

Creating a kinder world

What's special about the second week in February? It's Random Acts of Kindness Week – a time when people **1**........ others and are, well, kind. The Random Acts of Kindness Foundation (RAK for short) is the organisation behind the idea. They have set themselves the **2**........ of making the world a kinder place.

It's understandable that we prioritise our family and the people we **3**........ with most. But RAK thinks we can spread kindness so that it becomes part of everyday life. And don't be **4**........ if you think it sounds expensive. Helping someone with their bags, complimenting someone, or simply smiling at a stranger are all free.

RAK believes that if you're kind to a person, they feel good and they also act in a thoughtful way. Giving someone a **5**........ just means that we can **6**........ a little better. So go on, take a deep **7**........ and try a random act of kindness today. You really have nothing to **8**........ .

	A	B	C	D
1	come across as	look up to	fill in on	reach out to
2	goal	intention	purpose	idea
3	hang on	hang onto	hang out	hang in
4	put down	put off	put out	put upon
5	hand	need	help	care
6	get down	get through	get along	get over
7	breath	smile	sigh	air
8	waste	pay	stand	lose

SPEAKING

1 Read the speaking task. Match the vocabulary phrases with the five points in the task. Some phrases can be used to describe more than one category.

be compared to each other   give up meat   not have your own space
make someone feel isolated   cook separate meals
hurt someone without realising   keep in touch   lack your own identity
have nothing to do with someone   not be able to invite friends over
owe someone an explanation

becoming a vegetarian	**How might these situations cause relationship problems for a young person?**	sharing a bedroom with a sibling
unfriending someone on social media	being a twin	changing schools

2 🔊 8.4 Listen to students talking about the task in Ex 1. Match the students' conversations (1–3) with the problems (A–D). There is one extra problem you do not need.

A reading out the whole task aloud ....
B not sounding very interested ....
C not discussing the topic together ....
D not deciding on the first topic together ....

3 🔊 8.5 Two students are discussing the task. Choose the correct words to complete the conversation. Then listen and check your answers.

A: ¹**Shall / Let's** we start with sharing a room?

B: Yes, sure.

A: Well, in this situation, there are often a lot of arguments about dividing the space fairly and who has more stuff. And if one brother or sister is more untidy than the other, then there can be a lot of disagreements. What do you ²**agree / think**?

B: Yes, ³**you have / you're** right. I think it's a very common problem. It can also be difficult for the young person and their schoolmates. If there isn't a private space where they can hang out after school, then the group might not spend so much time together.

A: That's a good ⁴**point / topic**. Or that teenager might even become less popular.

B: Hmm. OK, so how about ⁵**going along / moving on** to being a twin? I think people like this are often very close, but then that might make life really hard when they argue. I mean, it could take longer to get over a disagreement if they had a special relationship before.

A: I know what you ⁶**say / mean**, but I think the biggest problem for teens in this situation is being yourself. I know two brothers and everyone sees them as a pair. It must be annoying for them when they have different personalities and their own hobbies. ⁷**Are / Do** you agree?

B: Yes, I hadn't thought of that. It could drive you crazy if people say, 'You're just like your brother.' all the time. So, ⁸**let's / shall** talk about …

4 🔊 8.6 Listen to the students discussing their answer to the next part of the task. Which situations in Ex 1 are discussed and which two are chosen?

5 Put the words in the correct order.

1 to / quite / decide. / It's / difficult

....

2 sure. / quite / not / I'm

....

3 changed / mind. / I've / my / Sorry,

....

4 the / choice / one. / best / wasn't / that / maybe / Yes,

....

6 Are the sentences (1–8) used for making a suggestion (S), giving an opinion (O) or reaching a decision (D)?

1 As far as I'm concerned, sharing a room isn't that big a problem. ....

2 Personally, I don't think that being a twin creates too many difficulties. ....

3 Shall we move on to a different topic? ....

4 I'd go for moving to a new school as the most problematic. ....

5 It seems to me that giving up meat wouldn't cause many problems. ....

6 Let's start with unfriending someone. ....

7 I think being a twin is probably more difficult than sharing because you can lose your identity. ....

8 We both think that unfriending affects a relationship, don't we? ....

7 Read the options in the task in Ex 1 again. Imagine you have a partner and you need to discuss this task with them. Which questions or phrases from Ex 3 could you use to involve them in the discussion?

8 🎙 Record your answers to the task in Ex 1. Then listen to your recording and answer the questions.

1 Did you give reasons to support your answers?

2 Did you use appropriate phrases to change topics or change your mind? (e.g. So moving on to…)

3 Did you use questions to involve your imagined partner in the discussion?

WRITING

a letter

Read the task and choose the correct option (A–D) to complete the sentences.

Community Centre
Countdown

It's just 100 days until YOUR centre reopens. We're inviting people in the local area to come up with suggestions for classes and activities that will put the centre at the heart of the community. Ideas that appeal to different generations and across cultures are welcome.

Write an email with your suggestions to:
Ms Gemma Hillier, Community
Centre Manager

In this task ...

1 you are writing to someone you:
   A don't know.
   B know quite well.

2 the style should be:
   A very formal.
   B very chatty and informal.
   C more formal than to a friend.

3 the reader will be expecting:
   A a long list of ideas and suggestions.
   B three or four ideas with relevant reasons.
   C the names of people who will help out.
   D reasons for working at the centre.

Choose the correct words to complete the sentences.

1 Why don't we **set up / setting up** a computer club?

2 How about **to create / creating** craft days?

3 It might be a good idea **we having / to have** a space for dance and exercise.

4 You could think about **introducing / introduce** live performances.

5 It would be a good idea **to put together / putting together** a programme of outdoor events.

6 I recommend **provide / providing** facilities for preparing food.

Match the suggestions (1–6) in Ex 2 with the reasons and examples (A–F).

A Crafts are popular and objects could be sold to raise money.

B Cookery is an important skill and it's fun to try different dishes.

C It would be good to show local talent through concerts and plays.

D Using the centre's outdoor area would bring the community together.

E It's important for people of all ages to increase their levels of activity.

F Technology is part of everyday life and we all need to update our skills.

Complete the sentences with these words or phrases.

---

so few   so little   so many   so
such a lot of …   such an … that   that

---

1 Using technology is .... important skill .... everyone needs it.

2 It was a shame that .... people used the old centre.

3 Students have .... free time in summer .... they need a programme of activities.

4 Cinema is .... enjoyable!

5 With .... space in town for people to meet up, the centre will be important for everyone.

6 I'm sure it will be important for .... people.

Choose the correct options to complete the email.

[1]**Dear Ms Hillier / Hiya Gemma**

[2]**This email / I'm writing** to give you some suggestions for the new community centre. It [3]**will / could** be great to have it open again.

As food is [4]**so / such** an important part of everyday life, I recommend a food festival. You [5]**could have had / could have** regular stalls too.

Secondly, how about setting up a cinema club? It's [6]**such / so** entertaining to watch a film as a group and this would help people to get together. People's own videos could also [7]**show / be shown**.

[8]**Final / Finally**, there are [9]**so few / so little** dance opportunities in town it would be a good idea [10]**to introduce / introduce** regular dance days, with a range of styles to appeal to different age groups.

I think the important thing is that we [11]**reach / push** out to different parts of the community and that the centre benefits everyone. I hope my ideas are helpful.

[12]**Cheers / With best wishes**

Gita Rai

You see this announcement on a school noticeboard. Write your email in 140–190 words, in an appropriate style.

Fundraising ideas needed!

We need fundraising ideas for the new centre so that we can reach the amount required. Please send your suggestions for events or activities that would appeal to local people and raise the most money possible.

Write an email with your ideas to:
Mr Adrian Leeson, Community Advisor

UNIT CHECK

1 Complete the girl's comments with these verb forms.

---
can be fixed   have to unfriend   'll be able to   might have been delayed
must have got   ought to   should be   shouldn't have been

She **1**... my text. I sent it ages ago. And she
2... back from school by now. Why hasn't she
replied? I guess she **3**... on the way – yes, that's
a possibility. But it doesn't take much time to text. I guess she's angry
with me. And I don't blame her. I **4**... so horrible.
Perhaps I **5**... go round to her house. That way I
6... apologise face to face. Yes, that's the answer.
Any problem **7**... with a chat and a hug. Oh, my
phone! … Oh, no! Did she really **8**... me altogether?

2 Choose the correct words to complete the sentences.

1 We hardly ever saw each other despite **to live / living** in the same street.
2 She was **so / such** possessive that she created problems for my other friends.
3 Not only **he borrows / does he borrow** it, he forgets to ask first.
4 My brother and sister turned up at the party despite **weren't / not** being invited.
5 **In spite of / In spite** our differences, we can agree sometimes.
6 Why are you in **so / such** a good mood today?
7 Despite the fact **of / that** we get on well, we're quite competitive.
8 I have so **little / few** time to hang out with friends.

3 Complete the chatroom post with one word or a contraction in each gap.

●●● ▮ ▶   🔍 🏠

I'm not proud of it, but ...

We all do things to people that we regret. What have you done
that you really **1**... have? Be honest!

Suzi	Add message | Report

A schoolfriend was **5**... hooked on
chocolate biscuits with cream in the middle that she would
never share them with us. One day, we bought a packet
and replaced the cream with toothpaste. Hiding behind
the door, we didn't **6**... to wait long
before she opened the packet and took a big bite. It must
7... tasted disgusting! 😖 And she
8... have guessed it was us because
she's never mentioned it.

4 Which preposition can complete the sentences in each set?

1 ....
A Do you have difficulty .... managing your time?
B Who do you hang out .... most after school?
C Money has nothing to do .... being happy.

2 ....
A Do you have much .... common with your brother?
B Can you fill me .... on all the gossip?
C Please keep .... touch while you're away on holiday.

3 ....
A I wish I hadn't taken .... with a bad crowd.
B Regular exercise will help to build .... your strength.
C How do you put .... with his negative attitude?

5 Complete the tips with the missing words.

●●●   🔍 🏠

How to be BFF
Want to be best friends forever?
Here are our top do's and don'ts.

👍 **DO**

✓ be loyal and **1**...
up for your mates.

✓ reach **2**...
to friends when they're in trouble.

✓ **3**... up
misunderstandings quickly.

✓ keep your **4**...
shut if told a secret.

👎 **DON'T**

✗ pay **5**... to
your friends' faults. No-one's perfect.

✗ keep people **6**... .
Being late is just annoying.

✗ **7**... time being
childish. Accept apologies with a smile.

✗ **8**... across
as arrogant.

READING

Complete the sentences with these words.

---

a split second   beware   filter   founder
gets crammed   poised   short-sighted   skip

---

1 Evan Spiegel, the .... of Snapchat, became a billionaire at the age of twenty-five.

2 To spend the whole budget in the first weekend was very .... of us.

3 I took a shot at goal and .... later the final whistle blew.

4 .... of making decisions without thinking things through.

5 Start with as many ideas as you can think of and then .... them down to the best ones.

6 Don't .... breakfast or you'll be starving by eleven o'clock.

7 A simple meditation can help when your head .... too .... with thoughts and ideas.

8 He stood on the board high above the water, ... to take the dive.

Read the article and choose the correct answer (A, B or C).

1 Who was the article written for?

   A psychology students

   B general readers

   C the unemployed

2 What was the writer's main aim?

   A to give advice on how to make decisions

   B to summarise a scientific paper

   C to talk about a topic that affects most people

3 What is the main tone of the article?

   A academic and scientific

   B neutral and at times more personal

   C informal and chatty

Read the article again. Choose which sentence (A–G) best fits each gap (1–6) in the article. You do not need one of the sentences.

A This was true after both the two- and six-month periods had passed.

B Most featured unimportant choices like changing hair colour or joining a gym, but a third dealt with serious issues.

C In fact, other psychology studies suggest we have an inbuilt preference for the status quo.

D As strange as it seems, nearly 4,000 people used the site for help with those problems.

E So volunteers who were having difficulties with a potentially life-changing decision agreed to take part in an intriguing experiment.

F Even Levitt himself recognises that his experiment wasn't completely scientific in its approach.

G Then having chosen the question that reflected their current dilemma, each volunteer flipped the virtual coin on the website.

Extend

Complete the phrases with words from the article.

1 a tried and .... something (introduction)

2 .... life choices (introduction)

3 act .... something (para 4)

4 .... a change (para 4)

5 .... with difficult decisions (para 6)

6 turn something .... in your mind (para 6)

7 work .... (para 6)

Choose the correct words to complete the sentences.

● ● ●

Dealing with decisions

Are you someone who ¹turns / tests a question over and over in their mind before deciding? Or do you just flip a coin? Just what *is* the best way to make a decision?

| Nicky | Add message | Report |

At thirteen, I haven't been faced ²with / from too many major ³life / live choices, but I do think flipping a coin can help. The test isn't how the coin lands, but your reaction to it. Imagine you decided that heads would tell you to give up playing the guitar. If it's heads and you feel disappointed, you know you shouldn't ⁴make / act on the result because you secretly want to keep up playing. Simple!

| Ash | Add message | Report |

My ⁵trial / tried and tested method is to write a list of points for and against the decision. It's immediately clear which list is longer and that helps me ⁶do / make the change. Not terribly scientific, but it's always ⁷worked / become out fine up to now.

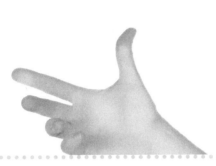

Can't decide?
Just flip a coin

Flipping a coin is a tried and tested method of coming to a decision over something fairly minor: such as what to watch on TV, who buys lunch, or whose turn it is to wash up. But what if you were to make major life choices in the same way? Heads I do it, tails I don't.

This is exactly what a study by Steven Levitt of the University of Chicago got people to do. He says that very few studies have been done to find out whether people are good at making important choices. [1] .... Its aim was to assess whether change would play a role in making people happier.

Participants were invited onto a website set up by Levitt and were asked to choose one of thirty questions. [2] .... Examples included leaving a job, breaking up a relationship or going back to full-time education. The first two of these were in fact the most responded to questions in the whole experiment. 'Should I change my job?' was the subject of 2,186 coin flips alone.

So how did it all work? The participants gave an assessment of their level of happiness on a scale of one to ten. [3] .... Heads meant go ahead and make the change; tails stick with the status quo. Levitt followed up with each participant at two- and six-monthly intervals after the initial experiment. He surveyed them to find out if they'd followed the result of the coin flip and how happy they were with their choice. People the volunteers knew were also invited to give feedback on their level of wellbeing before and after the experiment.

In total, the coin was flipped in the experiment over 22,000 times. Of course, not every question answered was a life-changing one and not every participant acted on the result of the coin flip. However, over half in the serious question category did. In Levitt's summary of his findings he states that the people who had made a change were 'substantially happier' than those who had done nothing. [4] ....

What does this mean for the average person trying to navigate a complex world? Well, it isn't an invitation to leave every serious life decision to the flip of a coin. [5] .... The fact the study group were volunteers means that it wasn't fully representative of the general population. Having them self-assess their happiness level also leaves their conclusions open to interpretation.

However, what the experiment does show is how much help we need when faced with difficult decisions. The thought of major change is both exhilarating and terrifying. Despite the countless hours spent turning a decision over and over in our mind, the end result is often to do nothing. [6] .... Also, research into regret shows that we are more likely to feel negative about inaction than action. You regret what you *don't* do, not what you do. So if Levitt's work teaches us anything, maybe it's to take a leap into the unknown. It might just work out fine.

GRAMMAR

relative clauses

1 In which sentences can the highlighted text be removed and the sentence still make sense?

1 That's the decision that I regret most.
2 When you are making up your mind, don't be rushed into a decision.
3 The person whose advice I listen to most is my older brother.
4 People who are faced with too many decisions often don't decide anything at all.
5 The problem page, which is part of my favourite magazine, often has useful tips.
6 I don't want a friend who isn't there for me during the bad times.

2 Complete the sentences with the correct relative pronoun. Put the pronoun in (brackets) if it can be left out.

1 I'm a person .... finds making decisions really hard.
2 Do you remember .... we first met at school?
3 That was the moment .... I decided my future career.
4 Millie is the girl .... brother invited me to the party.
5 I'll never understand the reason .... he didn't keep in touch.
6 She told a joke .... made everyone laugh.

3 Join the pairs of sentences with relative clauses. Use a relative pronoun only where necessary.

1 Do you remember that time? We took the wrong road and got lost.
   ....

2 These are the trainers. I wish I'd never bought them.
   ....

3 Max is the student. His twin brother decided to dye his hair purple.
   ....

4 My friend has been a vegetarian for five years. She decided to eat meat again.
   ....

5 This is the café. It serves over 100 different drinks.
   ....

6 I went to the school. My mum had been a teacher there.
   ....

4 Choose the words from each sentence that can be removed to form reduced relative clauses.

1 The players who are on a team need to work together.
2 I didn't recognise the person who was waving at me from across the street.
3 The number of choices that were included on the pizza menu made it impossible to choose.
4 We spent a day clearing up all the litter which had been left on the beach.
5 The train that is just arriving is the express service to Edinburgh.
6 People that had been waiting in the ticket queue for hours gave up.

5 Complete the sentences with a past or present participle of these verbs.

| come | encourage | impress | pack | try on | wear |

1 .... by her presentation, the teacher chose her to lead the debating society.
2 .... five different outfits, I decided not to buy any of them.
3 .... a uniform for school, I don't have to make clothes choices during the week.
4 .... by their success in the early games, the team went on to win the tournament.
5 .... from a big family, I'm used to making group decisions.
6 .... far too much stuff, he promised to travel light in future.

6 Complete the blog post with a relative pronoun or a participle in each gap.

• • •

How *crazy* is that?

I was looking at a website [1] .... has information about the age [2] .... you can legally do different things in England. Everyone [3] .... is over eighteen can vote, but I was surprised that you can actually stand for election at that age too. I don't know anyone [4] .... life experience at eighteen would make me want to vote for them.

Another limit set at eighteen is getting a tattoo. [5] .... seen some awful results, personally I don't know [6] .... anyone would want one. But what seems odd is that there is no legal limit for piercings. People [7] .... up their mind to have a piercing need as much protection as those having body art, don't they?

As a fifteen-year-old car fanatic, I also find these age limits confusing: you can fly a glider solo at fourteen and it's possible to get both a driving *and* pilot's licence at the age of seventeen. These rules, [8] .... I guess are made with safety in mind, just don't seem to add up.

VOCABULARY

knowing, thinking and deciding

🔊 9.1 **Listen to five short conversations. Complete the sentences with the correct form of these phrases.**

---
be torn between two choices
have a Plan A and a Plan B   have second thoughts
sleep on it   speak out about

---

1 The boy ....
of what to buy.

2 The girl wants to
.... before
making a decision.

3 The girl ....
about a promise she made.

4 The boys
.... for
getting to the match.

5 The students intend
.... the
reintroduction of school uniform.

Complete the puzzle and find the mystery word.

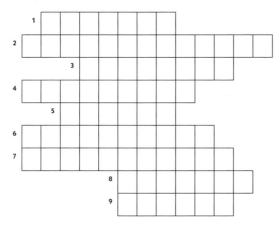

1 suggest
2 the noun from *consider*
3 assess
4 the noun from *judge*
5 choose
6 the noun from 3
7 a noun from 1
8 discuss with someone
9 the verb from *intention*

Choose the correct words to complete the conversation.

A: Welcome to today's debate club. For the next hour, we encourage you to [1]**talk / speak** your mind and then we can all [2]**go / come** to a decision after hearing all your opinions. So today's question is: Is it better to be decisive or to consult other people?

B: Decisive, definitely. People who know their [3]**own / self** mind very often become leaders in business or politics. And being able to make up your [4]**decision / mind** quickly is an important skill.

A: But what if your first thinking isn't right? It's better to [5]**change / adapt** your mind than base a decision [6]**for / on** something that's wrong or incomplete.

C: [7]**According to / Carrying out** research, decisiveness is a characteristic that is looked for in a leader, so I agree with the first point. But no one in a big company or government should decide everything independently. You need to [8]**imply / involve** others in a decision to get the best information.

A: Yes, research also [9]**discovers / reveals** that asking for other people's ideas helps you [10]**make / do** better decisions in the long run.

D: Can I just say that in organisations it's important to be able to [11]**challenge / argue** a decision that you don't agree with?

A: Yes, that's right. The power shouldn't be with just one person. One other thing is …

Complete the article with one word in each gap.

Decision time

Imagine you have to make a big decision. If you are torn [1]... two choices, typical advice might be to [2]... up the pros and [3]... of the different options. But does the time of day have anything to do with good decision-making? Research carried [4]... by a team of psychologists suggests it does.

A group of online chess players [5]... at the centre of the study. This allowed the researchers to investigate decision-making in a large number of people throughout the day. Put simply, the research revealed that in the morning, the players [6]... to a decision more slowly, but more accurately; later in the day they made up their [7]... with less thought and less accuracy; by the evening all players made faster and riskier choices.

So if this research [8]... any weight, it seems decision time should definitely be before lunchtime.

LISTENING

🔊 9.2 **Listen to an interview with a young person who has made a change. What did she do?**

A give up social media permanently

B give up social media temporarily

C use social media just at bedtime

🔊 9.3 **Listen again and choose the correct answer (A, B or C).**

1 Why did Lucy give up her phone?

  A her family and school got her to take part in a trial

  B she was worried about the time she spent online

  C her teacher told her parents she was exhausted

2 At the start of the scheme Lucy missed

  A her phone only for a few minutes.

  B only some of the apps on her phone.

  C being part of online interaction.

3 How did Lucy's family react?

  A They punished her for being in a bad mood.

  B They offered her alternative activities to social media.

  C They told her she couldn't leave home to use her phone.

4 How did life improve for Lucy?

  A She had more spare time to do different things.

  B She replaced social media with former hobbies.

  C She was able to fall asleep more easily at bedtime.

5 There has been a benefit to Lucy at school in that

  A it's easier for her to revise for exams.

  B she now listens to what the teacher says.

  C she can keep her mind on her work.

6 When advising someone to give up social media, Lucy recommends

  A letting the person make the decision to change.

  B telling the person they have to turn their phone off.

  C getting them to admit they don't enjoy social media.

7 What's Lucy's attitude to social media now?

  A She wants to stop using it altogether.

  B She's scared of being pulled back into it.

  C She feels she has it more under control.

Extend

Match the phrases (1–8) with the definitions (A–H).

1 a digital detox

2 didn't know what to do with myself

3 bit their head off

4 take my mind off something

5 had a spare moment

6 no wonder

7 know in your heart of hearts

8 reach for something

A had no idea how to keep busy

B it wasn't surprising

C had a little free time available

D stop me thinking about something

E a period without going online

F put out your hand or arm to get something

G responded in an aggressive way

H really believed deep down

Complete the blog post with the correct form of words from Ex 3.

My dad asked if I could help him move some furniture as soon as I had a ¹ .... moment. I told him I was busy waiting for a friend to message me. In fact I ² .... his head off. I felt bad, but then a few seconds later my phone beeped and I was back online. I could hear my dad moving stuff around and I ³ .... in my heart of hearts I should offer to help. But I kept ⁴ .... for my phone and checking for the next message. It seemed to take ages and I didn't know what to do with ⁵ .... between texts. I put on some music to ⁶ .... my mind off my friends and what they were doing. Maybe they were out having a good time without me? Still no message, but I spent the rest of the afternoon checking. No ⁷ .... I felt tired and fed up. It was then I came across an article headed: Do you suffer from Fear of Missing Out (FOMO)? Maybe I did have FOMO and maybe it was time for a digital ⁸ ....

USE OF ENGLISH 1

Match the sentence beginnings (1–6) and endings (A–F).

1 I think it was my sister
2 What's most challenging is
3 What happened
4 What he did in reply to my question
5 It was about three weeks ago
6 I must admit what frustrates me

A when she last got in touch with me.
B to arrive at a decision that suits everyone.
C was that the box was sent to the wrong place.
D who sent me the Valentine's card.
E about them is their childishness.
F was to just look at the floor.

Rewrite the sentences starting with the words given.

1 My battery ran out so I couldn't text. (What happened)
   ....
2 I received the invitation just yesterday. (It was)
   ....
3 I don't understand their way of thinking. (What I don't)
   ....
4 My parents pay for most of my clothes. (It's my)
   ....
5 I'm surprised how much everything costs. (What surprises me)
   ....
6 I wasn't allowed to stay over at my friend's until I was sixteen. (It wasn't)
   ....
7 We weighed up the pros and cons and then decided. (What we did)
   ....
8 You should think things through before you make a choice. (What you should do)
   ....

Complete the second sentence so that it has a similar meaning to the first sentence using the word given. Use between two and five words, including the word given.

1 I really like giving people nice surprises.
   IS
   What .... giving people nice surprises.
2 We got separated and couldn't find each other.
   HAPPENED
   What .... we got separated and couldn't find each other.
3 My parents make the final decision on where we go on holiday.
   WHO
   It's .... make the final decision on where we go on holiday.
4 I dislike their attitude.
   ABOUT
   What I dislike .... their attitude.
5 I made a stupid choice.
   DID
   What I .... a stupid choice.

Complete the article with one word in each gap.

In search of surprise

It seems that we could do with more surprise in our lives. At least, ¹..................................... to 'surprisologist' Tania Luna. (²..................................... surprises me is that such a job exists!) Tania has studied the importance of surprise in everyday life today. She says ³..................................... is now more than ever that we need to make things less predictable and accept change. But why?

In one way, life is under more control than it used to be. For example, what we all ⁴..................................... before a new experience is to Google information about it. So the surprise and delight in the experience are lost. In another way, we live in a world ⁵..................................... is more uncertain than ever before. The people ⁶..................................... have the skills to deal with surprise and change will best survive the challenges of the future.

Certainty makes us comfortable, but change makes us feel alive. Tania, ⁷..................................... personality naturally made her want to stay in control, has learned to enjoy change. What she advises ⁸..................................... to let life surprise you. Don't do research into experiences, live them! Actively look for new activities to do and people to meet. Surprise others.

USE OF ENGLISH

🔊 **9.4** Listen to six short conversations about fashion and style. Number the sentences that describe each conversation (1–6).

He/She:

has a crazy dress sense. ....

is obsessed with style and image. ....

looks as if they have thrown on their clothes. ....

is happy to follow the crowd. ....

wants to wear a particular brand or label. ....

is good at picking up bargains. ....

Choose the correct words to complete the text.

Have your say: *fashion*

There's so much fashion advice out there it's easy for your head to get crammed with ideas about what you should and shouldn't wear. What do you think?

Tanya
I wear a uniform five days a week so I love to [1]**experience / experiment** with new looks outside school. It takes me a while to [2]**put / make** an outfit together.

Ali
Don't feel under [3]**stress / pressure** to wear something you don't want to. The same goes for make-up and tattoos. YOU decide what [4]**looks / shows** really cool.

Josh
I have an [5]**issue / objection** with the fashion industry and that's how silly some of the clothes are. It's great to stand [6]**up for / out in** a crowd, but no one wants to look like a clown.

Complete the sentences with the correct form of the words in brackets.

1 I like to be .... (imagination) with my clothes, but I often get funny looks. People can be very .... (judgement) about people who look different from them.

2 My mum used to be quite .... (boss) about my clothes, but now she lets me be a lot more .... (independence) in my choices.

3 I'd be .... (suspicion) of anything with a designer logo bought on a market. Even if it looks .... (style), it's likely to be fake.

4 Getting a piercing isn't the most .... (intelligence) thing to do. In fact, it can be pretty .... (risk) if things go wrong.

5 I like to be more .... (ambition) with my style, but I don't really feel .... (confidence) enough.

6 All the smart watches were .... (fault) and so had to be returned. There must have been a problem during the .... (develop) stages of the product.

7 My dad is .... (obsession) with cybersecurity. He's always looking for ways to keeps his personal data .... (confidence).

Read the article and complete it with the correct form of the word in capitals.

Wear me / or / share me?

Are the clothes that don't fit into your wardrobe in a [1]................................ pile on the floor? **MESS**
Are your parents losing [2]................................ **PATIENT**
with you for buying clothes you don't wear? You're not alone. It's estimated that there are 3.6 billion items of clothing unworn in the UK alone. Even if you don't collect clothes [3]................................ , you're likely to **OBSESSION**
buy more than you wear. But there might be a solution. Academics are working on the [4]................................ of a connected **DEVELOP**
wardrobe. A system of micro-chipped tags in the clothes and a reader work together to monitor how long the clothes are left. The system is also [5]................................ , tweeting a reminder **INTERACT**
to the owner to 'wear me!' If not worn, the clothes then contact a charity shop for recycling or put themselves up for auction on eBay. This [6]................................ would help the biggest **INNOVATE**
fashion fan to keep track of their clothes, but would also have [7]................................ **ENVIRONMENT**
benefits. Reducing the overproduction of clothes is [8]................................ to prevent them **ESSENCE**
ending up in landfill.

SPEAKING

1 Look at the photos and read the task instructions. Tick (✓) the sentences that describe the task .

> Compare the photos and say why you think the people have chosen to shop in these ways.

In this task you need to:

1 describe the pictures in detail one at a time. ☐

2 say what is similar and different about the pictures. ☐

3 answer the question before talking about the pictures. ☐

4 talk about a time when you did the activity in the photos. ☐

5 answer the question after talking about the pictures. ☐

6 speculate about their reasons for shopping in this way. ☐

2 Are these phrases used to say something is the same (S) or different (D), or to give an opinion (O)?

1 Both pictures show … ....

2 For me, … ....

3 Another similarity is … ....

4 In the first picture, … whereas in the second picture, … ....

5 Another difference is … ....

6 I'd say that … ....

7 On the other hand, … ....

3 🔊 9.5 Listen to a student answer the question in Ex 1. Which of the phrases from Ex 2 do they use?

4 Choose the correct words to complete the sentences.

1 They look as **though / like** they're enjoying shopping and have noticed something that they might want to buy.

2 They **may have / may** want to buy something special for someone, so they've gone out to see what they can find.

3 There **should / could** be a problem with the site – maybe what they wanted sold out at the last minute.

4 I'd say that they're shopping in this way **so / order** that they can see and touch the items they're interested in before they buy.

5 **Perhaps / Possible** they're trying to get something you can buy only online, like tickets for a concert.

6 They might **be going / going** on to do something else in town, like have lunch or see a movie.

7 They look really disappointed at what's gone wrong, so the item **can't / must** be important to them.

8 I think they might have chosen to shop in this way **whereas / because** it would be quicker than going to a mall.

5 Match each sentence beginning (1–3) with two endings (A–F).

1 I'd prefer ....

2 I know I'd rather ....

3 If I had a choice, ...

A meet my friends in town because we enjoy looking round the shops.

B I'd buy everything on the internet because I don't like going shopping.

C to shop on the high street because you don't have to wait for delivery.

D search online to see what's available, but then buy in an actual shop.

E I'd shop in both ways to get convenience online, but also the fun of real shops.

F to buy things like books and games online because you get a better price.

6 🔴 Record your own answer to the task in Ex 1. Listen and check if you used any of the phrases from Ex 2.

WRITING

an essay

Read the task and underline the key words.

> In your English class you have been talking about decision-making. Now your English teacher has asked you to write an essay.
>
> Write an essay using all the notes and giving reasons for your point of view.
>
> Teenagers should be able to make their own choices. Do you agree?
>
> **Notes**
>
> Write about:
>
> **1** clothes and appearance
>
> **2** free time
>
> **3** .... (your own idea)

Which two of these ideas would not be suitable for the third point in the essay? Why?

---

image and style   friendships   daily routine and times
TV and films   leisure activities   food   spending money

Read one student's introduction to the essay. What is the problem with it?

> Making their own choices is part of growing up for teenagers. However, it's too simplistic to say that teenagers should always make their own choices. It depends on their age and the type of choice they have to make.

Replace the highlighted text with the correct referencing words.

1 Teenagers need the freedom to choose their own clothes because choosing their own clothes helps teenagers develop a sense of identity.

2 Managing money is an important life skill, so managing money is something all young people need to do.

3 Younger teenagers have less experience. In spite of younger teenagers having less experience, younger teenagers should still be given some independence.

4 Young people want to be free to choose their own clothes. In addition to choosing their own clothes, young people want to choose how to spend young people's free time.

5 Deciding for yourself might sometimes lead to mistakes, but mistakes can also give important learning opportunities.

How can you say the phrases (1–5) in a different way? Choose the correct answer to complete phrases A and B.

1 make their own choices

   A choose for **their** / **themselves**

   B **make up** / **make** their own mind

2 a teenager's appearance

   A the **way** / **how** a teenager looks

   B the image a teenager **predicts** / **projects**

3 be allowed to

   A have the **free** / **freedom** to

   B be **let** / **given** permission to

4 make a mistake

   A **become** / **get** something wrong

   B fail **in** / **at** some way

5 have your own identity

   A understand **what** / **it** makes you unique

   B be **whoever** / **whichever** you are

Rewrite the introduction in Ex 3 without any repetition.

Write your answer to the task in Ex 1. Write your essay in 140–190 words, using an appropriate style.

UNIT CHECK

1 Choose the correct words to complete the sentences.

1 These jeans, **which / that** I've only just bought, have a hole in them already.

2 **Being / Been** very tall and only thirteen, it's very hard to get clothes to fit.

3 That's the girl **whose / who's** older brother wants to be a model.

4 I finally got the trainers I'd been saving **up / up for**.

5 **I was bored / Bored** with all my clothes, I decided to design my own.

6 **After / Having** looked round the shops for hours, I was tired.

7 Do you know the reason **which / why** the shop's closed.

8 We're the same size, **which / whose** makes sharing clothes easy.

2 Put the words in the correct order.

1 exchanged not refunded. / only / can / bought / Items / in the sale / be

2 jeans and a top / works / in the local music shop. / wearing / The boy

3 I / is / about shopping / What / trying stuff on. / hate

4 It / I / last week / started / was / my part-time job. / when

5 in / It's / my circle of friends. / Annie / the most clothes / has / who

6 borrow / did / What / without asking. / I / was / my brother's jacket

3 Complete the article with one word in each gap.

Why buy when you can hire?

An online scheme **1**... is helping teens resist overspending on clothes is gaining popularity in Australia. For Lily Habel, seventeen, from Adelaide it all started **2**... she posted a picture of her dress on Instagram. The next thing she knew she was approached by a girl **3**... wanted to know if Lily would hire it out. Since then the idea of hiring clothes has become the norm.

4... happens is quite simple. If there's an event that you are looking forward **5**..., you simply check out what clothes are for hire on Instagram and make a choice. **6**... contacted the owner and agreed a fee, you can get the item in time for the event.

Lily's sister Eve, fifteen, is also a hirer, but **7**... is her school that's at the centre of everything. **8**... setting up a shared clothes hiring page, the students make deals online and then use the building as a collection point.

4 🔊 9.6 Listen to a girl talking about her friends' dress sense. Match the names (1–5) with the descriptions (A–G). There are two descriptions you do not need.

A has an issue with the overproduction of clothes.

B knows how to put an outfit together.

C always wears a particular brand of jeans.

D feels under pressure to wear expensive clothes.

E experiments with new looks.

F likes picking up bargains.

G never stands out in a crowd.

Ellen ....
Tim ....
Katrina ....
Simon ....
Melanie ....

5 Complete the blog post with these words.

base   coming   decision   involve   make
mind   pros   reveals   sleep   torn

The power of numbers

It's good to **1**........................... on it when you have a tough decision to **2**........................... . But what if you still can't make up your **3**........................... the next morning? **4**........................... to a decision can be a lengthy and lonely process, so why not try these tips?

TWO

Two heads are better than one. So always **5**........................... at least one other person in an important decision. They can help you see things from another perspective and weigh up the **6**........................... and cons.

THREE

If you are **7**........................... between two choices, add a third. Research **8**........................... that people feel more satisfied about choices that are made from several options. So don't **9**........................... a big decision on just A or B. Broaden your options to make it easier.

TEN

Try the ten, ten, ten strategy. Think about the consequences of a decision over time, not just what will happen immediately afterwards: What will happen in ten hours? Ten months? Ten years? Thinking longer term can help you challenge a **10**........................... and make a better choice.

PART 1

Read the text for questions 1–8 and decide which answer (A, B, C or D) best fits each gap.

When **emojis** joined the **opera**

Many teens would **0** <u>think</u> twice about entering a competition to win opera tickets. But what if the competition involved understanding the complicated **1**....... of an opera told only in emojis? This is exactly how London's Royal Opera House celebrated World Emoji Day. Some people might be **2**....... at this idea. After all, many would say that these fun icons have nothing to **3**....... with the more formal world of opera.

Its work can **4**....... across as rather challenging and complex, so the Royal Opera House wanted an entertaining way to **5**....... out to a new audience. They translated the stories from twenty well-known operas and ballets into a series of emojis. These were tweeted on World Emoji Day and the public were invited to guess the correct opera or ballet and also take **6**....... in the competition to win tickets.

Emojis are a quick and easy code to show how you feel across social media. Opera is all about people singing at the top of their **7**....... and expressing emotion. Perhaps popular culture and high art **8**....... something in common after all.

0	**A** dream	**B** wait	**C** think	**D** imagine
1	**A** plot	**B** twist	**C** scene	**D** plan
2	**A** concerned	**B** surprised	**C** confused	**D** interested
3	**A** take	**B** get	**C** do	**D** make
4	**A** come	**B** go	**C** move	**D** carry
5	**A** hand	**B** arrive	**C** get	**D** reach
6	**A** part	**B** place	**C** position	**D** role
7	**A** music	**B** voice	**C** song	**D** sound
8	**A** get	**B** keep	**C** take	**D** have

PART 2

For questions 9–16, complete the text with one word in each gap.

Spread the love

If someone suggested **0** ....<u>giving</u>........ a Valentine's Day card to everyone at your school, you might think it was a mad idea. But this actually happened in a school in Ohio. Not only **9** .... the student make 13,000 cards, but she also used origami, **10** .... is the Japanese art of paper folding, to create them. And **11** .... made them perfect for Valentine's Day was that each one was in the shape of a heart. This creative and caring girl, **12** .... hasn't given her name, didn't leave anyone out, even the teachers! It must **13** .... been a challenging task because she started making the cards the previous September to get them ready in time. And in **14** .... of the huge number of cards, each one had a handwritten message 'you are loved'. The head of the school said that it was amazing to have a student **15** .... dedicated to other people. And I think, although I don't even know her name, she sounds a lovely person to hang **16** .... with.

PART 3

For questions 17–24, read the text below. Use the word given at the end of some of the lines to form a word that fits in the gap in the same line.

Can **friends** be categorised? ☒

I was reading an article about
friends playing different roles in
relationships. At first, I thought that's
0 ....nonsense............. – you can't   **SENSE**
stereotype. And then after thinking
about my own little group and their
17 .... , I found   **BEHAVE**
that these roles rang a few bells.

The joker ▶

This is Josh. He can make you
smile even when things seem
18 .... Though   **HOPE**
he has been known to act a little
19 .... When he   **RESPONSIBLE**
changed the signs on the toilet doors
at the youth centre, I must admit I ran
out of 20 .... !   **PATIENT**

The talker ▶

Suzanne doesn't need any
21 .... when it   **ENCOURAGE**
comes to talking! She's brilliant at
putting people at their ease and with
her around the conversation never
dries up.

The thinker ▶

Ali is the quieter one. He's
22 .... , but   **COMMUNICATE**
doesn't need to be chatting all
the time. Ali's the one to go to
for advice, too – he's the least
23 .... person   **JUDGEMENT**
I know.

The fixer ▶

I guess this is me, the planner.
Not that the others are
24 .... , but   **ORGANISE**
whenever something practical needs
to be done, I tend to do it.

PART 4

For questions 25–30, complete the second sentence so that it has a similar meaning to the first sentence, using the word given. Do not change the word given. Use between two and five words, including the word given.

0 We have only a few euros left to last the rest of the weekend.
MONEY
We have only ....a little money............ left to last the rest of the weekend.

25 Eating my main meal at lunchtime always seemed strange to me.
USED
I never ....
eating my main meal at lunchtime.

26 The memory of winning my first trophy will stay with me forever.
NEVER
I'll .... my first trophy.

27 You must return all books to the library within a month.
BE
All books ....
to the library within a month.

28 I'm lucky because my mother taught me to speak German.
IT
I'm lucky because ....
taught me to speak German.

29 Without building a new power station, the city won't meet its energy needs.
UNLESS
The city won't meet its energy needs ....
.... a new power station.

30 The dog bit me after I stepped on its paw.
GOT
I ....
after I stepped on its paw.

10 Practice Test

READING AND USE OF ENGLISH

Part 1

For questions 1–8, read the text and decide which answer (A, B, C or D) best fits each gap. There is one example at the beginning (0).

A shorter school day

Teenagers should start school later than 8.30 a.m., **0** according to experts at the American Academy of Sleep Medicine. Earlier start times can **1** ...... to young people not getting enough sleep and this sleep loss can **2** ...... a negative effect on their lives. Poor performance at school, weight problems and depression are **3** ...... of the problems teens can experience.

Young people in the thirteen to eighteen age group are advised to get eight to ten hours' sleep a night to be **4** ...... their best the following day. However, many say that they get about just seven hours on school nights. Inevitably, teachers have to **5** ...... tiredness and poor concentration in class.

Although most UK schools start between 8.30 a.m. and 9 a.m., British experts have suggested students would **6** ...... from starting later – at 10 a.m. or even later. Parents may well have an **7** ...... with this as they themselves usually have to be at work by nine. However the school day is organised, it's difficult to get it **8** ...... for everyone.

	A	B	C	D
0	corresponding	agreeing	following	(D) according
1	lead	result	involve	mean
2	give	have	get	take
3	regular	common	usual	typical
4	in	on	at	for
5	catch up on	put up with	stand up for	run out of
6	succeed	benefit	improve	encourage
7	objection	obstacle	issue	excuse
8	right	appropriate	satisfactory	acceptable

Part 2

For questions 9–16, read the text and think of the word which best fits each gap. Use only one word in each gap. There is one example at the beginning (0).

Designers are constantly coming up **0** with gadgets to make our lives easier. CES, which stands **9** .... Consumer Electronics Show, has been described as the biggest technology event in **10** .... world. Here are a few of the latest innovations **11** .... offer.

A smart bed could be the answer if you're getting too **12** .... sleep and are waking up tired. One model can even warm your feet up on chilly nights. And if you're not the best cook ever, how about trying a smart frying pan? It can calculate **13** .... much food is in the pan and even give you cooking instructions.

There's also the first listening hairbrush. **14** .... makes this brush different is the built-in microphone and sensors. The brush 'listens' as you tidy your hair and then sends information to an app on your smartphone **15** .... that you can look after your hair better.

I'm the first to admit that technology has improved our lives, but do we really need to **16** .... taught how to fry food or brush our hair?

Part 3

For questions 17–24, read the text below. Use the word given in capitals at the end of some lines to form a word that fits in the gap in the same line. There is one example at the beginning (0).

The colour the world likes best

The world's favourite colour has been chosen, but the **0** ....surprising....... thing is that people   **SURPRISING**

can't decide if it's blue or green. The **17** .... name of the shade is 'Marrs Green'.   **OFFICE**

Colour experts have said that despite this name, it wouldn't be **18** .... to call it   **CORRECT**

blue. People often disagree about colour, particularly on computer screens where it's difficult to

reproduce shades with **19** ....   **ACCURATE**

So how was Marrs Green chosen? The **20** .... was made after a six-month survey   **SELECT**

online. It asked people to choose their favourite colour from a huge range. Results from 30,000

21 .... in 100 countries were analysed. Annie Marrs from Scotland took part   **PARTICIPATE**

and the colour she chose was closest to the most popular one and so it was given her name: Marrs

Green. She said that it felt **22**'................................. amazing' to have a colour named after her.   **ABSOLUTE**

A **23** .... of objects have already been reproduced in the new colour. Who knows?   **VARIOUS**

A young woman from Scotland may change the **24** .... of our world forever.   **APPEAR**

Part 4

For questions 25–30, complete the second sentence so that it has a similar meaning to the first sentence, using the word given. Do not change the word given. You must use between two and five words, including the word given. There is one example at the beginning (0).

0 The pilot announced a problem during our flight to New York.

   WERE

   While ....we were flying........... to New York, the pilot announced a problem.

25 Paul is so good at singing that he could turn professional.

   SUCH

   Paul is .... that he could turn professional.

26 School won't organise the trip if students don't pay some of the cost.

   LONG

   School will organise the trip .... pay some of the cost.

27 After leaving college, she became a personal trainer.

   WENT

   After leaving college, she .... a personal trainer.

28 The walk took six hours so they were exhausted.

   WALKING

   They were exhausted because they .... six hours.

29 They believe that the storm winds reached over 100 kilometres an hour.

   BELIEVED

   The storm winds .... over 100 kilometres an hour.

30 'You won first prize – that's fantastic!' my sister said to me.

   CONGRATULATED

   My sister .... first prize.

Part 5

You are going to read an article about clothes. For questions 31–36, choose the answer (A, B, C or D) which you think fits best according to the text.

Pink for a girl, blue for a boy?

Walk into any high-street shop and you don't need signs to show you the clothes aimed at girls and those at boys. Just look at the colours. There's a rainbow of bright shades for girls, while the boys' range is usually darker and more limited. With clothes for younger children, the difference is even more obvious. A top covered in pink princesses is marketed for girls, while it's silver spaceships for boys. The girls' department is also where you'll find the skirts and dresses, but couldn't they just appear alongside the jeans, hoodies and other unisex items? Do we actually need different departments according to gender?

A British retailer recently decided to get rid of separate sections for youngsters' clothes. This was met with mixed reactions. Some parents welcomed the unisex approach while others threatened to stop using the store altogether. One parent said, 'I feel high street stores need to develop new ranges offering teenage clothing which can appeal to both genders.' Another felt there was a practical advantage to having clear sections for gender and age, to speed up the shopping process. This is particularly true online. If all the male and female ranges were put together, it would take a lot longer to make choices.

So is the world of clothes for older teenagers more equal? Girls are no longer expected to look neat and well-styled, as they were in the 1950s. And you could say that there's already a unisex look of jeans, a top and trainers that's worn all over the world by girls and boys alike. However, the range available online and on the high street suggests that the same colours and symbols are used for girls of all ages. There's still a lot of pink to be seen, along with images of fantasy creatures like unicorns and mermaids. Tops with messages suggest that the girls are interested in being 'cute' while for boys it's more about being 'cool'.

What about what some young people wear all week: school uniform? Traditionally, this has worked according to gender, with girls in dresses or skirts and boys in trousers, though some schools have a 'trousers for all' policy, especially in the winter. The dress code at one school hit the news during a summer heatwave. Girls at an academy in the south of England are allowed to wear skirts all year, but a request for boys to wear shorts during this particularly hot period was turned down. The head teacher jokingly said, 'You can wear a skirt if you like.' So a group of boys did just that on the hottest day of *line 48* the year. After their protest, the head teacher said she might consider changing the uniform in the future.

It isn't just young people's clothes that are under review. In the last decade, gender-neutral clothes for adults have seen a rise in popularity as both fashion designers and high-street shops have created unisex ranges. One female designer, Melissa Clement, enjoyed borrowing men's clothes and so wondered why male and female categories couldn't be done away with. Her range of jeans offers the *line 58* same shapes for both men and women. She says it's more about getting the right style for the individual, whether male or female.

So does it matter if we see male and female clothes as different? For adults and older teenagers, each person can choose how they want to look, but it's important to think about the messages young children receive. While the last thing we want is kids all dressed in identical clothes, a recent example reveals the difference in marketing across the genders. A T-shirt for boys went on sale with the slogan 'Little man, big ideas'; the corresponding top for girls read 'Little girl, big smiles'. In a world where little girls can grow up to be astronauts and boys hairdressers that just seems rather behind the times.

31 In the first paragraph, the writer suggests that

    A people need clear signs to help them find the clothes they want.

    B dividing clothes into male and female categories is unnecessary.

    C there should be a clearer difference between clothes for younger and older children.

    D it's unfair that clothes for boys are more limited than clothes for girls.

32 When a store put children's clothes together in one department

    A parents stopped using the store and shopped online.

    B the clothing appealed to both boys and girls.

    C it speeded up the shopping process.

    D not all parents agreed it was a good decision.

33 What does the writer say about clothes for older teenagers?

    A More teenagers in the world should dress in a unisex way.

    B Girls are expected to be neater and more stylish than boys.

    C Clothes marketing for girls is similar whatever their age.

    D Boys think it's cool to buy tops with messages on them.

34 What does 'did just that' in line 48 refer to?

    A came to school dressed in a skirt

    B stayed away from school on the hottest day

    C asked to wear shorts to school

    D protested about the change in uniform

35 What does 'done away with' in line 58 mean?

    A made to suit the individual

    B made more popular for everyone

    C made into different categories

    D made to disappear altogether

36 What is the writer's main purpose in the final paragraph?

    A to encourage readers to choose how they want to look

    B to support the idea of identical clothes for boys and girls

    C to disapprove of stereotypical images of young children

    D to advise readers to see male and female clothes as different

Part 6

You are going to read an article about a new type of scientist. Six sentences have been removed from the article. Choose from the sentences A–G the one which fits each gap (37–42). There is one extra sentence which you do not need to use.

The rise of the citizen scientist

If the word 'science' makes you think of dull experiments in the school laboratory, you might want to think again. There's a new category of scientist around, not a trained professional, but a keen amateur –someone who gives up their time to contribute to a real research project with real goals. Welcome to the world of the citizen scientist.

Volunteers of all ages are taking part in science investigations on everything from wildlife to weather. Working from their own computer anywhere in the world, they make a significant contribution to academic research without needing formal training or specialist knowledge. And the benefit to the science community is that they get the data for studies that they wouldn't normally be able to collect. **37**

One way of finding out about a citizen science project is through the platform Zooniverse. Set up in 2009 and with a wide range of subjects on offer, this site aims to get measurable results from the volunteers' work. **38** The projects they have worked on have resulted in a number of published papers and sometimes they themselves have made significant discoveries across the world of science.

An example of citizen science set up by Zooniverse is 'Penguin Watch', which involves the public counting different species in online photography taken across Antarctica. So how does this help the scientific community and the birds themselves? **39** This in turn provides valuable data for the conservation of these much-loved animals and their environment.

Dr Tom Hart from Oxford University is a member of the Penguin Watch team. He says that it's important to check how the penguins are surviving at different locations in Antarctica. Only by comparing several groups of penguins can we understand where environmental changes are taking place and what dangers the birds are facing. **40** People are needed to analyse the images and this is why the volunteers are so important. Every time they add data, it increases the scientists' understanding of each species.

Another organisation that has already benefited from citizen scientists is the space agency NASA. During the 2017 solar eclipse in the USA, sixty-eight teams of teenagers set up cameras in remote areas to collect images of the moon covering the sun. **41** It was their opportunity to contribute to a project that aims to increase understanding of the solar system itself.

This collaborative effort was set up to get as much data as possible from locations across the country. Trained astrologists were on hand with professional equipment to help the young starwatchers get the best results. And the teenagers didn't disappoint. In total, they collected more than 4,000 images, which will provide NASA with more information than in previous studies. **42** This is because the project director wants to encourage their interest in science far into the future.

A Not only did these amateurs take part in an amazing study, they also got to keep the cquipment.

B The information collected in such a project will allow specialists to measure changes in habitat and behaviour.

C Despite lasting only two minutes and twenty-seven seconds, it was viewed by millions all over the world.

D Although there are a number of cameras already in place across the region, this provides a challenge.

E It's the hundreds of thousands of people who come together to assist researchers that make this possible.

F Some groups went on a ten-hour drive to reach the perfect location, but all agreed it was worth it.

G So the amateurs aren't just playing at being scientists.

Part 7

You are going to read an article about four young entrepreneurs. For questions 43–52 choose from the four entrepreneurs (A–D). The entrepreneurs may be chosen more than once.

....

Which teenager:

43 didn't make a conscious decision to be in business? | 43 |

44 feels irritated at the suggestion that commercial life gets in the way of being young? | 44 |

45 expresses a desire to help people of a similar age understand business? | 45 |

46 thinks carefully about how much to charge customers? | 46 |

47 developed a business idea out of problem people had? | 47 |

48 mentions that people do not always believe they are the boss? | 48 |

49 had to use an alternative way of doing business from older people? | 49 |

50 gave a talk without the help of written text? | 50 |

51 says they didn't expect to make many sales? | 51 |

52 made use of a skill that others didn't have? | 52 |

Meet the 'teenpreneurs'

We feature four young entrepreneurs who really mean business.

A Henry Patterson

Henry is the director of the online gift retailer Not Before Tea. In many ways he comes across as a typical entrepreneur: ambitious, outgoing and full of self-confidence. When he made a recent presentation to 200 conference delegates, he didn't bother with notes. What makes Henry a little different is the fact he's only twelve. He's actually been interested in business since the age of five and he launched his online shop when he was just ten. He started by making and selling sweets, but this worked out too expensive so he switched to story-writing and self-published a book. After sales of 3,000 copies, Henry saw the opportunity of exploiting the story characters on bags, pictures and other gift items. With income of £80,000 in his first year of trading, Henry has featured regularly in the press and on TV. And he only gets annoyed when people say that business must be interfering with his childhood.

B Sky Ballantyne

This young entrepreneur got into the world of commerce almost by accident when she was given homework to invent something for a competition at school. She came up with a device that helps parents teach young children to ride a bike. Inspiration struck after watching a father struggling to help his young son on his bike in the park. Sky admits that she didn't imagine the product would be successful at all, but her invention, named Crikey Bikey, is now manufactured in China. The business has two stockists in the United Kingdom as well as online sales. Working alongside her older sister Kia, who's fifteen, Sky, thirteen, has made the most of technology by using social media to boost the brand. The sisters have made £5,000 up to now, but are not in any hurry to spend it. They're putting it away for when they get to university.

C Matthew Bridger

At the age of eleven, Matthew took full advantage of technical knowledge that older people lacked – he was asked by his neighbour to fix a computer. After Matthew got it up and running, the neighbour offered to pay for the work and his business idea soon followed. Matthew's company, Whisper Media, gives digital media and web advice to customers in Europe and the USA. Now fifteen, Matthew says there are pros and cons to being a young entrepreneur. He can market himself as a new person with fresh ideas, but he sometimes gets mistaken for just a junior in the company rather than the owner. However, this has in no way limited Matthew's ambition. He hopes to help make the commercial world more accessible for other teenagers. And when he's finished his school exams, he intends to work full time and turn Whisper Media into a leading company in his sector.

D Katie Mortimer

It was the sale of her unwanted jewellery that got Katie thinking commercially. Too young to use eBay, she turned to Depop, a trading platform set up for teenagers. After making money from items she no longer needed, Katie chose to use her monthly pocket money to build up her business. Phone cases and clothes were the first things she ordered from China and sold at a profit through Depop. Now sixteen, Katie specialises in accessories, clothes and stationery, selling mainly to other girls of her own age. And she has a keen eye for pricing. She makes sure she knows what people are willing to pay, but also how she can make a profit. Most of the money is invested back into the business, but by the time she's old enough to take her driving test, Katie hopes to have enough saved to buy a Fiat 500.

WRITING

Part 1

You **must** answer this question. Write your answer in 140–190 words in an appropriate style.

In your English class you have been talking about the importance of managing money. Now your English teacher has asked you to write an essay for homework.

Write your essay using **all** the notes and giving reasons for your point of view.

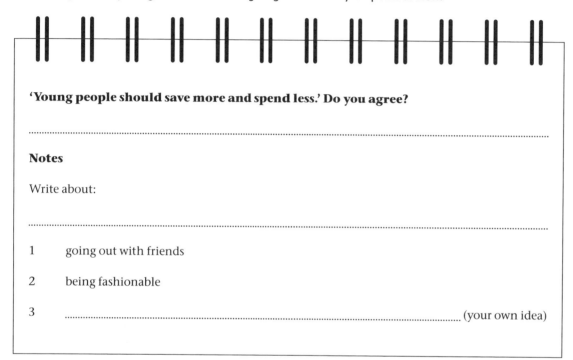

'Young people should save more and spend less.' Do you agree?

Notes

Write about:

1   going out with friends

2   being fashionable

3   .... (your own idea)

Part 2

Write an answer to one of the questions 2–4 in this part. Write your answer in 140–190 words in an appropriate style

---

2   You see this advertisement in a magazine for learners of English:

Reviews Wanted

English language websites

We are looking for reviews of a website for young people who are learning English. Your review should include information about the content of the site, what is good about it and how it could be improved. Would you recommend this website to other people your age?

The best reviews will be published in next month's magazine.

Write your **review**.

3   You have received this email from your English-speaking friend, Chris.

From: Chris

Subject: Help with a project

Could you help me with a class project? I have to write about food and eating habits around the world. What do people typically eat at different times of the day in your country? Do people eat a lot of fast food? Thanks for your help.

Chris

Write your **email**.

4   You have seen this announcement in a new English-language magazine for young people.

Stories wanted

We are looking for stories for our new English-language magazine for young people. Your story must **begin** with this sentence:

As soon as Amy saw the competition advertised on the noticeboard, she knew she had to enter.

Your story must include:

- an accident
- a surprise

Write your **story**.

LISTENING

Part 1

🔊 10.1 **You will hear people talking in eight different situations. For questions 1–8, choose the best answer (A, B or C).**

1 You overhear a girl talking about a fast-food restaurant on her phone.

She wasn't very impressed by

A the food on sale.

B the interior and the choice of colours.

C the cost of her meal.

2 You hear a boy talking to a friend about a football match he played at the weekend.

What problem did he have?

A He was embarrassed by a relative.

B He was sent off by the referee.

C His team lost three-two.

3 You hear a teacher talking to his class about a competition.

What is the teacher doing?

A reminding the students to finish their designs

B encouraging the students to win for the first time

C explaining the rules of the competition

4 You hear part of an interview with a young artist.

What is he going to do next?

A change his style of painting

B go abroad for a year

C go to a photo exhibition

5 You hear a man talking about a young singer.

What does he say makes the singer special?

A She is an amazing performer.

B She can play a range of instruments.

C She writes her own songs.

6 You hear two friends talking about a music festival.

How does the girl feel about it?

A nervous about the journey there

B worried that it might be boring

C happy to be going with her brother

7 You hear a news report about a new sports stadium.

What is the most surprising point about it?

A how many people it will hold

B how attractive it will look

C how quickly it will be finished

8 You hear two friends talking about their first day at a new school.

What do they agree about?

A the rooms are comfortable

B the teachers are supportive

C the food is enjoyable

Part 2

🔊 10.2 You will hear a student called Jessie talking about film-making. For questions 9–18, complete the sentences with a word or short phrase.

A young film-maker

Jessie says that she decided to work a camera rather than perform because she lacks
9 ....

Jessie says she thinks a good film-maker is a person who **10** ....

The type of film Jessie got first prize for when she was thirteen was a
11 ....

Jessie says she felt **12** .... by older people's low expectations of teen movie-makers.

Jessie explains that her inspiration comes from **13** .... in everyday life.

When choosing her cast, Jessie avoids **14** .... because they don't act in a very natural way.

The main characters in Jessie's current film are **15** ....

Jessie reminds the audience that you can't make a successful film without an interesting
16 ....

Jessie advises people who want to make films to show their work to
17 .... in order to get direct criticism.

Jessie's next step is to start a course in **18** .... at university in a month's time.

Part 3

🔊 10.3 You will hear five short extracts in which people are talking about a news website for young people. For questions 19–23, choose from the list (A–H) what each speaker says about the site. Use the letters only one. There are three extra letters which you do not need to use.

A There is too much information on it.

B My favourite thing about it is its international perspective.

C It would be better if it had more product reviews.

D I liked it when it started, but it isn't so good now.

E The articles on it aren't informative enough to help with schoolwork.

F The amount of advertising on it spoils my enjoyment.

G Its content needs to be simpler for younger people to understand.

H It has influenced the job I might do in the future.

Speaker 1 **19**

Speaker 2 **20**

Speaker 3 **21**

Speaker 4 **22**

Speaker 5 **23**

Part 4

🔊 10.4 You will hear an interview with a teenager called Marc Clements, who's talking about becoming a cookery writer. For questions 24–30, choose the best answer (A, B or C).

24 Marc says he got interested in food because of
   A his French family's influence.
   B his health problems after eating certain foods.
   C his love of food from across the world.

25 What did Marc often eat for his main meal?
   A pizza with extra cheese
   B salad and organic fruit
   C white meat and vegetables

26 Why did Marc invent different recipes?
   A He wanted variety in his diet.
   B He needed to lose weight.
   C He stopped enjoying his mum's food.

27 Marc started writing a food blog because
   A it will help him become a professional chef.
   B his friends from school asked him to.
   C he needed a place for people to find his recipes.

28 Marc says that the success of his blog is mainly due to
   A the appeal of his dishes to a range of people.
   B his entertaining writing style.
   C the great photography of the food.

29 When asked about cookery demonstrations, Marc says he
   A suffers from nerves before he does each one.
   B dislikes seeing himself in front of the camera.
   C appears with other young chefs to cook a dish.

30 Marc advises young people who are into food to
   A enjoy cooking and follow their own tastes.
   B only use the best ingredients to stay healthy.
   C work hard if they want to earn a lot of money.

SPEAKING

Part 1

🔊 10.5 The examiner will ask you and the other student questions about yourselves. Listen to the questions and then answer them.

Part 2

🔊 10.6 The examiner will give you two different photographs and ask you to talk on your own about them for about a minute. You will also have to answer a question about your partner's photographs after they have spoken about them.

Listen to the recording and answer the questions.

Student A

What are the friends enjoying about spending time together?

Student B

Why might the people have chosen to stay in these places?

Part 3

🔊 10.7 The examiner will ask you and the other student to discuss something together for about two minutes. Read the task and listen to the examiner's instructions. Discuss the task.

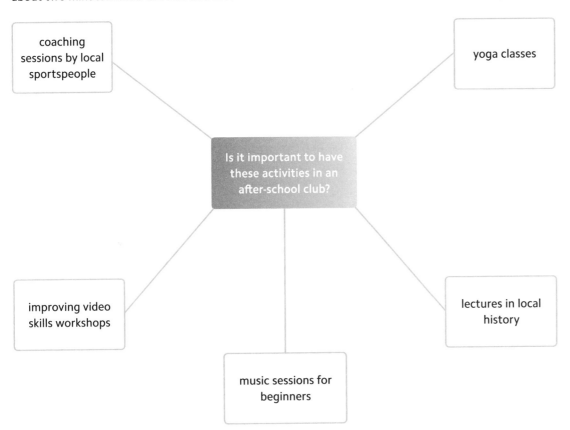

coaching sessions by local sportspeople

yoga classes

Is it important to have these activities in an after-school club?

improving video skills workshops

lectures in local history

music sessions for beginners

Part 4

🔊 10.8 The examiner will ask you and the other student questions related to the topic in Part 3. Listen to the recording and answer the examiner's questions.

AUDIOSCRIPTS

1.2

1 Have you hurt yourself? Come on, you'll be OK. Let's go and see mum.

2 Oh, no! St-o-p! Help! I want to get off! I want to get off!

3 Why are you doing that? At least let us play one song. You might like it!

4 Come on now, you can you do this. You are going to win this point. You are going to win this match.

5 And that's the end of my presentation. Thank you for coming today. Phew! I'm glad that's over. I was so nervous at the start, but I think it went OK.

6 Oh, that's awful! I really hoped it would all work out for them, but it didn't. I feel really sad for that girl. I wonder what will happen to her.

7

A: No, not good enough … Next!

B: Oh, no! They're really hard on everyone. I don't think I can do this. I'm so nervous. What if I forget my steps … or fall over? I feel sick.

8 Yes! The winning basket with just seconds to go! That's a fantastic result for us! The best result ever!

1.3

Hi and welcome to this week's Science for Life podcast. In the first talk in the series on senses, we looked at sight. Today, it's all about taste.

Have you ever eaten or drunk something and just thought 'Yeuch! That is disgusting!'? You must have tried my cooking. Sorry, stupid joke. Do people think you're a 'fussy' eater – someone who refuses to eat different foods? Well, you might just be a supertaster.

This is someone with a higher density and number of taste cells compared with the average. That must be great, right? To be better than average means you must really enjoy your food. Wrong! Supertasters can't stand a whole range of foods, including green vegetables like broccoli, sour fruits like lemons or grapefruit, hot and spicy dishes with lots of chillies, and coffee. Some supertasters are also sensitive to sugar. Imagine that – missing out on your birthday cake because it tastes too sweet! This was the biggest shock for me when researching this talk – that being a supertaster can actually limit the range of foods you enjoy.

So how do you know if you're a supertaster? A test was developed using a bitter-tasting chemical. The population varies in its ability to taste this chemical. Surveys suggest that approximately fifty percent of people can detect the taste, but not very strongly; about twenty-five percent cannot taste it at all; that leaves about a quarter of us who have a very strong reaction to the bitter taste. These are our supertasters.

As you might expect, non-smokers and those who don't regularly drink tea and coffee are more likely to be supertasters. Across the population in general women are more likely to be supertasters than men, and young people more likely than adults. Although the receptors for taste and smell are replaced regularly, something like every ten to thirty days, as we get older the total number of these receptors drops. So our sense of smell and taste fade over time, especially after reaching about seventy.

In fact, smell plays a huge role in our perception of flavour. Yes, smell. Sure we eat with our mouths and the taste buds are located there, but the nose and mouth work together. What most people don't realise is that we need the receptors in the nose to work with the taste buds to produce the sophisticated range of flavours we get from our diet. Think about what happens when you have a cold. You can't taste anything, right? In fact, try this test. Hold your nose and eat a strawberry. It tastes just like water – not sweet, not fruity, just watery.

The tongue can pick up only five main taste categories: sweet, salty, sour, bitter, and 'umami'. This is a Japanese word to describe savoury foods like soy sauce, dried meats and strong cheese. It's the nose that's really doing the hard work in making your food taste good. Humans have about 350 different receptor genes for smells. Their job is to recognise the chemical pattern given off by different foods. Estimates vary as to how many individual smells humans can detect, but one study suggests it's as many as one trillion. Amazing.

Many people from the team here at the Science for Life office tried the test. I was really hoping to get supertaster status, but I'm sorry to say I was the worst taster of the whole group. Must be all that black coffee I drank at college! Anyway, that's all from me for today. There'll be more from us on senses in next month's podcast, so don't forget to join us then.

1.5

1

A: Do we go left or right here?

B: Left, no right. No good asking me. I get lost in my own living room.

A: Excuse me? How do we get to the … ?

2

A: Starting on the right, and two and three and four. Step, turn and one and …

B: Sorry! Ooops! Which foot are we on?

C: Ow!

B: Sorry!

3

A: So the patient says 'Doctor, I have a pain in my eye whenever I drink tea.' And the doctor replies: 'Take the spoon out of the cup before you drink.'

B: That's so silly, but funny.

C: What? I don't get it. Why would anyone leave the spoon in when they're drinking tea?

A: It's because the spoon gets stuck in their eye …

C: Hmm?

A: Oh, never mind, it's not important.

4

A: Hey, look at this. We have got to try this new climbing wall at the activity centre. It goes up four metres and you can have races to the top. Let's put our names down.

B: Erm, I'm not sure. I'm quite busy just now.

A: Yeah, but they open seven days a week. We could go one weekend.

B: Thanks, but I'm not sure it's for me. I think I'll stick with my chess club.

5

A: And first over the line it's Mel Fisher. Gold for Mel in the 500-metre sprint.

B: Well done, Mel. You must be thrilled with that result.

C: I don't know. I think I could've done better really.

B: You got gold, Mel. You won. You should be enjoying this moment.

C: Yeah, but I might get beaten in the next race.

1.6

I'd like you to talk about your photographs on your own. Here are your photographs. They show young people enjoying themselves in different places. I'd like you to compare these two photographs.

1 I'm going to talk about just this photo because I prefer it. I can see some people skating. Maybe it's the first time that they are trying this activity because they don't look very happy. One girl has fallen over.

2 OK, so let's talk about the pictures. What do you think is happening in this one? To me, it looks like they are trying a new challenge. Do you agree?

3 The people in the two pictures are in very different places. In the first photo, they are outside and it's early morning, whereas in the second they are in a club at night. They are on the … er, oh, I can't remember the word, sorry, how do you say, this thing in English?

4 Er, OK, what else? … I'm not sure. In both pictures, the teenagers seem – er – seem to be having a, a fun time. Perhaps they are celebrating something like er, er …

5 OK, so both pictures are very nice. The people look happy. It's a nice day and they are having a nice time. I think they are happy because they are at a party.

1.7

So I'm walking home and this girl calls my name. The next thing I know she's there in front of me and she's shouting. She wants to know where her iPad is. And I say to her, "I don't even know you. What are you talking about?" So then she just runs off. And I'm standing there thinking, "What has just happened?"

2.2

1 Oh, everything! School, homework, money, football. I've got so much schoolwork to do and nothing to look forward to. It's ages until the end of term.

2 Not 'it', 'she'! She's just so beautiful. I knew I had to have her as soon as I saw her. She's exactly right for me, in size and character. We can be out riding for hours and she never gets tired or complains. The best friend a girl can have!

3 Quite a while. I didn't know anyone when I started there, so it was hard walking into class as a stranger. Everything was different – the class sizes, the timetable, even the food! It's fine now, but I didn't make a lot of friends on day one.

4 It was such a surprise. I wasn't expecting the team to play with such determination. It was a tough match, but they never gave up. They played for each other and for the crowd. I'm so proud to wear this shirt.

5 My parents have finally agreed I can have a scooter. I've wanted one for ages, but they were worried about the amount of traffic on the roads. No more asking for lifts or standing around at the bus stop. I can't wait.

6 Having time to hang out with my friends from home. I go to boarding school, so I don't see them much in term-time. We've got a trip to Amsterdam planned and then the rest of the summer just to catch up and have fun.

2.3

I = Interviewer   S = Samira

I: I'd like to welcome Samira Kahn from a local book club who's joined us to talk about reading lists. So how do most of these lists work, Samira?

S: The majority of them have fairly typical categories. You know, like the signs in a bookshop – books for under-fourteens, books for fourteen to sixteen-year-olds. Or like the lists on a website: stories for animal-lovers, books about aliens, or whatever.

I: But I see from the book list you sent me that your group has done things differently. Can you tell us about that?

S: Yes, my book club has been following a reading project called 'Around the world in eighty books.' The eighty books have different themes and ideas, but what brings them together is a very strong sense of place. Each book is set in a different part of the world, so as you read, you're taken to the far corners of the globe. It's like a round-the-world trip, but you don't have to pack your suitcase or even leave home!

I: So tell me, how do you select the order of books?

S: Well, we thought of different ways of organising the list. For example A–Z by country, so starting in Australia and ending in, I don't know, Zimbabwe. In the end we just voted for the first book as a group and since then each person has chosen a story and so the next destination. We could have grouped them by region, I suppose, but just didn't do it that way.

I: So looking at your list here, the first two titles were Life of Pi and The Old Man and the Sea.

S: That's right. We began our adventure in India with Life of Pi. It's the magical story of a teenage boy who survives in a boat with a group of wild animals. It turned out to be a great starting point. It's so thrilling that everyone loved it! The next story took us to Cuba with The Old Man and the Sea. This is a classic, but it kind of divided the

group. Some members enjoyed it, but others felt it lacked plot. There isn't much real action in a lot of the story.

I: And the next one is a book I haven't read, called First Light. What can you tell us about that?

S: The main character, Peter, is a young guy who joins his parents on an expedition to Greenland. Peter is looking forward to having adventures on the ice, but he meets the mysterious Thea, who has never seen the sun. Er, I don't want to say too much more in case your listeners are reading it or want to read it. But I really enjoyed it. It's a clever mix of mystery, science and adventure in a place few of us will ever visit.

I: Sounds great, There's just time to mention your favourite story – why did you like The Shadow of the Wind so much?

S: Ah, this story brings us back to Europe, Barcelona in fact, and the discovery of a forgotten book. We follow the hunt for an author who may or may not be alive. It's translated from the original Spanish, which is a good thing as my language skills are hopeless! I just couldn't put this one down despite it being a lot longer than the other books. The plot was so thrilling I had to read right to the end in a single weekend.

I: Sounds like a good read. And, finally, what for you is the key thing about the eighty books reading list?

S: The descriptions of the different places are fantastic, but what matters to me most is that you get to understand the experiences of people you would never meet, no matter what language the original books are in. You really do get a global view.

2.6

1 Excuse me, Sir. Excuse me. But you haven't settled your bill. You had the two-course lunch and a bottle of water. So will that be cash or card?

2 That was rubbish! The ad said 'the most thrilling ride on earth', but it was ancient and so slow.

3
A: You can't take all that stuff! You've got more than half of the space already.

B: But I need different outfits. What if we go clubbing?

A: It's a walking holiday, Amy. You won't need going out clothes.

B: Yeah, well. I still don't see why we have to share a suitcase.

4 You won't get me anywhere near that water. I heard someone say a swimmer was bitten last year. Terrifying!

5
A: Right, so what's the plan for today? How about a walk round the Old Town?

B: Boring! We haven't been to the beach yet.

C: Oh, I hate the beach. All that sand and sticky sun cream.

D: You said we could go to the water park. Can we?

E: The market is on today. Why don't we start there and then do something different this afternoon?

B: Oh! No! Why?

2.7

1 No, I don't.

2 What do you mean? What is camping?

3 Yes, I think it's great fun because you don't have to stay in the same place the whole time.

4 No, I don't very much, to be honest. We tried it two years ago and it was awful! It took a long time to put up the tent and it rained all week.

2.9

1 I'm sorry, I didn't quite catch that.

2 Would you mind repeating that?

3 Sorry, can you say that again, please?

4 That's an interesting question. I'm not really sure of the answer, but I think I'd say flying is the best way to travel.

5 To be honest, I've never been abroad, but I'd like to go to New Zealand because my favourite movie was filmed there.

6 I used to love just playing on the beach, but now I prefer spending time in cities.

7 I'm not really sure which school I'll be at, but I'll still be studying English.

2.10

Which part of your country do you like best for holidays?

Would you prefer a winter skiing holiday or summer beach holiday?

Which country would you most like to visit next?

What did you like doing on holiday when you were a young child?

How would you feel about a holiday without your family?

3.1

1 Don't touch any of the equipment. Please just watch and listen. I'll demonstrate and then you can all work in groups and try it for yourself. You'll need to keep a record of your results to add to this worksheet for homework.

2
A: Have you heard about the new history teacher? He's so strict.

B: I know. He kept three kids back after school for not turning their phone off in class. And they had to do an hour's extra work.

3
A: Did you know the head was thinking of employing a teacher of Mandarin next year? We already do Spanish, German and Russian here.

B: Actually, it might be a good idea. Relationships with China are getting more and more important. But what other class would we lose to fit in Mandarin? There are only so many hours in the week.

4
A: Josie, I just wanted to say well done on your change in attitude this term.

B: Thank you, Miss Clarke.

A: You haven't missed one day so far, which is brilliant. And your homework and test results have improved enormously. Keep it up!

B: I will, thank you.

AUDIOSCRIPTS

3.3

1 I wasn't that keen on the idea. I mean, my dad works for local government and so I thought it was going to be a bit dull really. Sorry, Dad! But it turned out a lot better than I expected. The staff had been part of the scheme before, so they were used to having teenagers around the office. But what I really liked was that they'd planned the day. I wasn't just sitting at a desk and I wasn't stuck with my dad all the time. I worked on reception and sat in on a planning meeting in the morning. But the best part was writing a job advert. That really helped me see what skills you need to get an interview.

2 At first I thought I was going to miss out on the scheme, as my mum works from home! But I got a place where my aunt works. She's an engineer in a local company, but to be honest, I wasn't really sure what that meant day to day. Seeing her in her place of work really opened my eyes. The work is a lot more varied than I thought. She works with the highways team, so they're responsible for the construction of new roads. The team talked me through the key stages – from the basic map stage, through a computer simulation and then an actual visit to the construction site. It was amazing to see work starting on the road – from a safe distance!

3 My mum dropped me off at reception before she headed out to see some clients. Her colleagues were expecting me, but it was pretty clear no one knew what to do with a thirteen-year-old. I'd really been looking forward to seeing life inside a magazine studio. OK, so it's not fashion, but it's still part of the media and an area I'm really interested in. By eleven o'clock, I hadn't really done anything. Then a woman came over to me, handed me some old copies of their magazines, and said, 'Here you are, in case you're feeling bored.' What a waste of time!

4 My dad doesn't talk about his job as a food scientist much and this was the first time I'd been inside his lab. It all started well when I put on a white coat, hat and protective glasses. I was sure we were going to see some cool experiments and try some of the latest food. We did have a go at a taste test, but it was something I'd already done at school. What I really wanted was to see some of the food under development, but that wasn't possible. They have to keep it all a secret because of competition. No wonder Dad doesn't tell us much.

5 The law is an important part of my mum's life. Her dad represented people in court too. I think she'd like one of us to follow in her footsteps, but my dream is to do something creative. But I was happy enough to go along. I knew the work wouldn't be anything like you see in TV dramas. My mum refuses to watch them! But I didn't expect to find it all so fascinating. Talking to my mum's colleagues showed me how important their work is. We discussed a fictitious case in the office and then even went to the court to watch part of a trial. I might even be changing my mind about my career. But it's still early days and please don't tell my mum!

3.5

1 What on earth have you got in here? They weigh a ton!

2 Why are all these empty bottles and empty bags on the seats? Please collect them up.

3 How was everything? Did you land on time? And was the flight OK?

4 What's the dog doing on there? Move him off to make space for grandma. She'll be here in a minute.

5 How can you have run out already? I gave you £10 just the day before yesterday.

6 It's all about IT and coding now. And languages are important too.

3.6

A: Shall we start with this one?

B: OK. Tell me what you think.

A: Well, if you do things like picking up bottles and cans, the whole town benefits. It makes a better environment for everyone. Don't you agree?

B: Yes, what else?

A: I suppose another benefit is a better sense of community. When you care for where you live, it brings people together.

B: Yes. Right, this one next. I don't see the benefit of talking to people about history. That's just boring. I'm right, aren't I?

A: I'm not sure I agree with you. You might be doing different things in a place like this – giving people advice and directions, selling things in the shop or serving people in the café. That would all help your people skills.

B: I think you're wrong about that.

A: OK, we can disagree on that. What about this next point? Do you want to say something about …?

3.8

1 That's not a very kind thing to say. Say sorry!

2 I think there are two possible options, but I don't know which to go for. There's either working in the local shop on Saturdays or babysitting two nights a week.

3 I can't really say what I'll do next. I need to see what grades I get and what courses are on offer. I like the idea of a gap year, but we'll have to wait and see.

4 I can't start now, no way! I'm not ready. I need to put my lucky sweater on. And I always start at seven minutes past. If I don't, it'll be bad luck.

5 It was good. We were all feeling a bit lost and in need of help with the same questions. We worked through old exam papers together and I learned a lot that way.

6 Yes, it works! It took me ages to work out the coding and I nearly gave up, but I'm glad I didn't. This animation works really well with the sound now.

4.1

1 When you press this button, …

2 If tourism to the city falls, …

3 You'll get thrown off the bus …

4 I wouldn't buy food from that market …

5 What would you have done …

6 If you hadn't been wearing your headphones, …

4.2

1 We interrupt this programme to bring you warnings of storms leading to flash flooding right across our area. Expect very hazardous driving conditions with some roads becoming unpassable very quickly. More updates to follow as soon as …

2

A: Thanks for making time to see me.

B: No problem. So what's this about needing more staff before the launch of the new designs?

A: Yes, we're definitely going to need more people. The current team is too small to sell all the new products we'll have into our key markets. If we don't take on some new reps, we won't reach our target for year one.

B: OK, well let's talk to each team leader and see how many people they think they'll need.

3 Hey, this is amazing. Just think they've surrounded this place for centuries. You can see for miles across the countryside and I can just make out my parents standing back down in the street. You should come up here … No, wait, I forgot you don't like heights ….

4

A: I hope they do it again next year.

B: Why, what was it like?

A: Well, they closed off the whole area to traffic and organised a big event for the festival. They built a stage where the food is usually sold. There were street performers, and some really cool stuff for sale. The atmosphere was so different from when you come and buy just fruit and vegetables or some bread.

5

A: Shall we get the bus into town later?

B: Hmm, I'm not sure. I haven't got much money, to be honest.

A: We don't have to buy anything. We can just have a look.

B: I'm not very keen on looking round when I'm short of money. Sorry.

A: No worries. We can go another time.

6

A: What do you mean you've fallen off your bike? What happened?

B: Well, I was on a street I don't know very well and it was getting dark.

A: You had your helmet and lights on, didn't you?

B: Yes, Mum, of course I did. Please listen! All that happened was I didn't stop in quite the right place because the lines weren't clear. They had faded a lot and you couldn't see them. I braked really hard and fell off, but I'm fine. I've just torn my trousers, so …

4.3

1 Hi, it's dad. Just to say I'm sitting in traffic. There are roadworks all the way along the bypass and every set of lights seems to be stuck on red. Please wait at school and I'll get there as soon as I can. Get a friend to wait with you if you can. Whatever you do, don't start walking or we'll miss each other. And don't bother going to the bus stop because the buses are also delayed along this road. Looking at the traffic, I think I'll be another twenty minutes OK? Bye.

2

A: Hey, have you seen this? Lucinda has just updated her profile. Check out the pictures she's uploaded.

B: Wow! That's like in a celebrity show home. I knew she was moving somewhere big, but I didn't expect that.

A: I know. All that space for just her. That's like all the rooms in this house put together.

B: Has she posted anything else?

A: Just a few more images and a note to say 'come and see me soon'. Would you go?

B: Yes, if she invited me. It would be great to live like a king for a weekend.

A: Hmm, just imagine. But I hope there's a map. If you went upstairs, you might get lost and never come down!

3

A: So, tell us Ryan, how have you found your first month?

B: It's been good. The course is more or less what I expected and I'm getting used to being away from home. But the one thing that was a bit difficult was getting student accommodation.

A: Oh?

B: Yes, I was going to be sharing a flat with some friends, but then I thought I'd better be near college, you know, closer to all the amenities.

A: Yes, I think that's wise in your first year. So you have a room on campus?

B: That's right. I don't have to travel far to lectures, but it's only twenty minutes into the centre by bus.

4

A: Excuse me, can I just tell you about …? Sorry, but would you like a leaflet about this …? I don't suppose you would like a leaflet about a games fair?

B: A games fair? Here today?

A: Yes, it's on in town, in a hall just off the main square. Only about ten minutes from here. They've got demos, competitions, an interview with a games designer and stuff for sale.

B: Sounds cool. Have you been over there?

A: Yes, I was there earlier. I got a free pass for the morning in return for handing out 250 of these leaflets.

B: How many have you done?

A: About thirty.

B: I'd offer to help, but I'd like to see what the fair's like myself.

A: No problem. Have fun!

5 Save our village! Save our village! The council has refused to listen to our concerns about the plans for the new road so join us this Friday morning for a peaceful demonstration outside the council offices. We need to make our voices

heard: NO NEW ROAD! Join us in the main square at 8.30 on Friday. We will then march to the council offices to hand in our petition. Thank you to everyone who signed. The petition is closed, but you can still join us on the march. Don't forget 8.30, Friday morning. Save our village! Save our village!

6

A: So how was your weekend with Auntie Em?

B: Yeah, it was OK, I guess.

A: Only OK? Didn't you have enough to do?

B: No, we were busy all weekend. Just not in a good way. I mean, why do people in the country get up so early? It's not like they have less time than us! There are still 24 hours in a day.

A: Yes, I can't argue with that.

B: So there wasn't time to get bored. Up at seven, seven thirty horse-riding, which was awesome. Then an hour looking after the horse before going to town food shopping. All that before lunch. I fell asleep on the sofa in the afternoon.

A: Hmm, all that country air.

7

A: Do you fancy coming to that urban farm near here?

B: Actually, I went last weekend while you were away.

A: Oh, what's it like?

B: Well, I was expecting it to be a bit dull. I only went along because my brother was going –he's thinking of working in farming. Anyway, it was actually really good. You can see what it's like to work with animals in the fields, but there's also a high-tech information centre.

A: So it's not full of little children looking at baby animals?

B: There is a play area for little kids, but I spent most of the time at the 'farm to fork' exhibition. What I enjoyed most was finding out how what they grow gets from the farm to our plate. It was really interesting learning from the interactive screens and the staff there were really helpful.

A: And did you get to try any of the food?

B: Not on the day I went, but I've heard they do some great food tasting days. You should go.

A: Yeah, I think I will.

8

A: So what bus shall we get to town later? The film starts at six.

B: The bus drivers are on strike today, remember?

A: But I'm desperate to see that film. It's the last screening today so we can't see it tomorrow. Could your dad give us a lift?

B: He's working late, sorry. I suppose we could walk in and get a lift back.

A: What, all the way into town?

B: Hmm, otherwise it means a taxi and I can't afford that.

A: No, me neither. OK, let's go in on foot. Everyone at school has loved the film so I really don't want to miss it. And I guess it's not that far into town.

4.5

1 Oh, no not again! For the last time, stop barking, will you?

2 Right, phones off, sit down and be quiet! No talking and that means everyone.

3 We're moving to a great big house with five bedrooms and space for three cars. I'm going to have my own horse and …

4 There's no vegetarian food left, only burgers and chips. Do you want that?

5 Oh, no! The tent's full of water. My back's all wet.

6 Look at you! Haven't you grown! You're nearly as tall as your brother now. And you're helping your mum with the shopping, isn't that nice?

7

A: Come on, slow coach. We're getting behind. I don't want to be last.

B: You go on, I need to stop for a bit.

8

A: Hurry up! We're going to miss the train. Quick!

B: I can't! My feet hurt.

4.7

Speaker 1

I don't know. I haven't thought about that.

Speaker 2

As I see it, being a good neighbour is really the same as being a good person. I mean, you put others first, you help people if they have a problem and you look after shared spaces.

Speaker 3

I'd definitely say that city life is preferable for young kids. Of course, there are also things to do in the country, but life is slower and there's less variety. I can't think of many big events that take place outside the city where I live.

Speaker 4

I'm not sure. I can't really think of any examples.

Speaker 5

Cities have a lot to offer, but they can also be challenging for elderly people. They may feel isolated if they have no family or insecure if they live in an area with a lot of crime. I think it's important for older people to feel included in a community.

Speaker 6

To be honest, I don't think it matters if you live in the capital or not. So many people travel now that you can visit it more or less whenever you want. And social media keeps you connected to big cities even if you don't live in one.

4.8

What makes a town or city a good place to live? Why?

What should the government do to improve towns in your country?

How do you think living in the country is different from living in a city? Why?

Do you think that living in the country is better for older or younger people? Why?

Should all young people get to know their capital city well? Why?/Why not?

If you could live anywhere in the world, where would you choose? Why?

5.1

1 A good win for us today, but it certainly wasn't a walk in the park! City High School really challenged us. After forty-five minutes, we knew they would come back fighting in the second half. All credit to the High School team – they played really well here today.

2 People always say to me 'You make it look so easy' and I think 'I wish!' The first time you do any new jump or routine, it's a challenge. Of course, your body knows what to expect, but you'll never get it completely right first time. To achieve excellent control and performance takes repetition. But all the early starts and late nights are worth it when you do get it right.

3 It's been a hard-fought competition, with each team really pushing to get their hands on the cup. It was five years ago that it was last in pride of place in the school hall, so I am delighted to ask the team captain to come and accept it here again today. Well done, Jessica and all the team.

5.2

I = Interviewer   N = Nathan

I: Hello and welcome to this week's 'Hooked on Sport'. And we're kicking off today with something a little different. With me to tell us all about it is Nathan Miller. Now, Nathan the name of your chosen sport is floorball – a cross between ice hockey and field hockey. I must admit, that's a new one on me. So how do people react when you first tell them about floorball?

N: Well, I've been playing floorball for a while now and so everyone I know understands about the game. But a lot of other people say they've never heard of it. In fact, I've had conversations where people have thought I've said football and they launch into a long description of Liverpool's latest match. It's funny to see their face when I say, "Not football, floorball!" They just look blank!

I: And how is floorball different from other similar sports?

N: Well, the first thing to say is that it's played only indoors, so it makes it a perfect all-year-round sport. You won't find us freezing to death on an outdoor hockey pitch or having a match cancelled because of winter weather. Each team has only six players in the game at any time – five on the field and a goalkeeper. Having so few players makes each game really fast.

I: So would you call floorball an exciting sport?

N: Definitely! A game consists of three twenty-minute periods of play, but in that time team members are coming on and off the field at any moment. You may do only a short turn in the game, score, but then come off and be replaced with someone with different skills and more energy. This is what makes the sport so thrilling because you can change the style of play at any time. It's very different from the one or two substitutions you might get in ninety minutes of football.

I: That is different. And what makes a good floorball player?

N: Well, the stick and the ball are much lighter than in field or ice hockey because they're made of plastic. So you need a lot less power to get across the field of play. This means a successful player relies more on tactics than strength in floorball. A good job because I'm not exactly Superman! The other benefit is that people of all ages can play – we have teenagers and people over fifty in our squad.

I: Interesting. So, what made you want to try floorball?

N: We had the usual sports on offer at my youth club – you know, football and basketball. But then they started looking for something that would appeal to as many kids as possible. What got me interested was the fact that we can play in mixed teams. I think it's really old-fashioned to divide up sports, you know, with the lads playing football in one place and the girls netball in another. We're all teammates in floorball and we all bring skills to each game to help us try and win.

I: Hmm, but it'll never be as popular as more established sports. What's your reaction if people call floorball uncool?

N: Of course I'd like floorball to have as many fans as football does, but it doesn't upset me if people think it's uncool. To be honest, it doesn't really bother me what other people say. It suits me to do my own thing and not to play the same old games as everyone else. And since when do we need a popularity contest for sports anyway?

I: Good point. And finally, what do you think is the future for floorball?

N: Actually, it's already more popular than you might think. Since the Swedes set up the IFF – the International Floorball Federation – in 1986, there are sixty member associations from all continents, so it's pretty much international. I can see it continuing to grow where there are already a number of established clubs and fans. But although we'd like to see it at the Olympics, there's no sign of it becoming an Olympic sport any time soon.

I: Thank you Nathan for telling us all about the sport that hooked you and …

5.4

1 What's your best sporting memory?

2 Why you didn't tell me you were going swimming?

3 Here, have some chocolate for energy.

4 Can I borrow your exercise DVD?

5 That wasn't very nice. Why did you call the other team 'losers'?

5.5

1 Unlike the friends, who are not competing with each other, the team are probably thinking about the score.

2 Both groups may spend a lot of time together, but for different reasons.

3 The team might be worried about making mistakes in front of spectators whereas for the friends it doesn't matter if they do something wrong.

4 As they're playing to win, the team may not enjoy the activity as much as the group of friends.

5 In the second photo, the friends are actually using the equipment, but in the first it could be half-time or during a pre-match talk.

6 Perhaps the friends don't need to think about motivation whereas for the team that's an important part of the activity.

6.1

1 Sound of a ball being kicked

2 Hey, let me in. It's freezing out here!

3

A: What was that? We need to get out of here!

B: Relax. It's only an owl. And it's a long way yet. It's going to take us an hour to get out the other side.

4 Oh no! Please! Come on, open, open! Can anyone hear me? Help!

5 And it's down to the final thirty laps in this Grand Prix race here at Le Mans.

6

A: Is this the bus to the city centre?

B: No, sorry, I'm not in service right now. The next one for town leaves in five minutes from stand twelve.

7

A: I bet I can get to the other side of the field before you.

B: I bet you can't. Ready. Three, two, one, go!

8 Look where you're going! My phone's covered in water now.

6.2

Today I'd like to tell you about my hobby, making sound maps. Quite simply, a sound map is an online map with audio recordings added to it. This can be people's voices, songs, wildlife – anything that gives extra information about a place.

I first got into sound maps when I was at school – surprisingly not in geography classes or even music sessions, but as part of a drama course. We were studying different accents and I wanted a way of adding a recording of each speaker to a geographical map. So you would click on the city of Liverpool and then hear someone speaking in the accent of that city. Sadly, back then the process wasn't very simple so it was a huge amount of work. But I'm happy to say that now the technology has really moved on, so today anyone can add sounds to a map.

So to begin with, why put sounds into a map in the first place? Well, it's a way of adding to the practical and visual information already contained in the map. It adds another perspective. But the thing that I find fascinating is how sound helps you to remember. People often say that a sound recording of a place brings back stronger memories than looking at a traditional map or photo.

I've already said you don't need to be an expert to get started. The audio quality on most modern smartphones is good enough, so there really isn't any need for costly equipment. And just one piece of very basic advice: the key thing is to know what you've got, so don't forget to include a brief description for every audio file. It's surprising how a sound out of context and without a label can be confusing!

And for people new to sound mapping, I would start simple and work your way up to something more sophisticated. One of the most user-friendly tools is called, appropriately, Map Maker. It uses Google Maps that we're all familiar with. First, you find the location of your recording on the map and add a place marker. Once you've given the marker a title, you can click on 'embed' to link the sound file to that place on the map. I've found that the majority of people take up sound mapping in their spare time after producing recordings of their own street. Though of course, they could start anywhere – in the city centre, or the countryside near their house.

So, let's say you've mapped your neighbourhood and you want to try something else. A fun way of customising a traditional map is to create a sound walk. This is where you choose a route and add in recordings to enrich the walkers' experience. The most valuable information I've ever got on an area has been in interviews with residents who live at different points along the route. They know their region better than anyone and so can really bring the place to life and take you off the beaten track to hidden spots.

But you don't have to keep it local. I can't get over the number of maps that offer a global sound tour. It's unbelievable how a quick search online will take you to maps from all over the world with everything from the sounds of a market to a beautiful singing voice. And don't forget that you too put where you live on the map, quite literally!

And people with specialist interests are also catered for: animal and birdsong recordings, poetry, and regional languages have all been mapped. Among the most visited wildlife sites are Animal Archive and Sounds of the Jungle. But the one I go back to, almost on a daily basis, is Nature Zone. The range of animals and locations is so wide, you could never get bored.

So, what's to stop you having a go at sound mapping? Check out my website for …

6.4

1 When I look at the board in class, the letters are all blurry, not at all clear. I can hardly read the smaller text.
2 It's Chris's sixteenth birthday in a couple of weeks so we should do something nice.
3 I have a Saturday job in a café, so I'm always washing up. It wouldn't last more than a day. Plus I think it looks a bit silly.
4 Don't laugh, but I've got one foot bigger than the other, so it's a nightmare getting the right size. After a match, my feet really hurt.
5 Mum will go crazy if she sees it. Please tell me it's a fake!
6 I was too self-conscious to smile in pictures, but I'll be able to again soon.

6.5

A: So then, which two activities do you think are best?
B: Well firstly, I don't think leaflets are very interesting. Sometimes it's useful to pick up leaflet on a local event, but most young people get information in different ways nowadays. What do you think?

A: I agree. And then I think signing up for a charity is definitely less appealing than a wildlife walk because the information they give you might not be relevant to where you live.
B: Absolutely. So, that leaves the talk, the walk and the competition. Let's make up our minds about this. A talk could be interesting, but it would depend on the speaker. If the talk was optional, I wouldn't go to it. Would you?
A: No, I don't think so. Basically, I think young people enjoy learning by doing things and being active. So, the wildlife walk is my first option, plus the competition because it's a creative task and competing for a prize is motivating. Are we both in favour of the walk and the competition?
B: Yes. OK, so we'll go with the walk and the competition as the best two options.

7.1

A: Thank you, Gina. I'm sure we all can't wait to find out what happens next. Now I know the people here would like to ask you some questions, so let's see who's first? Yes, the guy here at the front.
B: Thanks. So, Gina, why did you choose to write graphic novels?
C: For me, words and pictures go hand in hand. Every time I drew a picture as a little girl, I made up a story to go with it.
D: And is it really true that you illustrate the books yourself?
C: Yes, it is. I'm very lucky in that way. I can get the exact feel that I want in each image. Sometimes that's a lot easier than the words.
E: Do you ever run out of ideas for your novels?
C: To be honest, I don't. That's the advantage of writing adventure stories, I think. Each one can go in a number of different directions. And I often have more than one possible ending.
E: How long does it take to finish each book?
C: It's a long process – getting the ideas and characters, then planning the story before you even think about the pictures. So I guess about nine months to a year.
F: And might you start writing different types of novels, I don't know, like love stories?
C: Nahh,… I don't think so. All that romantic stuff isn't really me.
G: When are your books going to be made into films, Gina? They would make great movies.
C: Thank you. Sadly, there are no plans as yet, but it's something that I'd be really happy to …

7.2

1
A: Do you feel like seeing the new Bond movie at the cinema on Saturday?
B: Er, no thanks, Dad. It'll be available to download soon, so why bother going all the way out to the leisure complex when we can watch it here?
A: It's not the same. Action movies are made for the big screen. You need a group reaction to the moments of suspense to really feel them and to appreciate the special effects. You'd never get all that on a computer screen.

B: But you can't stop and start the movie like you can in your own living room. If people start talking, you miss some of the dialogue and you can't go back to listen to what they said again.
2 I've read this particular reviewer several times before. Unlike other journalists who seem to take delight in being extreme, his opinions always seemed pretty balanced and fair. So I've no idea what happened this time. I couldn't figure out why he took an instant dislike to the book. I was left wondering why it was all so one-sided. And I pity the poor writer who must have been so upset to read his criticism. There is always something positive you can say about a work even if you don't recommend it overall.
3 I've got a sinking feeling in my stomach and I keep going all hot. I don't know why I feel so bad. It's not like I haven't performed on stage before. But I'm more worried about this than being in a play. What if I mess up and I can't remember the words? Or I get the notes all wrong? The band have been rehearsing for weeks and they sound amazing. I come on at such an important part in the whole show and I don't want to let anyone down. I just keep imagining opening my mouth and no sound coming out.
4
A: So what would you say is the best advice you can give to an up-and-coming young writer?
B: Gosh, there is so much to learn about writing, it's hard to sum it up in a single tip. And there's no such thing as the average writer. Each person who creates stories does so in a different genre and for a different audience. But what's helped me is just being myself. There are so many talented writers out there, it's tempting to imitate their style, but you really have to create your own voice. Yes, that would be the main thing to remember when you're first starting out.
5 So I've had a look at all your short stories and I must say they were pretty good. Most of you remembered the techniques for getting the readers' interest right from the start, which is really encouraging this early in the course. However, there was one big problem that was common to everybody: the length of your conversations. This is a short story so you can't have line after line with people just chatting. I've made individual comments to each of you on characters and plot. Generally, these were quite well done, so let's have a look at a few examples now and see how we can improve.
6
A: Don't tell me what happened in the last episode. It's downloaded and ready to watch as soon as I get in from school.
B: I've got news for you. It's going to be continued!
A: You're kidding! So they're carrying on all the storylines and making another series?
B: Yeah. There was nothing about it on the programme website, so it came as a complete surprise. But there were complaints all over social media as soon as the programme ended. How come you didn't see that?
A: I've kept off social media all weekend so as not to find out the ending. What a waste of time!

7 And just before we finish, I'd like to give you some information on our story competition for this year. It's open to the same age group as before – fourteen to sixteen-year-olds – and we're looking for the usual length, that's an upper limit of 1,000 words. The difference this time round is that we want to encourage fresh talent, so if you've entered before, I'm afraid you won't be allowed to compete this year. But if you're new to the contest, aged fourteen to eighteen and wanting to make an impact with a one-thousand-word story, please do send us your entry.

8

A: Hello, City Theatre booking line. You're through to Natalie. How can I help you?

B: Oh, hi. I booked four tickets for the play on Saturday, but now my friend can't come. Would it be possible to get my money back on the extra ticket?

A: I'm sorry, but it isn't our policy to accept a single returned ticket. It's very difficult for us to sell one seat on its own.

B: But I can't use the ticket and no one I know wants to buy it, so it seems unfair that we pay for four seats, but use only three.

A: I can see your point, but it's just the way we do things, so I can't reimburse the cost of an individual ticket. I'm sorry.

7.4

1

A: Do you feel like going to the cinema later?

B: No, not really. Why bother travelling all the way into town when we have Netflix? Let's have a look at what's on. How about a vampire story?

A: You're kidding! I'm not sitting through another one of those!

2

A: How was the audition?

B: Not great. I messed up and had to repeat the lines three times.

A: Well, there's no such thing as a perfect reading.

B: Yes, but I really got it all wrong – the character, the voice, the timing, everything.

A: Could you try for another part?

B: I doubt it. I think the director took an instant dislike to me right from the start.

7.5

1

A: Yes, I completely agree with that. It can really help with listening and vocabulary. And you can understand a lot more because the images make it easier.

B: I agree with you up to a point, but not all films or programmes are helpful. You get a lot of new vocabulary, which can be confusing. And the grammar isn't always correct.

A: Hmm, I have to admit, you have a point. Not every programme is useful, but I still think TV and movies are enjoyable. Students just need help to choose the right programme.

B: Yes, I think so, too. If the language isn't too difficult, watching a video can be a fun way to learn.

2

A: No, I don't really think so. Many people sit in front of the TV together to watch a movie or sports for example. It's still a good way for people of different ages to spend a Saturday evening.

B: I couldn't agree more. And now there's TV on demand, there's a lot more choice.. So a family can watch a cartoon with younger children and then maybe a film with older teenagers.

A: Yes, you're absolutely right. Although we all have computers, my parents like us to spend family time together. And I can't watch whatever I want anyway.

B: I know what you mean.It's the same for me.

7.7

Which age group do you think enjoys reading more? Why?

Is anyone you know good at writing stories?

We can all watch films and programmes on screen any time nowadays. Is this a good thing?

Would you prefer to be in a film or behind the camera?

What can you learn about a country by watching films about that place?

Do you think printed books will disappear completely one day?

7.8

1 You got into drama school! That's fantastic news. Well done, you!

2 I'll come and see you perform on stage.

3 OK, yes, it was me who dropped your book in the bath.

4 Do you fancy coming along to the story group after school?

5 If I were you, I wouldn't pay to see that movie at the cinema.

8.2

Speaker 1

The unusual thing about us is the age range. At sixteen, I'm the youngest by two years and the oldest player is in her fifties. You might think this would cause problems, but our love of the game brings us together. As the 'baby' of the team, the older members have kind of taken me under their wing, you know, really taken care of me. Winning is important, but we also have fun. After every game, we give an award for something silly. One player usually falls over on the pitch and so she often wins it! I also learn all sorts of things from overhearing the older women's conversations!

Speaker 2

I was asked to join the team to represent our class in a tournament. To be honest, I wasn't very keen, but the others stressed how much they needed a fourth member, so I gave in. It turned out that the team's general knowledge was really broad. We won by miles and then I got hooked and we haven't looked back. We now compete once a week. Older teams are surprised at how much we get right, not just the stereotypical teen stuff on music or sport. We've been very successful and that's down to training. Yes, when our classmates are running around outside we're asking each other questions!

Speaker 3

My first love was gymnastics so I've always had a sense of rhythm and timing. Then two years ago I was at a festival and I saw this group perform live and I thought, 'I have got to do that!' As soon as I arrived home, I found a local club and asked if I could join. They were a talented and established team and there I was a complete beginner, so the answer was no. I was desperate to be allowed in and eventually the director agreed to let me join. After hours of work and dedication, I'm a regular performer with the club now.

Speaker 4

Everyone thinks that teens are glued to their screens all day zapping aliens or zooming round a racetrack. Sure, I enjoy online gaming, but it can be a bit solitary. You can spend hours without speaking to anyone. That's why I formed the club, to bring people my age together to have fun in a different way. And we don't play just chess or cards. There's so much on offer now – it's not just moving a counter round a board and scoring points. I enjoy the more strategic challenges, where you need to come up with a solution to a problem and create a win-win situation.

Speaker 5

The group is run by a lady who was a professional, so we take on quite ambitious projects. She pushes us hard, but then we get very good reviews. At first, I joined just to help out with costumes and lighting, things like that. It was just something different to do at weekends and in the holidays. And then someone dropped out and they needed a stand-in. It was only a small part, but I found I really enjoyed it and now I'm a regular on stage. I don't think I'd ever want to do it as a career, but it's really helped build my confidence.

8.4

Now talk to each other about how these situations might cause relationship problems for a young person.

1

A: OK, you start.

B: Oh um, sorry. I don't know which one …

A: Well, let me choose then. OK, the first topic I want to talk about is being a vegetarian and I think that …

2 OK, so we have to look at these five situations and talk about how they could create relationship problems for a young person. So the first one here is about becoming a vegetarian, the second one is.

3

A: Ah, the topic if being a vegetarian is important to me. I gave up meat last year and my family weren't happy about it. They didn't understand that it was a very important decision for me. Are you a vegetarian?

How might these situations cause relationship problems for a young person? Talk together.

8.6

B: So then, which two situations do you think would cause the most problems?

A: It's quite difficult to decide. They could all make life difficult in different ways.

B: Hmm, well, I'd say moving to a new school involves so many different relationships that it could cause a lot of problems. You know, keeping in touch with old friends and making new ones.

A: Yes, you're right. And maybe becoming a vegetarian could affect friends as well as family.

B: Er, I'm not quite sure.

A: Sorry, I've changed my mind about that option, being a vegetarian.

B: Yes, maybe that choice wasn't the best one. I'd say than unfriending causes more problems for people.

A: Yes, I'm happy with changing school and unfriending.

9.1

1

A: Oh, I don't know which one to choose. It's so difficult.

B: Well, you tried them both on so which did you prefer?

A: I really like this one … and this one.

B: Yes, but if you can only choose one, you need to make up your mind.

A: But I don't know which one to have! That's the problem.

B: Oh, please. You're only buying a T-shirt, not negotiating world peace! Just decide!

2

A: Grace, I have a proposal for you. How would you feel about taking part in the regional music competition?

B: Gosh, I'm not sure. Do you think I'm good enough?

A: Absolutely, but I don't want to push you. Do you want to some time to think about it?

B: Yes, I'd rather not come to a decision straightaway. Can I let you know tomorrow?

A: Of course, tomorrow's fine.

3

A: Oh, why did I say I would do that?

B: What's the matter?

A: My neighbour asked me to look after her little boy after school tomorrow. I said yes, but now I wish I hadn't. I've got so much project work to do, I can't really spare the time.

4

A: OK, so my older brother has said we can travel with him by car to the match, though he wasn't too keen on the idea.

B: Oh, that's good, but what do we do if for any reason he can't go? It's the final and we can't miss it. Perhaps we need an alternative if the worst comes to the worst.

A: OK, well we just get the train. It's only a short walk from the station to the stadium.

B: Great. It's good to have a back-up just in case.

5

A: Why are they doing this now? I haven't worn a uniform since I started at this school.

B: I know. It seems crazy to make us buy new shirts, ties and everything else.

A: And I think they're talking about the girls having to wear skirts, not trousers.

B: You're kidding! We can't have that. Skirts in the winter when it's freezing.

A: I know. We need to have our say about this. If we survey the rest of the school, we can tell the student council exactly what we think.

9.2

I = Interviewer   L = Lucy

I: Today we have Lucy who did something that would make most teenagers shake with fear. She gave up using her phone. So my first question, Lucy, has to be why?

L: Well at the start, it wasn't actually my decision. My parents had been worried about how much time I'd been spending online. Then the head wrote to the parents of everyone at my school to say that students were turning up to class exhausted because of overuse of social media. The school wanted to trial a period of no-phone use at home and needed students in different years to take part. So my parents put me on the scheme: a so-called digital detox.

I: So what was the first day on the scheme like for you?

L: Horrific! I didn't know what to do with myself. Before I'd be checking my phone every few minutes, moving across different apps to keep up with who was saying what. My phone was like an extension of my hand. Without it, I felt that life was empty. It was as if the world was going on and I was missing out.

I: And what about the rest of the people at home?

L: Oh, I was in such a bad mood that first day. If anyone spoke to me, I bit their head off! I thought my parents were punishing me and that it was so unfair. I must have threatened to leave home about fifty times! The reality was that everyone was trying to take my mind off my phone by suggesting nice food, games, or walks. But that first day I really didn't want to know.

I: And did things improve for you?

L: Yes, it did get easier. The key thing was to always have something to do. As soon as I had a spare moment, I would think, 'I need my phone. I need to know what's going on.' So to fill the time, I went back to things I used to enjoy like drawing and painting. As long as I had something to do with my hands, I was fine. And a good book at bedtime saved me! I always used to fall asleep with my phone in my hand. No wonder I was tired at school.

I: Would you say your performance at school benefitted?

L: I'd have to say it did. Apart from sleeping better because I wasn't waking up to check my phone ten times a night, the key thing was being able to concentrate more. Now I'm able to keep focused on what I'm doing for longer and the teacher says I'm making a better contribution in class. I know that some of the students doing important exams this year have found their revision a lot easier being phone-free.

I: So would you advise other people your age to give up social media?

L: To be honest, I think that depends on the person. You can't say to anyone who's addicted to being online, 'Just turn your phone off.' It doesn't work that way. They need to want to cut down. In my case, I knew in my heart of hearts that I wasn't enjoying social media, I just didn't want to admit it. So school and family did me a favour, I guess.

I: Finally, Lucy, the big question: what's your attitude to social media now?

L: Well, I'm back on it now, but I'm pleased to say it doesn't rule my life like before. I don't reach for my phone the moment I wake up. But social media is very seductive so it's easy to get pulled back in. I keep a check on how long I'm spending online and if it gets past twenty minutes, I stop and do something else. Social media is always going to be with us, so we all need to set limits to balance the online and offline worlds.

9.4

1

A: Have you noticed how Liam never stops looking in the mirror?

B: I know. He doesn't think about anything, but his clothes and hair. He even checks how he's looking when he walks past a shop window!

2

A Oh, that belt's really nice. Is it designer? It looks expensive.

B You'll never guess what I paid for it – just £5 in the sale.

A You lucky thing! But then you always were good at spotting a great deal.

3

A: You're not going dressed like that, are you? It must have taken you all of two seconds to put that outfit together.

B: Why? What? Jeans and a top are OK to wear to auntie Sue's.

A: No, that top hasn't even been ironed. You need to go and get changed. And choose something a bit smarter, please.

4

A: Have you seen how that new girl dresses - all those bright colours and weird shapes?

B: Yes, her style certainly gets her noticed.

A: Hmm, it's a bit too much for me. Wearing a purple and pink hat to school is just a bit strange.

5

A: Dad I need some new trainers. I've found some online that I like. Look.

B: How much? That's twice the price I pay for mine. Sorry, but I'm not giving you the money for those.

A: But they're by my favourite designer. And all my friends have them. I'm not wearing any old pair from the sports shop.

B: Fine. If you want that particular make, you pay for them.

6

A: Have you seen this fashion feature in the magazine? It's the latest looks for guys your age.

B: Well, this stuff looks great on the models in a fantastic location, but I'm not sure it would work for me.

A: Hmm. You're more of a jeans and T-shirt type, right?

B: Yeah, just like most of my friends and I don't mind that. Not everyone wants to look different. And at least I know I won't get strange looks.

9.5

Both photos show people shopping, but in different ways. In the first picture, the couple are in a shopping centre. It looks as though they've been there for a while because they're carrying things they've already bought. In the second picture, the girls are at home and they're trying to shop for something online, but perhaps there's been a problem. Another similarity is the relationship between the people. Both pictures show people who know each other well. However, the main difference is how they are feeling. The couple in the first picture are smiling and they seem to be having fun. The boy is pointing at something in the shop window and they may be about to go in and take a closer look. On the other hand, these girls are having a much less enjoyable experience. The girl holding the card appears confused and her friend looks upset. Perhaps there's a problem with the card and so they haven't been able to get what they wanted. For me, the boy and girl probably chose the shopping centre because they prefer to look at things before they buy them. I'd say the two girls might have wanted to book something like festival tickets and so they chose the internet.

9.6

My circle of friends are quite a mixed bunch and we all have a different attitude to clothes. I'd say my best friend Ellen is the most adventurous of us all. You never see her in the same thing twice and she often gets complimented on her different looks. Then there's Tim. He's a jeans and hoodie type of guy so isn't likely to get noticed. I don't think I've even seen him wearing anything unusual, but he still looks good. Katrina is our very own eco-warrior. She's passionate about the planet and has been speaking out against fast fashion, you know the way that styles change so often that we all end up with a pile of stuff we never wear. Oh and Simon. His mum used to be a model and I think he's inherited her style. It's nothing out of the ordinary, but everything he wears just works. It's like it all belongs together some how. And last, but not least, Melanie. No jeans and T-shirts for her, unless they're designer of course. She reads all these fashion blogs and then she's pushed into buying stuff that costs a fortune. I don't get it. I wouldn't be forced into wanting something just because it was in a blog.

10.1

1

Do you know what's really nice about about it? It looks very inviting from outside. They've used a really lovely bright turquoise, which makes you think of blue skies and holidays. And the furniture is comfortable and there's enough space to put all your stuff. They haven't put the tables too close together either. What let it down for me was the menu – all they had were the usual dishes when I was hoping for something a bit more imaginative. You know, maybe a salad with some new ingredients. But at least it's a lot cheaper than some of the other places in town so I guess that's something.

2

A: Hey, how was the match on Saturday? Did you lose like you thought you were going to?

B: No, actually we won for once. We beat them three-two.

A: Excellent. You must be really pleased with that result.

B: Yes, apart from what happened in the second half.

A: Why, were you asked to leave the pitch again? You really must listen to the referee!

B: No, nothing like that. I scored in the fiftieth minute and my aunt ran on and gave me a kiss. I went bright red and now it's all over social media.

A: Sorry, but I really wish I'd been there to see that.

3

Before you all head home today, I want to say a few words about this year's technology competition. As you know, the final date for entries isn't for another six weeks, but you need to get started on your designs. This time you have to work in teams of four, that's both boys and girls working together. Your designs need to be in the form of an online project, with drawings, but not a model. We've had several winners from this class in the past so I hope to be congratulating four of you very soon. Thanks for your attention and now off you go. See you all tomorrow.

4

A: So, Adrian, tell us something about your plans for the future.

B: Well, having just finished an exhibition in my local town, I'd really like to take a break from painting for a while. It's easy to get repetitive and come up with the same type of work if you keep going. But that doesn't mean I'm going to give up art altogether. My plan is to go travelling for twelve months and see something of the world. I'll be taking loads of photos and doing sketches of course. So I hope when I get back, I'll have plenty of ideas for new paintings and who knows possibly a bigger exhibition.

5

The first time you listen to singer Kerry Sanders, it probably won't change your world. Her voice is pretty average and she couldn't be called the most exciting performer in the world. Unlike some of the other artists around now, she isn't gifted at the piano, drums and saxophone. But what makes her stand out is her ability to create her own lyrics. In a world where companies employ professional songwriters to create tracks for artists, it's good to know that Kerry can do this herself. Let's hope she keeps producing wonderful words and putting them to music for years to come.

6

A: So you're coming to the festival next month after all?

B: Yes, I was lucky. I got one of the last tickets on sale. I wasn't sure about it at first, I thought the bands sounded a bit dull, but then they announced some extra acts so it looks really good now.

A: Yes, it should be good fun. I'm looking forward to it. Have you been to a festival before?

B: Yes, but only with my older brother so I'm a bit concerned about getting there by myself this time. It's quite a long way.

A: That's no problem. My dad's taking us so you can get a lift in our car.

7

And finally in today's sports news, an update on the city's planned stadium development. As you may remember, the design of the new building has already been approved and it's generally agreed to be more attractive than the one we have now. The final funding needed has been raised, but the most unbelievable thing is that the completion date has been brought forward and the whole thing will be ready in less than eighteen months. So all 20,000 spectators will be sitting in brand new seats and cheering on our local teams sooner than any of us thought.

8

A: So, that's the first day done, I'm happy to say. The new building's great, isn't it?

B: Oh, do you think so? I thought all the classrooms were a bit dark and airless.

A: Really? Maybe you were on a different floor from me.

B: Maybe. But I can't complain about the staff.

A: Me neither. They've all made us feel really welcome.

B: I know. It really helped me get over my first-day nerves. I really didn't know what to expect.

A: We've still got horrible food in the canteen, though. No change there.

B: Oh, I enjoyed mine. It was quite tasty – much better than at our old school.

10.2

Hello, everyone and thank you for coming today. My name's Jessie Mitchell and I'd like to talk to you about my hobby and passion – film-making.

Most people are curious about why I chose films as my hobby and I always say it's because of my character. People associate the world of films with people who are outgoing and who like being the centre of attention. I'm just the opposite. I chose filming instead of acting because I don't have much confidence in myself. So, as a child, while my brothers and sisters were putting on little plays, I would just stand and watch. But that actually was a very good thing for me. You see, I believe that to produce a successful movie you need to be someone who notices details. To me, this is much more important than being assertive or even creative.

I actually started getting serious about film at the age of twelve, when I won a competition. You might think that a person of that age would go for a simple cartoon or a comedy as their first film, but I wrote and directed a thriller about two boys who hack into a computer. It was fantastic to win at such a young age, of course, but what irritated me a little was that the adult judges thought young film-makers wouldn't achieve much. Just because we're starting out doesn't mean we're unambitious.

Another thing people want to know is where I get my ideas from. The truth is I use other people a lot. I don't mean I borrow other directors' ideas – that would be cheating! No, my imagination often gets working when I overhear conversations in day-to-day situations. So, I'll be on the bus sitting behind two people and one of them will spark an idea just by a simple comment.

I've actually met some pretty cool performers that way too. Of course, I don't have access to famous stars or award-winners, though I hope to one day! But for now, I tend not to use trained actors. Once they've had drama lessons, they aren't so spontaneous and instinctive as people I just meet by chance.

In fact, that's exactly how I met the people for the key roles in the movie I'm making now. I was walking down a street where I'd never been before and twin sisters were walking towards me. They're perfect for the short comedy I'm doing where they take each other's identity. They fool the teachers and even their own parents!

And if there are any budding film-makers in the audience today, please think quality, not quantity. Today everyone has a video camera on their smartphone, so it's tempting to shoot anything and everything. Fine if you want to just have fun, but remember, the best films all have an absorbing story. You can't say you've really made a movie if you've just done an interview with your mates for your video blog.

And one other tip – don't get your friends and family to look at your movies. Of course, they will say they're brilliant! Upload them onto a film-makers' forum as strangers will always give you a more honest opinion. It can be hard, but if you want to make it in the movie world, you'll need to please a wider audience one day.

Which brings me to my own future. You might think I'm about to take my place at an international film school or take a course in camera work or special effects. Actually, I'm about to start my English degree in about four weeks. That's going to give me a great background in understanding narratives for the future and I'll keep up with my film-making of course. But I'll also have something to fall back on.

10.3
Speaker 1

To be honest, I didn't look at the site for ages. There are so many ways for us to access news nowadays, I just thought, 'Why bother looking at another one?' But then I started getting into writing myself – blogging about the problems that everyday teenagers come up against. I started to get a positive response to my blog, so I didn't hesitate when I saw that the news site was asking for young reporters to submit articles. I sent one

in to the editor and now I'm a regular contributor. And it's really helped me decide what career I'd like to do. It's journalism for me – strange really after I'd ignored the website for so long.

Speaker 2

I always try to keep up with what's happening in other countries. I'm in the school debating club and it's good to be well-informed for different discussions. So I signed up immediately to the news site and got regular updates through to my phone. But after a while, I was finding there was too much to get through. You know, with the amount of schoolwork I have, it's hard to do a lot of extra reading. Don't get me wrong, the articles were great, just too long and dense. So I just get shorter summaries from a different site now. I can always go back to the original one when I have more time.

Speaker 3

A friend recommended the site to me and I was more or less hooked the first time I saw it. Great variety, contributors of my own age, a really cool design all made for a great package. But what I've noticed more and more is the amount of sponsorship there is now. You start to read a great-sounding article and then you get pop-up after pop-up trying to sell you stuff. Some of the products aren't even relevant to my age group. And what gets me is that the teen reviewers are all paid to give their comments. How can that be fair? Give me good articles online and leave the promotions for when I go shopping.

Speaker 4

Our teachers encourage us to discover what's happening abroad so that we can link it with what we do at school. But I've often found it difficult to find out about people my own age who live on the other side of the world. This is where this new site has been brilliant. The editor often takes a topic and get teenagers from different places to comment about their experiences. It's amazing how a range of opinions can really make you think. It's being able to access these ideas from young people from other cultures that I appreciate most about the site. And it's not just silly comments about stuff they like – they really think about their ideas.

Speaker 5

I was looking forward to seeing what this site had to offer. Most news for teenagers is a bit dumbed down – you know, over simplified, as if young people can't understand what's going on in the world. And at first, my reaction was positive. There were some really interesting articles written from a teenager's point of view – and not all about fashion and celebrity gossip. It went wider into world news, culture, business, everything you'd expect really. But I've found that over time, it's lost its appeal. There's less variety and some of the journalism is quite poor now. I know it's hard to deliver twenty-four-hour news, but I'd rather have less content, but better quality.

10.4
I = Interviewer   M = Marc

I: In the studio today, I have with me teenage cookery writer, M Clements. M, welcome. So my first question has to be: What got you into food?

M: Well I'd love to say it comes from my French background – my dad is from Paris – and that my grandmother taught me all I know. The fact is I suffered from different food allergies which affected what I could eat. I had to cut out sugar and dairy products like milk and cheese, for example. So it was more out of necessity than because I've travelled all over the world and developed a love of food.

I: That must have been tough. So what was a typical main meal for you?

M: Well, I'm happy to say it was more than just salad and organic fruit. I've never been that keen on red meat so an average evening meal might be chicken and broccoli. Of course, I couldn't go near pizza without getting an adverse reaction. That's such a shame as it's one of my favourite things and Italian food with dairy-free cheese isn't quite the same.

I: Sure. And what made you start coming up with your own recipes?

M: It was when my health was pretty good actually. My mum had worked out a food programme for me that meant I didn't get any severe reactions like losing a lot of weight. But the truth is I was fed up with eating the same thing every week. It can get pretty tedious when everyone else has a full range of ingredients to enjoy. But don't get me wrong, my mum is a fantastic cook. It was hard on her too having to stick to the same old things.

I: I can imagine. So why then start a food blog?

M: That's the funny thing, it kind of happened by accident. I took some cakes I'd made into school one day and suddenly everyone was asking me for the recipe. As I came up with more ideas, more people wanted to know how I'd made the dish. And in the end, I got tired of emailing recipes so I put them all into a blog. I try to be professional about the blog by updating it once a week. But the last thing I imagined a year ago is that I'd be a cookery writer!

I: But you've been a really successful blogger. Why do you think that is?

M: Well, I think my writing is quite entertaining. I try to make it fun by creating a story behind each of the dishes. But that isn't the main reason. I think I've achieved a large number of readers because my recipes work for everyone. So you can follow them because you need to in order to stay well or because you just want to cut down on fat and sugar. Having great photos of the food helps too, of course.

I: And you give cookery demonstrations. What can you tell us about those?

M: Yes, a food company has a website with up-and-coming young chefs showing people how to cook their favourite dishes. After seeing my blog, they invited me to give an online demonstration. I've already done five or six of them, but I never actually watch them myself. It's not that I get nervous, I'm just not very keen on looking at myself on screen. But I guess I'll need to get over that If I ever want to become a famous TV chef.

I: You're right there. So, finally, what advice would you give to young people interested in food?

M: Well, to be honest, there's a lot of nonsense talked about the glamorous life of a chef. It's very hard work and only the very best inventive cooks get to make a lot of money. So to any teenager who's into cooking, I'd say have fun in the kitchen and make what *you* like. We all need to stay healthy, but there are so many amazing ingredients out there now, if you can't use one, you'll find a good substitute and still make some delicious dishes.

10.5

Part 1

1   Do you prefer to spend time on your own or with other people?
2   Have you celebrated any special occasions recently?
3   Is there a sport you would like to try?
4   Where do you think you will be this time next year? will be this time next year?

10.6

Part 2

Candidate A, it's your turn first. Here are your photographs. They show friends spending time together. I'd like you to compare the photographs and say what you think the people are enjoying about spending time together.

Candidate B, how do you spend your free time?

Now, Candidate B, here are your photographs. They show people staying in different places on holiday. I'd like you to compare the photographs and say why you think the people might have chosen to stay in these places.

Candidate A, which of these places would you prefer to stay in on holiday?

10.7

Part 3

Here are some activities that many schools think are important to have in an after-school club and a question for you to discuss. First you have some time to look at the task.

Now talk to each other about whether it is important to have these activities in an after-school club.

Now you have about a minute to decide which two activities are most important to have in a successful after-school club..

10.8

Part 4

Do you think all young people should be able to go to an after-school club? Why? / Why not?

Do you think it's better for young people to take part in activities after school or to go straight home and complete their homework? Why?

What do young people enjoy doing after school where you live? Why?

EXAM OVERVIEW

The *Cambridge English Qualification B2 First for Schools Exam*, otherwise known as *Cambridge First for Schools*, is made up of four papers, each testing a different area of ability in English. The Reading and Use of English paper carries 40% of the marks, while Writing, Listening, and Speaking each carry 20% of the marks. There are 5 grades. A, B and C are pass grades, D and E are fail grades. Candidates also receive a numerical score on the Cambridge English scale for each skill. If a candidates performance is below B2 level but within the B2 range, the candidate may receive a Cambridge English certificate stating that they have demonstrated ability at B1.

Reading and Use of English: 1 hour 15 minutes
Writing: 1 hour 20 minutes

Listening: 40 minutes (approximately)
Speaking: 14 minutes for each pair of students (approximately)

All the examination questions are task-based. Rubrics (instructions) are important and should be read carefully. They set the context and give important information about the tasks. There is a separate answer sheet for recording answers for the Reading and Use of English and Listening papers.

Paper	Formats	Task focus
Reading and Use of English 7 tasks 52 questions	**Part 1:** multiple-choice cloze Choosing which word from a choice of four fits in each of eight gaps in the text.	Choice of vocabulary and relationships between words.
	Part 2: open cloze Writing the missing word in each of eight gaps in the text.	Grammar, vocabulary and knowledge of expressions.
	Part 3: word formation Choosing the form of the word given so that it fits into the gap in the text, with a total of eight gaps.	Grammatical accuracy and knowledge of vocabulary and expressions.
	Part 4: key-word sentence transformation Using a key word to complete a new sentence which means the same as the one given, with a total of six pairs of sentences.	Grammatical accuracy and knowledge of vocabulary and sentence structure.
	Part 5: multiple-choice questions Answering six four-option multiple-choice questions based on a text.	Reading for detailed understanding of the text.
	Part 6: gapped text Choosing sentences to fit into the gaps in a text, with a total of six sentences to place correctly.	Reading to understand text structure.
	Part 7: multiple matching Deciding which of the short extracts or paragraphs contains given information or ideas and matching these with ten prompts.	Reading to locate specific information, detail, opinion and attitude.
Writing 2 tasks	**Part 1:** compulsory task Using given information to write an essay of 140 to 190 words.	Focus on writing for an English teacher in a formal style.
	Part 2: producing one piece of writing of 140 to190 words from a choice of the following: an informal letter/email, an article, a story, a review, or an essay.	Writing for a specific target reader, using appropriate layout and register.
Listening 4 tasks 30 questions	**Part 1:** multiple-choice questions Eight short recordings, each with a three-option multiple-choice question.	Understanding gist, detail, function, purpose, attitude, etc.
	Part 2: sentence completion One long recording with ten sentence-completion questions.	Locating and recording specific information.
	Part 3: multiple matching Set of five short recordings on the same theme to match to one of eight prompts.	Understanding gist and main points.
	Part 4: multiple-choice questions One long recording with seven three-option multiple-choice questions.	Understanding attitude, opinion, gist, main ideas and specific information.
Speaking 4 tasks	**Part 1:** examiner-led conversation	Giving personal information, using social language.
	Part 2: individual long turn with visual and written prompts	Organising discourse in a 'long turn', describing, comparing, giving opinions.
	Part 3: two-way conversation between candidates with written prompts	Sustaining an interaction, expressing, justifying and exchanging ideas, agreeing and disagreeing.
	Part 4: discussion on topics related to Part 3	Expressing and justifying ideas, agreeing and disagreeing.

Pearson Education Limited

KAO TWO,
KAO Park
Hockham Way,
Harlow, Essex,
CM17 9SR
England
and Associated Companies throughout the world.

pearsonELT.com/goldexperience

© Pearson Education Limited 2018

Written by Amanda Maris.

First published 2018

Eighteenth impression 2024

ISBN: 978-1-292-19490-5

Set in Camphor Pro
Printed in Slovakia by Neografia

We are grateful to the following for permission to reproduce copyright material:

Text

Extract 2.5 after http://www.telegraph.co.uk/travel/news/The-worlds-coolest-passport/, copyright © Telegraph Media Group Limited (2017); Extract on page 25 from https://www.noisolation.com/uk/article/2017/marte-attends-classes-from-her-own-bed/ reproduced by permission of NO Isolation; Extract on page 25 after https://www.voanews.com/a/avatar-helps-children-recovering-from-illness-feel-less-lonely/3492212.html (c) Voice of America; Extract 4.3 from http://www.telegraph.co.uk/technology/2017/03/29/plans-unveiled-incredible-skyscraper-hangs-orbitingasteroid/, copyright © Telegraph Media Group Limited (2017); Extract 4.5 from https://www.theguardian.com/cities/2016/dec/02/cartube-tube-underground-cars-proposal-bury-traffic-next-best-thing-to-teleportation Copyright Guardian News & Media Ltd 2017 ; Extract 4.6 from https://www.theguardian.com/sustainable-business/2015/apr/16/ten-quirky-ideas-for-making-our-cities-more-sustainable Copyright Guardian News & Media Ltd 2017; Extract on page 57 from http://danielbritton.info/dyslexia reproduced by permission of Daniel Britton; Extract on page 57 from http://www.telegraph.co.uk/news/newstopics/howaboutthat/12186441/This-website-lets-you-experience-what-it-is-like-to-be-dyslexic.html, copyright © Telegraph Media Group Limited (2016); Extract on page 89 after http://nymag.com/scienceofus/2016/08/a-study-got-people-to-make-big-decisions-with-a-coin-toss.html reproduced by permission of Melissa Dahl/Science of Us; Extract on page 94 after http://www.telegraph.co.uk/science/2016/08/05/smart-clothes-of-future-will-auction-themselves-on-ebay-if-theyare not worn/, copyright © Telegraph Media Group Limited (2016); Extract on page 66 after http://www.telegraph.co.uk/news/2017/08/07/thieves-return-stolen-bike-awesome-apology-note/, copyright © Telegraph Media Group Limited (2017); Extract on page 98 from http://www.independent.co.uk/news/world/americas/student-13000-valentines-day-cards-schoolmates-teachers-ohio-troy-high-school-anonymous-a7584026.htm; Extract on page 100 after http://www.telegraph.co.uk/science/2017/04/14/teenagers-should-start-school-later-avoid-car-crashes-suicide/, copyright © Telegraph Media Group Limited (2017); Extract on page 102 from http://www.telegraph.co.uk/news/2017/06/29/results-worlds-favourite-colour-revealed-green-blue/, copyright © Telegraph Media Group Limited (2017); Extract on page 104 after http://www.telegraph.co.uk/women/family/gender-free-kids-clothing-way-forward/, copyright © Telegraph Media Group Limited (2017); Extract on page 104 after http://www.telegraph.co.uk/news/2017/06/22/boys-come-school-wearing-skirts-following-ban-shorts/, copyright © Telegraph Media Group Limited (2017); Extract on page 109 after http://www.telegraph.co.uk/women/family/meet-the-teenpreneurs-making-serious-amounts-of-pocket-money/, copyright © Telegraph Media Group Limited (2016); Extract on page 109 after http://www.telegraph.co.uk/money/consumer-affairs/child-moguls-started-selling-jewellery-online-aged-13-have-made/, copyright © Telegraph Media Group Limited (2017)

Gold Experience 2nd Edition B2 Workbook

Picture Credits

The publisher would like to thank the following for their kind permission to reproduce their photographs:

(Key: b-bottom; c-centre; l-left; r-right; t-top)